PROLOGUE TO MODERNITY:
EARLY MODERN EUROPE

PROLOGUE TO MODERNITY: EARLY MODERN EUROPE

JAMES D. HARDY, JR.
Louisiana State University

JOHN WILEY & SONS, INC.
New York • London • Sydney • Toronto

Cover Credit

Top: Bibliothèque Nationale, Paris
Middle: Ullstein, Berlin
Bottom: Diderot's Encyclopedia

Library of Congress Cataloging in Publication Data:

Hardy, James Daniel, Jr., 1934—
    Prologue to modernity.

    1. Europe—History—1492–1648. 2. Europe—
History—1648–1789. 3. Europe—History—1789–1815.
I. Title.
D228.H26   940.2   73–15579

ISBN 0-471-35139-3
ISBN 0-471-35140-7 (pbk.)

Printed in the United States of America

10 9 8 7 6 5 4 3 2 1

To Jo, Sarah, and Catherine,
who have had to put up with a writer in the house

Preface

This book is an essay more than a text. It is more essay than narrative, concentrating on why and how things happened in early modern Europe instead of merely citing the chronology and bare relation of events. It is certainly not a modern social science study, replete with statistics, jargon, and verbiage. And I have tried to keep the book from being a long editorial, although my opinions have not been omitted.

In an essay, some things stand out and others fall into the shade. I have given great weight to science and technology because they are the parents of modern life. There are two complete chapters (nearly one quarter of the book) that deal directly with these things and two other chapters that are concerned with the economic background of industrialization and technological change. The second main theme is the growth of the modern state, both in functions and power, from a ramshackle regime dependent upon the king to a bureaucratic government with vast power over the citizens. Four chapters have also been devoted to this theme. Thus, this book examines the factors of early modern Europe that characterize modern life, factors that have led from the Old Regime to our times. In the process, such interesting and important topics as philosophy, social patterns, and the fine arts have been rather neglected because they stood apart from the drift toward modernity. This procedure has defects, I am well aware, but I think it is genuinely superior to a chronicle of events and men, without any attempt to explain their meaning and indicate which were important for the future.

Finally, let me acknowledge the persons who contributed to this book. Professor Claude Sturgill read the manuscript and made several suggestions, which were followed. My

colleagues, Byron Davidson, Mary O'Quinn, Carol Waszkow-
ski, and Fr. William C. Morris made numerous comments
on the text and constantly prodded me toward what clarity
and precision this book possesses. Ms. Verson Alston did a
superb job in preparing the manuscript for the publisher.
Two history editors of Wiley, Carl Beers and Wayne Ander-
son, gave me generous support and if they were nagged
by doubts about the book kept it to themselves. Professor
C. Warren Hollister also read the manuscript and pointed
out several errors, since corrected. It may be, of course, that
errors still remain. If they do, I regret to say that they are
mine.

James D. Hardy, Jr.

Contents

PART I
MEDIEVAL SUNSET

CHAPTER
ONE
PROLOGUE : MIDCENTURY EUROPE

The Reformation, which convulsed Europe in the first half of the sixteenth century, was the last great wave of medieval reform, the legitimate successor to the Cluniac and Franciscan movements. It arose from much the same causes as did earlier reform movements. Anxiety concerning salvation, dissatisfaction with existing liturgical and sacramental forms, anger at the manifest corruption of clerics, dismay at the laxity of monastic life, and a genuine hunger for religious renewal all fired the zeal of religious reformers during the Reformation precisely as they had earlier. The goals of reformers, the spiritual needs of believers, and the articulation of issues followed a clearly medieval pattern.

In many of its characteristics, the Reformation resembled the earlier reform movements. As it had previously, the outpouring of religious concern began in the provinces, far from the great national and religious capitals. In the sixteenth century, religious renewal involved the bourgeoisie, artisans, and peasants far more than their betters, just as it always had. Once again, religious reformers demanded a sharp improvement in the conduct and morals of the clergy, and monarchs surveyed the religious upheavel searching for political and monetary advantage.

There were differences also, of course, and these differences have been most readily remembered. Previous waves of religious revival cemented the church more closely together, reduced regional differences in ceremony, organization, and practice, and enhanced the wide claims of the papal monarchy. The Reformation, however, split Christendom along its theological, national, liturgical, and linguistic fault lines. There emerged a plethora of churches, some hardly extending beyond a single congregation and others,

like the Lutherans, Anglicans, or Reformed, becoming large
national or multinational denominations. Universalism was
not the only casualty, although it was the most visible. Mo-
nasticism also suffered a partial repudiation. Earlier reform
movements had reinforced and enlarged the place of religious orders, and the Catholic Reformation moved strongly
in that direction. Protestant denominations, however, were
invariably hostile to monastic ideals and practice, and the
Protestants abolished them where they could. Finally, earlier reform movements had invariably increased the power
of the hierarchy over the parish priest and the authority of
the priest over laymen. Again, the Catholic Reformation followed this pattern, but Protestants reversed it. In many
Protestant sects, laymen gained control of their church.

By 1560, only one result of the Reformation seemed certain: Protestantism was going to survive, in spite of the Homeric efforts of the Counter-Reformation to lead the erring
brothers back. Other issues of the Reformation era still
sought solutions, however. European monarchs and statesmen knew that they faced the limitless catastrophe of civil
war. Religious passions had reached the dangerous tempera-
ture reserved today for race, and prevailing political doctrine and popular opinion denied that two religions could in-
habit one state. Although the bankruptcy and exhaustion
had brought the great powers to temporary peace in 1559,
no one thought it would last. Religious minorities were too
threatened and threatening. Nor were monarchs secure in
control over their own state church. Both pastors and cardi-
nals continued to argue for the superiority of religious over
secular concerns and demanded that the church be liberated
from state control.

The life of the mind, and its relationship to government
and society, was equally in turmoil. It was clear that the relatively free expression of ideas and opinion of the Renaissance was over. Philosophers also understood that the un-
leashed lust to save and convert was an enemy to thought
and reason. But, where were the bounds of heresy? Did heresy include only theological speculations and comments on

church government or clerical morals? Or were observations in astronomy or physiology also crimes against the Holy Ghost? No one knew. Priests and princes had not yet spoken.

Europe in 1560, therefore, was rather precariously balanced between the ecstasy of religious renewal and the travail of incorporating the new religious settlements into a stable political, institutional, social, and intellectual framework. The old, universal Christian church was gone. The new denominations were still volatile and unstable. New currents of thought disturbed ancient and comfortable verities. Renaissance monarchies, having survived reform itself, now faced the greater task of accommodating religion to the state. The future, viewed from 1560, was an incredible adventure for which few were prepared.

CHRONOLOGICAL CHART

Dates	England	France
1555		
1556		
1557	Major financial and banking crisis	Major financial and banking crisis
1558	Accession of Queen Elizabeth I	
1559		Death of Henry II
1562		Beginning of Wars of Religion
1563	Thirty-nine Articles of Religion	
1566		
1572		St. Bartholomew's Day Massacre
1576		
1581		
1589	Defeat of Spanish Armada	Accession of Henry IV
1598		Edict of Nantes
1603	Death of Elizabeth I Accession of James I	
1609		
1610		Assassination of Henry IV
1618		
1629		
1630		
1640	English Civil War	
1648		Treaties of Westphalia

Spain	Austria	The Netherlands
	Peace of Augsburg	
Accession of Philip II		
Major financial and banking crisis		Major financial and banking crisis
Beginning of Dutch Revolt		Beginning of Dutch Revolt
		Pacification of Ghent
Declaration of Dutch Independence		Declaration of Dutch Independence
Defeat of Spanish Armada		Defeat of Spanish Armada
Death of Philip II		
Truce with the Netherlands		Truce with Spain
	Beginning of Thirty Years' War	
	Edict of Restitution	
	Thirty Years' War becomes much wider as Sweden enters	
Revolt of Portugal and Catalonia		
Treaties of Westphalia	Treaties of Westphalia	Treaties of Westphalia

CHAPTER TWO

THE POLITICAL REFORMATION:
STATE CHURCHES AND RELIGIOUS WARS

"One Faith, One Law, One King."

French political proverb

"And the Lord said unto the
servant: Go into the highways
and the hedges and compel them
to come in that my house may
be filled. . . ."

Luke, 15:23 KJV

"We stand at Armageddon; we battle for the Lord," announced Teddy Roosevelt in the campaign of 1912. It was assumed he was speaking metaphorically. By the twentieth century, religious opinion was normally expressed in foreign missions, parochial schools, building programs, revivals, or vice crusades, not by burning at the stake. In 1560, Roosevelt would have been taken at his word. Reformation Christians were passionate believers in their faith, convinced that any deviation in word, deed, or dogma meant damnation. These attitudes encouraged religious persecution, which had the double virtue of being a respectable part of the Christian tradition and providing immense satisfaction to the persecutor. Hounding heretics did not remain a private recreation. It was elevated into an affair of state as kings organized the machinery of government to kill a Christian for Christ. The royal campaign for religious conformity went beyond defence of the True Faith; it also included the establishment of a state church. Religious dissent threatened the integrity of the realm and the authority of the king and, often enough, led to civil war. After midcentury, the politics of religion became more pressing than the definition of dogma and liturgy, as monarchs sought to control and direct their subjects' path to salvation.

Toward a State Church

In the sixteenth century, religious freedom meant that the Community of Saints who belonged to the One True Church would have to accept the open scandal of heresy, something clearly impossible. Theories of collective responsibility to God were still fresh. Could the Lord be expected to incline His face toward a community where many worshipped improperly? Were not heretics like the rocky ground wherein no good fruit could grow? Did not the king, who had sworn to uphold the True Faith, have the clear duty to lead his people to Heaven? He did, and most kings, frightened by the religious upheaval, attempted to fulfill this obligation by establishing a state church. Since no one could imagine the Church and state being separate, this was the only possibility.

The first modern state church was built in Spain and its American colonies by Ferdinand and Isabella, who combined genuine devotion to the faith with a high view of royal prerogatives. These remarkable monarchs foreclosed on the remaining autonomy of the medieval Roman Catholic Church and made it into a willing, and occasionally enthusiastic, partner in a general campaign to increase royal authority. Spanish monarchs had a dual program for the church. They used the power of the state to enforce a rigid doctrinal orthodoxy and used this same power to divest Catholicism of one of its main attributes—its ties with Rome and its international character.

The cornerstone of royal supremacy over the Spanish church was the royal patronage—the right of the crown to present to the major benefices. This was first wring from the papacy in 1486, as a reward for the conquest of Moorish Grenada. This initial grant was soon extended. In 1508 the crown received the royal patronage for its colonies and, in 1523, obtained the right to nominate bishops in all Spain. By

1560, no one but the king's friends held high church office in Spain, and loyalty to the crown was a major prerequisite for appointment. The crown was equally tenacious in squeezing taxes out of its church. In 1494, the crown obtained the royal third—one-third of all the tithes of Castile. This was supplemented by a crusading tax paid by the bishops. Beyond this, Ferdinand became the general of Castile's three crusading orders of knights—Santiago de Compostella, Alcantara, and Calatrava—and obtained these revenues for himself and his successors.

Spanish kings also became patrons of reform and renewal in the church. In 1491, the king received papal permission to reform the monasteries, which had fallen into a comfortable and civilized routine, dispensing with the primitive rigor of the monastic rule. This agreeable existence was destroyed when the crown drove the lax monks out, some to France where such reforms were not permitted and some to North Africa. Once begun, royal policing of monastic orders became sharper as Counter-Reformation zeal spread in Spain. Royal policing extended well beyond a single spate of monastic reform. The Inquisition was immensely expanded, and became the main vehicle for shielding the Spanish from impure notions by using methods common to a college dean or a policy spy. It was also the only institution that covered the entire peninsula, transcending the boundaries of the kingdoms that made up Spain. As an instrument of political control, the Inquisition was not as successful as it was in religious repression and persecution of Jews and Moors, but it still remained a valuable arm of secular power. The Spanish kings also aided new orders. The Jesuits, in particular, received royal patronage and aided in the pious program of reinforcing the Catholic faith and the king's authority. In the years after 1560, the number and variety of clerics in Spain grew enormously, until almost one-tenth of the nation were churchmen, and the church was the richest and largest and most privileged corporation in Spain.

In other states, this phenomenal clerical expansion would have been a distinct threat to royal independence. In Spain, it was not. Deep religious devotion and ferocious persecution were eminently compatable with Castilian character and mores, and royal patronage of the church won wide and genuine popularity for rather lackluster and unsuccessful Spanish kings. Beyond this, the crown shared in the increased power and wealth of the church, through clerical taxation, the royal patronage, and its support of reform. The alliance of throne and altar, a distant ideal in so many lands, was the basic political and psychological reality in early modern Spain.

The Spanish church, with its firm anchor to the crown and great wealth and piety, was the envy of princess and prelates elsewhere in Europe. It was a model of what could be done. Thus, the emperor, Charles V, who was also king of Spain, turned to the Spanish example when he tried to bring a quarter century of religious war to an end in Germany. Although Charles had won the battles, he could not win the war. The Lutheran princes would not give up their faith. Bankrupt and tired of fighting, Charles was willing to make peace on the basis of religious division. The Peace of Augsburg of 1555 enunciated the principle that the religion of the prince would determine the religion of his subjects. The formula was "cuius regio, eius, religio." This was hard on dissenters, particularly Calvinists and Radicals who were excluded from the settlement, but continuous war was worse, and the scheme won general approval.

The Augsburg settlement appealed to certain conventional political sentiments, as well as previous royal experience. Belief in the rights of kings was growing in the sixteenth century, and the Augsburg formula recognized it. The Peace of Augsburg also reaffirmed the ideals and reality of princely power within the Holy Roman Empire by giving the princes untrammeled authority over the greatest issue of the day. Finally, "cuius regio, eius religio" placed the responsibility for religious affairs safely in the hands of secular authorities where it obviously belonged. Priests and theologians had the unfortunate habit of dividing over trifles and then convincing segments of the faithful that their salvation hung on this nonsense. They were doing it now. Only the princes could squelch religious reformers and reestablish peace and order in the world.

In England, also, the crown and the people struggled toward a national church. In theory, at least, England had had one since the Act of Supremacy of Henry VIII in 1534. Henry himself desired as little actual reform as possible, but this desire had collapsed before the steady Protestant drift of English religious thought. By 1553, when Queen Mary came to the throne determined to restore England to papal obedience, it was too late. All Mary could do was establish formal acceptance of Catholicism and conduct an ineffective persecution of some salient Protestants. Her death in 1558 brought to the throne Elizabeth I, who was known to sympathize with Protestant opinion. The English church prepared for another shift in official doctrine.

Elizabeth I was far shrewder than her sister Mary, and her aim was not doctrinal uniformity but religious peace. She pursued this goal in partnership with Parliament, an echo of the politics of her father. The Parliament of 1559 gave Elizabeth the essential legislation she wanted. An Act of Supremacy reestablished the crown as the "Supreme Governor" of the English church, and an Act of Uniformity gave the Church of England a prayer book that was protestant in tone but made several concessions to Catholic opinion. In addition, Elizabeth halted the persecutions and allowed the exiles to drift home. In 1563 she issued the Thirty-Nine Articles of Religion, which stated the Anglican doctrine and ecclesiology in such vague terms that everyone but a Moslem could accept them. The aim of the Thirty-Nine Articles was to include as many shades of opinion as possible, and to soften hard doctrinal points of difference with vague and conciliatory language. Finally, Elizabeth cast a hard eye on the antics of Anglican bishops and priests, kept their zeal within reason, and treated Englishmen who did not support the state church as loyal subjects.

Although Elizabeth avoided civil war, and confined religious disputes within the bounds of good public order, she was not able to control the direction of religious thought in

England. Calvinist Protestantism grew in spite of the success of the Tudor monarchy and its established church. Protestant critics of the Anglicans were called Puritans because of their desire to purify Anglicanism of its faults and replace it with a communion both more coherent and far narrower than the existing establishment. Puritans wanted to rid Anglicanism of "Popery," which meant the bishops, the vestments, the Book of Common Prayer, the ritual, and the liturgical form of worship. The congregation would replace the parish, with the powers of the laity increased, sermons enhanced, and communion reduced in importance. Simplicity would replace elaboration. The doctrine also needed reform. Puritans opposed sacramental worship and wished to abolish the mass. Passages in the Thirty-Nine Articles on grace were insufficiently precise for the Puritans who wanted a clear statement of the predestinarian view. Such reforms would establish a Presbyterian doctrine, divine service, and form of ecclesiastical polity and, in the process, sharply reduce the powers of the crown over organized religion.

The Queen could never accept this. It would alienate too many people. Elizabeth I maintained a steady hostility toward the Puritans and, on occasion, harassed them. In 1573, she outlawed Puritan meetings and, in 1593, persuaded Parliament to pass a law against them. These measures, along with the Queen's great popularity and prestige, prevented the Puritans from unduly disturbing the established ways. Nonetheless, Puritan arguments became increasingly convincing and, by the reign of James I (1603–1624), Puritanism was accounted a serious menace to the stability of the state.

In some countries, monarchs failed in their efforts to found a national church, in spite of hard and persistent work. The salient case was France, where rising authority of the monarch in the early sixteenth century and the traditions of the Gallican church made royal control over religious institutions seem legitimate and proper. In 1516, Francis I signed the Concordat of Bologna and got the right to nominate all bishops and important abbots in France. This substantial addition to royal power was badly used. The

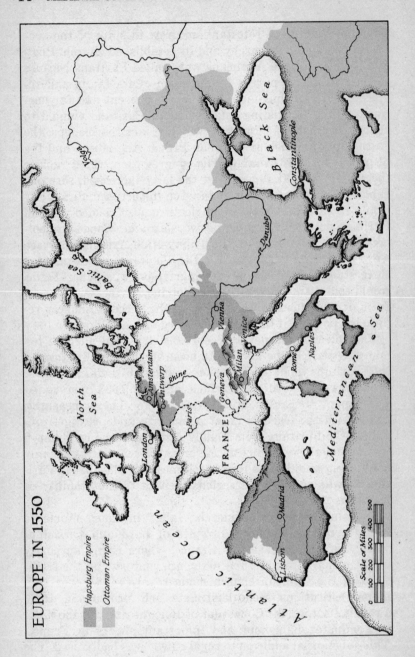

EUROPE IN 1550

Hapsburg Empire
Ottoman Empire

royal appointees were interested in the power, prestige, and revenues of their posts and not in reform. They tolerated wide abuses. Monks were allowed to ignore the rule, nuns were seen with men, priests were often absentee pastors, clerical ignorance was widespread, ecclesiastical justice was sold, and the bishops intrigued constantly to get new revenues and benefices and have their sons or nephews succeed them. The Cardinal of Lorraine held 14 major benefices, was absentee in all, and dispensed a vast amount of ecclestiastical patronage. His career was outstanding only in the size of his income and the number of benefices he accumulated. The crown did little to correct such clerical appointees. Instead of supporting church reform, French monarchs encouraged the same abuses that had led to the Reformation in Germany, England, Switzerland, and the Low Countries. Thus, the Concordat of Bologna was a mixed bargain for both sides. While it meant that France and her king would remain Catholic, it also meant that the French church would be unable to convert or destroy the Protestants. Such a stalemate could only lead to civil war.

In retrospect, it is clear that a state church was a reasonable solution to the alternatives of civil war only when accompanied by genuine religious reform, led by the king. Promises alone, in which French kings excelled, were insufficient. Persecution alone and the policy of the Spanish in the Low Countries only aroused the already dangerous zeal of dissenters. Anxious about salvation, Europeans of all classes demanded substantial religious renewal. People might be persuaded that this species of reform was better than that, but they were not prepared to accept no reform at all. This seems a simple lesson, even for kings and the reverend clergy. It was not.

Wars of Religion

Sixteenth-century monarchs strove to establish and protect their state churches with a kind of touching desperation because the consequence of failure was civil war. The heightened religious passions of the Reformation were not always amenable to royal direction, however. Many people preferred martyrdom to compromise. Monarchs frequently stung outraged zealots among their subjects to acts of revolt. In France and the Low Countries, and later in Bohemia and England, governments and peoples moved to this sinister form of confrontation. These confrontations in no way involved religious toleration, though the minority sect usually made some vague mention of that most untraditional virtue. Instead, religious warfare meant an armed attempt by dissident Christians to set up a state church, to which everyone must belong, different in doctrine and liturgy and organization from what the king had in mind. Such wicked enterprises normally failed, and the king, after some serious difficulties, put his own state church in power. In an age when church and state were inseparable, religious war only postponed the inevitable and prolonged the agony.

After 1560, major religious revolts were invariably the work of Calvinists. Lutherans, Anglicans, and Roman Catholics settled into patterns of the alliance of throne and altar with fairly good grace. Calvin's doctrine of the independence of the church from the state, and the fact that Calvinists were almost always a decided religious minority, demanded that Calvinists reject the concept of state church. Instead, they slowly elaborated a theory of the right of a Christian (Calvinist) to revolt against a godless tyrant. Moreover, the tight organization of the Calvinist congregation, bound together by common beliefs and policed in morals and doctrine by elected deacons and elders, made it an ideal revolutionary cell. This tight community life, combined with the exhalted feeling of being God's small band of elect, drew communicants to Calvinism. As the Calvinist minority grew in France, the Low Countries, England, or Bohemia, and as religious persecution grew with it, the more zealous Calvinists moved inexorably toward revolt.

In France, the wars of religion began with the confluence of several trends and events. Calvinism had grown so rapidly in the 1550s, particularly among the bourgeoisie and nobility, that Catholics were seriously alarmed and demanded that the king persecute the heretics. But the king could not. The years after the royal bankruptcy of 1557 were ones of decline. France lost the war with Spain, King Henry II got himself impaled on a lance in a tourney in 1559, and his sons and successors were not only children, they were stupid, sickly, ignorant, and weak. Royal authority, therefore, became the prize in a deadly struggle between the wily and corrupt queen mother, Catherine de Medici, and the three greatest families of France, the Catholic Guise, the largely Protestant Bourbon, and the religiously mixed Montmorency. Under these conditions, royal aid in the pious work of persecution could only be sporadic and ineffectual. Both Catholics and Calvinists, therefore, settled in to do the job themselves.

In spite of the frantic attempts by the crown to keep the peace, religious war began by private massacre in 1562. A group of Catholics at Vassy murdered about 30 Protestants. This naturally provoked counter atrocities by Protestants. Slowly, a war of pillage and butchery spread over France. The spread of religious mayhem and massacre, which disturbed the government as much as it soothed inflamed religious passions, held great political significance. War ended the drift toward Protestantism. Indeed, it reversed it. Slowly, families reassessed the implications of belonging to the religious minority and returned to the old faith. War also added treason against the king to the crimes of the heretic, and gave French Calvinism a suspicious, occasionally pathological republican flavor. Moreover, the crown swung back to loyal Catholicism and began to search for ways to end the war by destroying the Protestants.

Having abandoned hope for a diplomatic solution to religious war, Catherine de Medici threw herself into the hands of the ultra-Catholic Guise family, which was desperate to return to power. Opportunity came with the marriage of the Huguenot leader, Henry of Navarre to the king's sister, Margaret. Many Huguenots were in Paris attending the wedding and, on October 23, 1572, St. Bartholomew's Day, they were massacred. Of the Protestant leaders, only Henry of Navarre and his cousin, the Prince of Conde, survived. About 6000 others were butchered.

The massacre of St. Bartholomew's Day did not end the wars or eliminate Protestantism. The Huguenots closed ranks, with the ministers and urban bourgeoisie assuming the leadership. Moreover, not all French Catholics were enchanted by Catherine's program of slaughter. Many were outraged, and many others saw Catherine's policy leading to the partition of France or the domination of Spain. Moderate Catholics, who placed peace and their country ahead of religious passions took the name *politiques,* and rallied to the banner of Henry of Navarre. By 1575, the *politiques* and Huguenots controlled all France south of the Loire river, and had established their own government in defiance of the Queen Mother, who was now forced to grant limited toleration to Protestants. The policy of Catholic repression had failed.

Limited toleration of Protestants, desultory civil war, and widespread disobedience to the crown characterized French politics in the decade after 1575. This abruptly changed in 1584 when the Catholic crown prince died. Next in line was the Protestant Henry of Navarre, and Catholics faced the prospect of being ruled by a heretic. It was too much. The Duke of Guise formed a Holy League, financed by Spain and tied to Philip II's hopes of gaining the French crown for himself. Enjoying strong papal support, the Holy League soon grew into a major political force. It maintained an army, intimidated the king and Catherine de Medici, collected taxes, and conducted its own foreign and domestic policy. In 1585, Henry III was forced to revoke all edicts of toleration for Protestants and, in 1588, the League took over Paris, forcing the king into exile. Henry III struck back and had Guise murdered. Infuriated, the League partisans called for the assassination of the tyrant and, in August, 1589, Henry was stabbed by a Dominican friar. The new king, Henry of Navarre, was a Protestant.

Henry IV (1589–1610) was a welcome change from his incompetent, and sometimes degenerate, predecessors. He was strong and healthy, hunted and fought well, and enjoyed a degree of mental health that would astound a psychologist. He was amiable and generous and could hold his liquor. He chased women and caught them. Henry's shrewdness and good sense came through his most famous sentence:

". . . I hope to make France so prosperous that every peasant will have a chicken in his pot on Sunday"

He meant that, and everybody knew it.

Possessed of sound military talents and great political skills, Henry IV began to claim his country. He was the legitimate king, and Catholic nobles and towns slowly came over to his side. Frenchmen were ready for peace and the *politique* position. In 1593, Henry IV converted to Catholicism, remarking that "Paris is worth a mass." He entered his capital and began a systematic reduction of the remaining League fortresses. By 1598, it was all but over. The Spanish were driven out, the provinces pacified, and Henry issued the Edict of Nantes, an attempt to bring the religious wars to a political solution. In the Edict, Henry granted liberty of conscience to all Protestants, and liberty of worship to Protestants in selected towns. As a guarantee of their limited religious liberty, Huguenots were given the right to garrison about 400 towns, mostly in southern France, and Huguenot judges were placed on the major royal courts.

The Edict of Nantes ended the war. It acknowledged the basic Catholic victory by restricting the practice of Calvinism, banning it from Paris, and insuring a Catholic monarch. French Catholics, recently touched by the fervor of the Counter-Reformation, were more intent than ever on converting the Huguenots. For the Huguenots, Nantes was merely an armed truce. Faced with a reviving Catholicism and a Catholic monarchy, they could hope for no more than simple survival. They knew that Catholics, the overwhelming majority of France, would tolerate Calvinism no better after the Edict than before it. Thus, the real guarantee of the Edict of Nantes and religious peace was Henry IV himself. A strong king, intent on increasing royal powers, Henry refused to allow religious divisions to be the occasion for war. His successors departed from this pragmatic and secular policy and, within a generation, royal persecution of Huguenots had begun again. It did not end until after the middle of the eighteenth century.

Religious war in France had a parallel in the Low Countries. The religious zeal of a Calvinist minority placed insupportable burdens on the king, who was barred by both doctrine and inclination from toleration. As in France, many Catholics found the extreme measures of persecution abhorrent, and the heretics were joined by Catholics who wanted peace and compromise. Again, as in France, the war dragged on for years as both sides spurned compromise. There were also significant differences. In France, the Catholic and royal side won; in the Low Countries, the Calvinist, Dutch rebels defeated the king. In France, the war remained primarily a civil conflict, while the Dutch war for independence was an international struggle. In the Low Countries, an embryonic nationalism was added to religious passions. In such a conflict, exhaustion could be the only excuse for peace.

Until 1560, the Low Countries had enjoyed a general although unofficial religious toleration. Commercial interests had prevailed over religious ones, and the Spanish crown, anxious to tax and borrow money in the Low Countries, refrained from too vigorous a search for heterodoxy. The Spanish king also tolerated a wide measure of local self-government, inherited from the ramshackle rule of the Burgundian dukes. These two elements reinforced each other, as the nobility and urban patriciate of the Low Countries tended to equate royal persecutions with royal centralization and defended heresy under the banner of medieval privileges and legitimate government.

In 1559, Philip II of Spain had decided to reform the government of the Low Countries as his ancestors had done in Castile. He was going to hound Dutch and Belgian heretics with the same zeal and efficiency shown in Spain and Italy. He began with the church. In 1559, Philip II obtained a papal bull rearranging the diosceses of the Low Countries so that their territory would all be in Philip's domains and their superior would be the new Archbishop of Malines. For this post Philip had a devoted royal servant, Cardinal Granvelle. This measure provoked immense hostility, both lay and clerical. Popular outcry was supported by the overt disobedience of the magnates. It took the army to install some of the new bishops.

Anger over the bishops was reinforced by revamping the Inquisition. The Inquisition in the Low Countries had only limped along, overlooking the most obvious heretics, and totally without the obscene glee of its Castilian cousin. Philip pushed his viceroys in Brussels to pump some life into the Inquisition. When Granvelle and his subordinates tried, they ran into intense local hostility. Witch hunts were bad for business, reduced the confidence of the investor, and trampled upon local privileges. The Netherlanders were against it.

Philip also tampered with taxes and banking. In 1569 he instructed his viceroy, the Duke of Alva, to collect a new sales tax, the Tenth Penny, fashion on the Castilian model. In a region where commerce, not agriculture, supported people, the Tenth Penny would have been a dreadful blow. The towns and nobility of the Low Countries resisted its establishment and persuaded Alva to postpone it for two years. But they could not talk him out of it altogether. Netherlanders saw Philip II consistently sacrifice the interests of the Low Countries to Spanish religious prejudices. That led to revolt.

The first spasm of revolution occurred in the late summer of 1566. Calvinist cloth workers and petty bourgeoisie, goaded by their pastors, their zeal, their hatred of the Spanish, and their social grievances, sacked Catholic churches, destroying the statuary, communion plate, breaking up the altars, and murdering the priests. The furious destruction ended only when the symbols of the old faith lay in ruins.

The Calvanist Fury began at Poperinghe on August 14, spreading northward to the great cities of Antwerp, Ghent, Amsterdam, and Utrecht. A month later it was over. The mob simply went home to their jobs, their rage exhausted. Terrified, the government had done nothing.

Philip II was shocked and outraged. He sent the ruthless Duke of Alva as viceroy to Brussels with 20,000 Spanish veterans and instructions to crush foul heresy and revolution. Alva was a hard man, who combined aristocratic arrogance with a taste for blood. Alva moved at once to smash dissent. His Council of Blood dealt with the great nobility who had become Protestant or were lukewarm toward the government. The army marched against the towns. The Inquisition followed. Municipal privileges were destroyed. Heretics were rounded up. The new tax of the Tenth Penny was imposed. The Low Countries were at last being governed like Castile.

At first, Alva carried all before him. He struck with such force that no single town or noble could resist. But it was a transient triumph. Alva intimidated, but he did not convert. Opposition soon transcended Calvinism and became patriotism. As such, it was irresistible. When a group of Dutch Calvinist sailors captured the island town of The Brill in 1572, open revolt spread rapidly. Flushing fell next, and the Spanish garrison evacuated Middleburg, capital of the province of Zeeland. By 1574, the provinces of Holland and Zeeland were in the hands of Calvinist rebels, and the Spanish were in retreat everywhere. The Spanish sack of Antwerp and Ghent simply added to Dutch anger. By 1576, revolt was so general that all the provinces of the Low Countries signed the Pacification of Ghent, in which they pledged unity to drive out the Spaniards. Religious differences were submerged in an attempt at nationhood.

In this crisis, Philip II sent his best general to the Low Countries. This was Alexander of Parma, an Italian duke descended from popes, shrewd and subtle, as clever in dissimulation as he was decisive in war, far abler and more realistic than Philip himself and, incredible in a politician, he was a man of dignity and courage. As soon as he arrived in Brussels in 1578, Parma played upon the differences between the largely Catholic and Flemish provinces of the south and the more Protestant Dutch provinces north of the Rhine river. By promising southern provinces their political liberties, he was able to restore obedience to the King of Spain.

The Protestant north was not appeased by promises. In 1581, they declared independence from Spain, and made William of Orange, the leading Protestant noble of the Netherlands, *Stadhouder,* a sort of king. The war settled into conflict between Dutch and Fleming, between Catholic and Calvinist.

Parma had an excellent army, and he pushed campaigns for the conquest of the north. He enjoyed a certain success, recapturing Antwerp and confining the rebellion largely to Holland and Zeeland. This was good work, but it could not end the war. Parma could never capture the major Dutch cities, Amsterdam, Hoorn, Rotterdam, Utrecht, and Leyden, which were protected by rivers and the Dutch navy. The Dutch held absolute naval supremacy in the rivers and along the coast and, more and more, in the ocean as well. Thus, the Dutch held out, in spite of losing battles, in spite of losing territory. Time was a Dutch ally; they had merely to wait out the Parma cyclone and then win the war against his unworthy successors.

The decisive factor in the eventual Dutch victory was the war at sea. The conflict that thrice-bankrupted Spain (1575, 1595, and 1608) built the framework of Dutch wealth. The Dutch shut off Flemish commerce, and appropriated Flemish markets for themselves. Amsterdam replaced Antwerp as the market and banking center of northern Europe. The Dutch invaded Spanish markets in the new world, took over the slave trade, and gained a near monopoly in spices. They turned to commerce raiding and drove Spanish merchantmen from the seas. In the sixteenth century, war was an expensive business that ruined the greatest kings, but the Dutch grew rich from it, a phenomenon hitherto unheard of.

When the Spanish accepted a 10-year truce in 1609, they were so thoroughly beaten that Spain had begun its long descent from the ranks of the Great Powers.

The Spanish Habsburgs were not alone in being affected by religious dissent and allied political rebellion. Their Austrian cousins also suffered from these twin plagues. In Austria, Protestantism affected most of the crown lands and was a particular problem in Bohemia, where Calvinism grafted itself on the native Hussite heterodoxy. The Austrian emperors in the sixteenth century were unable to mount efficient and continuous programs against their Protestant subjects; the Turks were too close, the royal income was too small, and provincial privileges were too substantial. Thus, the Austrian monarchs slid into a sort of quasi-toleration. They did not like it, and various popes berated them for it, but it was the best they could do.

This began to change when Ferdinand of Styria became emperor in 1619. He was a strict Catholic and a strong believer in royal absolutism. As soon as he entered upon his inheritance, Ferdinand had both these values challenged. The Protestant nobility and gentry of Bohemia, anxious about the safety of their religion and privileges, revolted against the monarch. In 1618, they expelled the imperial officials from Prague and elected the Protestant Frederick, the Elector Palatine, as king of Bohemia. Aided by the Catholic League of German princes, Ferdinand invaded Bohemia and defeated the Protestant forces at White Mountain in 1620. He threw Frederick out, executed the leading rebels, destroyed provincial privileges, and began the elimination of Protestantism in Bohemia. It was the opening round in the Thirty Years War.

Had the war remained confined to Bohemia, restricted to hanging nobles who fought for provincial liberty or the butchery of Protestant peasants, the Bohemian episode might have remained a footnote in the annals of political rebellion and religious crimes. But Ferdinand pursued his enemy into Germany and involved both Catholic and Protestant states in an expanded conflict. Ferdinand's victory over

Frederick, and the consequent extension of Catholic power, brought Christian IV of Denmark in as the Protestant champion. The Catholic League, supported by the revamped imperial army under Albert of Wallenstein, routed poor Christian and drove him out of the war. Christian's collapse was followed by the Catholic conquest of most of northern Germany. The symbol of Catholic victory was the imperial Edict of Restitution of 1629, which declared that all ecclesiastical property secularized since 1552 must be returned to the church, and toleration would extend only to Lutherans. This threatened to so upset the precarious religious balance in Germany that many thought that Protestantism would not survive. It also reversed 300 years of German constitutional development, in which the princes had been getting stronger and the emperor weaker.

Such developments were impossible for two powerful neighbors of the Holy Roman Empire. France, a state rapidly gaining in internal coherence, could not allow Germany to be dominated by her ancient Habsburg enemies. Protestant Sweden, ruled by the warrior king Gustavus Adolphus, was unwilling to see a united Germany or a Catholic one. France, unready to intervene herself, was prepared to give Gustavus Adolphus financial and diplomatic support for a crusade that was anti-Habsburg and Protestant. With the entry of Sweden in 1630, the Thirty Years War turned from a religious conflict into one in which political motives counted for as much as the faith.

Gustavus Adolphus was a superior general, and he was able to defeat the troops of the Catholic League and the Emperor at Breitenfeld (1631) and Lutzen (1632), where he was killed. But the Swedish forces were too small to drive their enemies out of the war or conquer northern Germany. For their part, the imperial forces, particularly after the assassination of Wallenstein in 1634, were generally unable to win the battles. Even the entrance of the French into the war in 1635 did not change this strategic equation. The Habsburg emperors never regained the position of political and religious dominance they enjoyed in 1629, although the progress made in centralizing the Austrian crown lands and in eliminating Protestantism in Austria, Bohemia, and southern Germany was permanent. In northern Germany the Protestants survived, and the Edict of Restitution was never enforced. As for the German princes, they emerged from the Thirty Years War with their powers intact. Thus, the religious and political situation in 1648, when the Treaties of Westphalia ended the Thirty Years War, was the same as it had been in 1625 before the disasterous Danish intervention.

Although the last 23 years of the war had brought no changes in the ultimate form of the peace settlement, the various states had continued fighting. Monarchs and ministers were reluctant to admit their war aims could not be won. The religious passions inflamed in 1618 died hard and slowly. The political ambitions that swallowed them up were abandoned with even greater reluctance. The peoples of Germany paid for this. As the war spread over central Europe, the brutality and destruction grew with it. Unable to win victory in battle, armies tried pillage. Sacked in 1631, Magdeburg was completely destroyed, and 24,000 of its 30,000 inhabitants were butchered. Perhaps one-fifth of all Germans died of slaughter, disease, or starvation. Trade and agriculture collapsed. Whole villages were abandoned by their peasants. When peace finally came at Westphalia in 1648, it came from exhaustion and from the realization that Germany could not be conquered and religious uniformity could not be attained. Indeed, the Treaties of Westphalia were an explicit recognition that the religious wars were over. No one thought they were worth it.

In England, as well as in the Holy Roman Empire, a religious compromise, seemingly well established in 1600, broke down in the seventeenth century. The Anglican solution neutralized Catholic opinion but failed to stem or satisfy the Calvinist Puritans. The government and the Puritans were moving in opposite directions. The Puritans demanded greater simplicity in the liturgy, criticized the bishops, and insisted on the rigid enforcement of varous antisocial

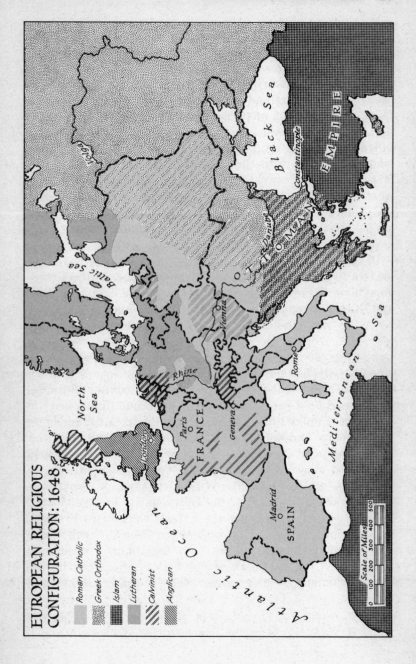

EUROPEAN RELIGIOUS
CONFIGURATION: 1648

Roman Catholic
Greek Orthodox
Islam
Lutheran
Calvinist
Anglican

"blue laws". The Anglicans were undergoing a liturgical revival and were moving toward greater uniformity of ceremony and discipline. The appointment of William Laud as Archbishop of Canterbury in 1633 brought the hierarchy of the Church of England into a total war with Puritanism. Laud's appointment was accompanied by increasing persecution. Authors of books denouncing the episcopacy were fined, jailed and, not infrequently, had their ears cut off. Priests who deviated from the prescribed forms of ritual were dismissed. Puritan conventicles, held in defiance of the law, were broken up. "No bishop, no king," James I (1603–1625) had retorted and, by 1633, Charles I (1625–1649) had staked the prestige, even the life, of the government on adherence to this formula and all it implied.

In 1637, Charles I began the final acts of religious folly that led to a civil war and his execution at the hands of the victorious Oliver Cromwell. Charles ordered the Anglican hierarchy and liturgy extended to Presbyterian Scotland. Attempts to read the English liturgy in Edinburgh moved the Scots to riot and then to war. Charles lacked the money to fight them, and, in 1640, he was forced to call Parliament, something he had not done for 11 years.

When Parliament met in April, 1640, it focused all the religious and political discontents of the nation in one body in one place. England had elected mostly Puritans to the House of Commons, and these were also the men who had most vigorously opposed Charles' attempts at personal rule and held the widest views of the prerogatives of Parliament.[1] Political issues, which revolved around Parliament's rights over taxation as opposed to the king's prerogative to govern as he wanted without consulting the nation, were more pressing and crucial in England than they had been in France, the Holy Roman Empire, or the Low Countries. Politics had clearly been present in these previous religious butcheries, but in England secular issues were probably paramount.

[1] Politics belongs more properly in Chapter 7 on the organization of the state and will be treated in detail there.

There were several reasons for this. Certainly, the existence and traditions of the English Parliament provided a focus for organized political opposition to the crown. There were representative institutions elsewhere, but only in the Netherlands were they strong enough to challenge the king successfully in an age of growing royal power. Again, in England, the religious confrontation came a generation later than it did in the Empire, and three generations than the confessional slaughters in France and the Netherlands. Religious passions had already begun to lose their pristine savagery. Furthermore, the war in England was between two competing brands of Protestants, one of which—the Puritans—howled as much for reforming the Anglicans as for obliterating them. English religious opinion never achieved that quintessential hatred so common across the Channel. So most Englishmen fought primarily for or against Parliament (or the king) and at one remove for or against the Church of England. Nonetheless, in spite of the above, godly grievances were bitterly real to seventeenth-century Englishmen, and the English revolution witnessed the temporary destruction of the Anglican church, thus fulfilling the prophecy of James I.

Conclusions

For more than a century and a half, Europeans fought unremitting and savage struggles over religion. Out of this vast and gloomy conflict emerged a compromise, differing from the religious configurations of 1565 only in detail. The haulings and tuggings, the mayhems and massacres, and the obscene bawlings of pastors over the course of an entire century had led to only fractional Catholic advantages. The principal sects of 1560—Anglicans, Calvinists, Lutherans, and Roman Catholics—still stood a century later. Although the Catholics had made gains in Bohemia, southern Germany, Hungary, and Poland, they had failed by a wide margin to achieve their announced aim of returning Europe to a single faith. Coercion had not worked.

After 1660, the grotesque passion to burn or convert ebbed rapidly in most Europeans of all classes, at least among the laity. There was a steady decline of belief in the idea that a single faith was necessary for political stability. Loyalty to religion became secondary to loyalty to a king or state. In many Europeans the idea took hold that religion was a private, not a public matter. Others simply cared less about it than their parents had. Ministers, seeing the useless wreckage caused by confessional strife, advised their monarchs against it. A few free and wicked spirits even began to suspect that the differences between the various Christian sects were minor, that no sect was susceptable to rational proof of superiority over another, that it was all personal preference, and that religious persecution was a low and un-Christian act. In 1660, this view was still quite rare, but its day was coming. Put simply, the compulsion to persecute was dying, the efforts at persecution were seen to be exhausting and unsatisfactory, and it was these reasons, more than some others, that signaled the end of an era of religious conflict.

BIBLIOGRAPHY

1. Reformation Background

J. Hurstfield, ed., *The Reformation Crisis,* is a series of short, simple articles on various aspects of the Reformation. They are invariably clear and easy to understand. Highly recommended.

2. General Political Accounts

Richard S. Dunn, *The Age of Religious Wars: 1559–1689,* is a short survey, part of a larger text. It is excellent and easy to read, with wide coverage and clear explanations. Highly recommended.

J. H. Elliott, *Europe Divided, 1559–1598,* is an excellent and detailed narrative of the politics, war, and diplomacy of the last half of sixteenth century. Highly recommended.

3. National Histories and Specialized Accounts

J. H. Elliott, *Imperial Spain,* is a superb book. It describes Spain from 1469 to 1700, with the main emphasis on the period before 1598. By far the best book of Spain, it is clear, balanced, with no heavy bias either for or against counter-Reformation Spain. Highly recommended and essential for the student interested in Spain.

Sir John Neale, *The Age of Catherine de Medici,* is also a marvelous book. Short and beautifully written, it deals with France from 1559 to 1589. Heavy emphasis on period before 1575. Highly recommended.

Charles Wilson, *The Dutch Republic,* deals with seventeenth century Netherlands. Good on imperialism and trade, weak on politics and diplomacy.

Pieter Geyl, *The Revolt of the Netherlands, 1555–1609,* is a detailed account of the Dutch revolt, with a heavy emphasis on the background of rebellion.

C. V. Wedgwood, *Richelieu and the French Monarchy,* is a good, short study of the end of religious wars in France, French participation in the Thirty Years War, and the development of French government.

31

C. V. Wedgwood, *The Thirty Years War,* is a long, detailed, and outstanding book on that dismal conflict. Heavy emphasis on the
period from 1618 to 1635. Highly recommeneded.

Garrett Mattingly, *The Armada,* a superb, beautifully written diplomatic and political account of the events of 1587–1589 and of the
tremendous Spanish defeat. Highly recommended.

A. L. Rowse, *The England of Elizabeth,* is an admiring portrait of
late sixteenth-century England. Highly favorable to Elizabeth.

Sir John Neale, *Queen Elizabeth I,* another favorable treatment, this
one by the leading Elizabethan scholar. An excellent, although serious and scholarly book.

C. Hill, *The Century of Revolution,* is a rather Marxist interpretation
of seventeenth-century England. This is a lively book and is easy
to read.

4. A Single Primary Source

Johann Jakob von Grimmelshausen, *Simplicius Simplicissimus* (1668),
is a picaresque novel by veteran of the Thirty Years War who
rose from private to regimental adjutant. In the novel, Grimmelshausen recorded some of his war experiences in colloquial and
brisk language. The novel goes beyond the anguish, atrocities, and
tedium of war. It is also a tale of the hero's spiritual development,
set against the endless war. The hero begins as a naive saint and
ends as one, while in between he is a rogue and soldier and a success. The zenith of his wordly success is the nadir of his spiritual
development. This is a major book and is highly recommended.

CHAPTER THREE

EUROPE OVERSEAS: THE GROWTH OF EMPIRE

"But I came to get gold, not to
till the soil like a peasant."

Hernan Cortez

"Colonies are the strength of the
Kingdom . . . while they are made to
observe the fundamental laws of
this original country, and while
they are dependent upon it."

Charles Davenant

On April 2, 1595, a modest fleet of four small vessels
sailed from Holland toward a far place. The captains had no
maps and relied for their route on hearsay, gossip, and speculation. They were to sail around Africa to the Indies and
capture the Portuguese spice trade. They hoped to make a
fortune and strike a blow at the Spanish who ruled Portugal
and were at war with the Netherlands. Conscience and inclination rode together, a happy circumstance all too rare in
human affairs.

The trip was a major turning point in European colonial
history. The Dutch, once embarked on colonial adventure,
created an immense empire of colonies and commerce. The
Portuguese and Spanish, once they had slipped into decline,
lost much of their empire and the profits from all of it. This
Dutch voyage was also symbolic of changing patterns of European power and prosperity, which was shifting from the
Mediterranean to the Atlantic. In the seventeenth century,
the Dutch, French, and English would rule Europe as the
Spanish had during the Reformation.

The commercial and colonial power the Dutch reached for in the first decades of the new century was a basic part of calculations about politics and diplomacy at home. Colonial empires had meant stupendous wealth. The river of silver that ran from Peru to Spain impressed Reformation statesmen as much as the wild howling of theologians and preachers. No one doubted that Spanish political predominance rested on America, or that the brief, bright glory of Portugal came from colonial trade. When contemporary statesmen analyzed Iberian decadence, they saw imperial defeat at the hands of the Dutch. When they meditated on Dutch power and prosperity, so maddening in a time of general distress, they saw the accoutrements of imperialism: colonies, joint stock companies, and fleets. When the statesmen advised their kings on the ways to wealth and power, they stressed the need to emulate the Dutch. "What we want is more of the trade that the Dutch have," said the Duke of Albemarle before the Dutch war of 1664. No one argued with that statement. It expressed the general view.

I

Portugal was the first European colonial power, acquiring some African islands and trading stations during the fifteenth century. After the voyage of Vasco da Gama to India in 1497, Portugal swiftly conquered an empire that stretched from Mozambique to Macao and included forts and trading stations in India, Ceylon, and Indonesia. At home King Manoel the Fortunate (1495–1521) presided over a genuine boom, as Lisbon became the western trade center for spices. A spacious prosperity and an exciting sense of power and optimism had rewarded imperial enterprise.

Though vast in extent, and potentially rich, the Portuguese empire had serious structural and economic deficiencies. Naval superiority in the Indian Ocean was maintained only because Portugal's enemies were so badly divided that they could never combine against her. Portuguese merchants never exploited the full trade possibilities in the Far East.

Even at their best, in the 1520s through the 1540s, the Portuguese seldom carried more than 15 percent of the spices. The rest went by Arab ship to Egypt. Nor did the Portuguese exploit the trade in silks and tea or calicoes and cottons, which were far more valuable than spices. These items remained in the hands of Asians and Arabs. The Portuguese simply did not have the ships to carry much beyond spices, which brought the highest profits. An additional problem was the Portuguese propensity to loot. The Portuguese never understood that loot and trade were incompatible, and they pirated Arab ships and seized the goods of Asian merchants as standard practice.

Economic difficulties were compounded by administrative ones. The Portuguese empire was not composed of colonies but of forts and trading stations. Most of these sheltered only a few dozen Portuguese, and at Goa, seat of the Viceroy, there were not more than a few thousand. These scattered stations remained alien outposts among the Arabs, Indians, or Indonesians, and the officials in them, unregulated on the spot, were equally beyond reproof from home. Portuguese officials carried corruption and graft to new levels of ingenuity and greed. They stole from the king, received bribes from merchants, cheated on taxes, and stole from the natives. "In India there is no justice," wrote the High Judge of Goa, "either in your Viceroy or in those who are to mete it out. The one object is 'the gathering of money by any means.' There is no Moor who will trust a Portuguese. Help us, Señor, for we are sinking."[1]

After the middle of the century, these disabilities combined to drag the Portuguese from profit to loss. After 1560 only one of three ships returned from the two-year voyage to the East, as opposed to better than half earlier. The reestablishment of the Venetian spice trade after 1550 cut into Portuguese profits at a time of general inflation and rising costs. The Portuguese also grew weary and conservative after the

[1] Letter of the judge and alderman of Goa to the king, November 25, 1552, in George Masselman, *The Cradle of Colonialism*, 221.

middle of the century. There was more profit in administration and graft, and the Portuguese had neither the money nor energy to set their imperial affairs in order. They did not develop the silk, tea, or calico trade, invest to expand the sugar or slave trades, or keep up the navy. These difficulties were compounded by the accession of Philip II of Spain to the Portuguese throne in 1580. Tied to the fortunes of Spain, Portugal became a prominent victim of Spanish decline. The Portuguese empire had been started by Prince Henry the Navigator, one of the genuinely original men of early modern Europe, who amply fulfilled the predictions of his astrologer, " . . . to engage in great and noble conquests, and above all . . . to attempt the discovery of things that were hidden from other men."[2] Now, it was falling into ruins. The Portuguese empire lay open to European conquest.

II

Viewed from the perspective of 1560, the Spanish empire was the wonder of the Western world. Spain and her empire were at the height of expansive vigor and prosperity. Beginning with the discoveries of Columbus, the Spanish had spread rapidly over the Caribbean and into Mexico and South America. Unlike Portugal, Spain established colonies instead of just trading stations. Spaniards cleared plantations and, using slaves, began to grow sugar, indigo, and tobacco. Small towns were built as sites for churches, government, markets, and soldiers. Boom towns near the mines, which produced the most desirable colonial product—silver —became the largest settlements in the new world. The population of San Luis Potosí grew to nearly 150,000 and attained a wild and gaudy lawlessness that was the envy and scandal of the colony. Thus, the Spanish empire attracted large numbers of settlers, over 150,000 from Castile in the sixteenth century alone. But the vast majority of the immi-

---

[2] Gomes Eannes de Azurara, quoted in Parry, *The Establishment of the European Hegemony.*

grants were black slaves and thus were reluctant partici-
pants in the Castilian effort to reproduce abroad the society
left behind in Europe.

The administration of the Spanish empire, both at home
and abroad, closely reflected the aristocratic domination of
Castilian society and the crown's fixed policies of increasing
royal power and showing great solicitude for the church and
faith. Definite institutional patterns developed as early as
the first decades of the sixteenth century. In 1503, the crown
established at Seville the *Casa de la Contratación*, a combination board of trade, mint, customs house, and joint stock
company, which was given a monopoly over colonial trade.
Fonseca's clerks and advisors grew into the Council of the Indies, which took its place in the highest levels of the royal
bureaucracy. A stable form of government also evolved rapidly in the colonies. In 1511, the *audiencia,* a tribunal of
judges, was formed to provide a court for the colonists and a
counterweight to the royal governor. The audiencia, however, proved to be an inadequate instrument of royal control,
so the crown sent a viceroy, with virtually sovereign powers,
to Mexico in 1535 and Peru in 1542. The viceroy system
worked, and the colonial empire was gradually but steadily
brought under an increasing measure of royal control. By
1560, both in Spain and overseas, the institutions of imperial
government were firmly established and working effectively.

Political absolutism was matched by vast royal control
over the church. The royal patronage made the colonial
church a department of state. Thus, the government rapidly
replaced the earliest missions with bishoprics and parishes.
These were followed by the Inquisition, established in Mexico in 1569 and Peru two years later. Missions, of course,
were not abandoned. They moved to the frontiers of colonization, where they performed the double role of converting
the Indians and extending the area of effective Spanish control.

A final function of the colonial church was to spread Hispanic culture and submerge the culture of the Indians. Although the missionaries and colonists were too few in num-

ber to eradicate Indian civilizations, they did apply a patina of Castilian mores over the Indian customs. Acculturation was carried out by means of language and art, as well as with religion and law, and the result was a huge caste of workers, peons, and slaves who were loyal to Spain. Thus, the Spanish achieved the goals of both civil and ecclesiastical administration to guard the power of the king and the glory of God.

In economic and commercial affairs, the Spanish were not so uniformly successful, in spite of the river of silver that made the Spanish empire the envy of the European world. In America, the colonial economy rested on the twin supports of plantations and mining, both providing goods that Europe could not do without. In spite of this immense advantage, the Spanish colonies did not grow as they should have. Fundamental errors by Spanish ministers led to serious economic mismanagement. Spanish officials thought the purpose of colonies was to bring profit to the king and merchants at home. Thus, they prohibited colonial manufacturing. Colonial merchants were sacrificed to those of Spain, as the *Casa de la Contratación* priced its goods at outrageous levels and paid less than market price for colonial products. This scheme to bilk the colonials could increase domestic profits only if trade flowed in official channels, if the colonies were dependent on European manufactures, and if Europe demanded colonial products. Only the latter continued indefinitely. By 1585 the Spanish were unable to (1) provide European manufactures in sufficient quantity or quality, (2) provide enough slaves, (3) stop the smuggling, (4) prevent colonial manufacturing, or (5) maintain their pricing policy. Spanish trade policies collapsed in the face of modest foreign competition and the inadequacies of the Castilian economy.

Serious as the trade losses were, the Spanish crown was far more concerned over the flow of treasure. In the 1590s, this flow reached its zenith, with the royal share coming to over two million ducats a year and private imports, both legal and illegal, probably eight times that. After 1605, howev-

er, the mines at San Luis Potosí were depleted, and specie
shipments dropped alarmingly. By 1615, the shipments were
less than half the 1595 total. This catastrophe cut to the core
of Spanish politics since power in Europe rested, to a large
extent, on shipments of silver.

In spite of these problems, Spain was in no danger of losing her empire altogether. There were too many Spaniards
overseas, and they were too well armored with cannon and
Hispanic, Catholic culture to be conquered by heretics from
the north. The losses aforesaid were real enough, but this is
to look at only two colors of the imperial spectrum: profit
and power. There were others. The colonial church continued to Christianize Indians and blacks. Hispanic culture was
permanently stamped on most of the new world. The Creole
gentry and the high colonial officials lived a spacious and noble life in pursuit of the aristocratic and Catholic ideals inherited from home. To the baroque Spaniard, these things
were more important than mere profit.

III

Trade was the opening wedge of colonial competition, and
the Dutch were prepared to sustain and extend overseas
commerce at a time when virtually all the rest of Europe
was suffering from a severe and prolonged depression. In
the early seventeenth century, the Netherlands became the
focal point of European trade and finance. The Dutch navy
dominated the oceans, and Admiral Tromp tied a broom to
the mast of his flagship symbolic of his determination to
sweep the seas clean of foreign shipping. Finally, the Dutch
state was dominated by merchant oligarchies from the major towns, who believed the proper end of government was
trade and profit, not war or glory.

In the first half of the seventeenth century, the Dutch
turned these advantages into a vast colonial and commercial
empire. The first ventures were in the Far East, where the
Dutch seized virtually all of the Portuguese empire. The
Dutch government moved quickly to organize the Eastern

trade, and Jan de Oldenbarnaveldt, the Grand Pensionary of Holland and real ruler of the country, brought the merchants and towns together in 1602, forming the Dutch East India Company.

The purpose of the East India Company was profit, not colonies. The company operated less as an arm of the state than as the agent of the shareholders. In the East, spices had been the queen of trade, but silks, tea, calicoes, jade, and ginger were also profitable, and the Dutch exploited them, too. Thus, the Dutch copied the Portuguese patterns of imperialism and improved upon the results.

This policy paid immediate and immense dividends. So large were the shipments that the Company's spices, stored in huge warehouses, gave a pungent odor to an entire quarter of Amsterdam. In its first years the Company paid dividends of 20 percent and, although the profits fell after 1650, they were still substantial. Moreover, the imports of the Company stimulated Amsterdam industry. Amsterdam merchants contracted with the Company for raw silk, to be woven at home, and the same thing was done with calicoes. Eastern woods were made into furniture, and drugs and dyes were processed from roots and herbs imported by the Company. In looking at their empire, from Capetown to the Moluccas, the 17 directors had reason to be content with their work and vision.

The West India Company was far less successful. It was founded in 1626, with the dual purpose of trade and war on the Catholic Spanish and Portuguese. War was expensive, even for the Dutch, and costs got out of hand. The Company lost huge sums trying to conquer Brazil from the Porturuese, and it lost New Amsterdam to the British. On a couple of occasions, the Company had to be reorganized, so uncertain had its solvency become. Even so, the Company had its moments. In 1628, Piet Heyn captured an entire Spanish treasure fleet worth 11 million ducats. The Company declared a dividend. It also made a steady profit from slaves and sugar, and sugar refining became a leading Amsterdam industry. There were over 50 factories in the city by the middle of the century, and the port handled about 10 million pounds of sugar a year. Nonetheless, the Company lost money, Dutch possessions in the New World remained meager, and the religious crusade was a distinct failure. For Amsterda merchants the lessons were clear: avoid war, avoid fanaticism, and keep the costs of imperialism low.

In spite of enormous initial success, the momentum of Dutch colonial expansion could not be maintained after 1660. The Dutch had grabbed their empire largely from the Portuguese and had done so when France and England were preoccupied with economic depression, foreign wars, and domestic revolutions. Such opportune times could not last forever, and their passing exposed serious weaknesses in the Dutch method of colonial administration. The Dutch had established trading stations—not colonies—to cut costs and increase profits. They discouraged emigration, and the outposts remained tiny and scattered. Moreover, the directors at home tried to rule the colonies from their desks at home and allowed too little initiative and discretion to their servants on the spot. This meant a narrow concentration on the known profits of traditional trade, and a marked reluctance to try something new. Such scrutiny of detail restricted commerce and harmed the colonies. A broader and more generous view would have paid off better in the end.

Beyond this, Dutch imperialism suffered from the decline of the Netherlands itself. The country was too small to compete successfully in both colonial and European politics, particularly against France and England. French and English economic recovery after 1660 meant that Dutch trade failed to grow as it had before, and war meant resources had to be diverted from trade and empire to defense at home. The Dutch lost Brazil and New York, suffered the French invasion of 1672, and fought almost constantly from 1689 until 1713. The English and French raised tariffs and placed all sorts of ingenious restrictions on Dutch trade. In these circumstances Dutch commercial supremacy faded and profits declined. Merchants shifted their capital from trade to investment banking, which was safer and paid better. By the end of the century the Dutch were a great power by courtesy only, and the age of expansion was over.

IV

During the sixteenth century, the French were too busy with domestic mayhems to pay much attention to the world overseas. But, when Henry IV cut confessional strife back to routine hatred, the French government was able to consider claiming its share of the non-Western world. An expedition was sent. In 1603, Samuel de Champlain landed on the Canadian coast and sailed up the St. Lawrence River, looking for gold and the Northwest Passage. He found neither, but the French settled in Canada anyway. French missionaries, explorers, and fur traders pushed up the river to the Great Lakes and into the heart of the American wilderness. La Salle followed the Mississippi River south and got to the Gulf of Mexico in 1682. Realizing this vast forest empire was vulnerable to the English, the French government tried to tighten its hold on the Great Lakes and the Mississippi valley. Forts and missions were established at Chicago and Detroit, and colonies were begun in Illinois and Louisiana. These struggling and starving outposts were to guard the flanks of empire.

French colonialism followed patterns already established by previous European conquerors. In the West Indies, the French established sugar plantations on the Spanish model, and were extremely successful. By the eighteenth century, French sugar, which was both good and cheap, dominated the European market. Slave stations in West Africa imitated the Dutch and Portuguese, and commercial outposts in India followed the Portuguese pattern of commercial exploitation without colonization. Frenchmen searched for gold, or were set to cultivating a cash crop in great demand at home.

This colonial domain was governed and exploited along definite principles articulated by clerics and officials who remained safely at home. French colonies were designed to benefit the mother country, both politically and commercially. Colonies were the result of government action, and royal control was extremely tight. Large commercial companies, on the order of the Dutch East India Company, were continually being organized to exploit the colonies and move colonial trade in the proper channels. Colonies were also to serve God. The Indians must be converted to the True Faith, and hundreds of missionaries, mostly Jesuits, were sent to the new world to serve their Lord by saving the noble savages. French officials made conscientious efforts to carry these principles from theory to action and tried to observe the letter of the law.

". . . The letter killeth, but the spirit giveth life," as St. Paul reminded us. French officials, observing the general ruin of their plans and hopes, forgot this and blamed the failures of colonialism on British and Dutch competition. There was some truth in that but not, I am afraid, too much. The basic malfunction of French colonialism occurred in France itself. The French restricted emigration to the colonies, for both political and religious reasons, and so the colonies never supported themselves. Canada and Louisiana were too big and empty to be exploited by a few fur traders. Furthermore, the French failed to grant sufficient self-government to the colonials. When it took six months to receive a letter, all decisions could not be made in Paris. Nor should they have been. Colonials deserved more from Paris than a constant stream of officials, letters, directives, orders, and reminders of their duty.

They also deserved more than expensive goods, irregular shipments from home, and low prices for their products. But the colonial economy took second place to the profits of merchants and commercial companies at home. French royal officials had a touching faith in the ability of commercial companies to bear the costs of colonization in return for trade monopolies. Sooner or later the companies always went broke, and they damaged the colony by discouraging investment and rigging prices. Beyond this, the crown consistently refused to commit sufficient resources to the navy and merchant marine.

French imperial ventures were not without success, particularly in the slave trade and the sugar islands of the West Indies, but they never justified the hopes and cash invested in them.

V

British imperial expansion did not begin until the seventeenth century, largely because Queen Elizabeth I was too cautious and inpecunious to seek a direct confrontation with Spain. By 1600, however, victory over the Spanish Armada, prosperity, and the optimism of the Elizabethan era had pushed the British to the brink of colonial establishments. The new colonies were still not government ventures. A residual diplomatic and financial caution remained. Private companies, such as the British East India Company (1602), the Virginia Company of London (1606), or the Massachusetts Bay Company (1629) carried the financial burdens of commerce and colonization in return for trade privileges and governmental powers. Upon occasion, the king granted a charter to a single proprietor, such as Lord Calvert (1632), who received extensive powers in exchange for planting a colony in Maryland as a haven for oppressed Roman Catholics. Thus, the king could support the companies or proprietors in their quarrels and petitions or not, as finances and diplomacy required. British colonization, like the Dutch, was the result of private enterprise.

This policy changed very slowly after the restoration of Charles II in 1660. The crown still made grants to companies and proprietors. In 1663, the Carolinas were given to eight proprietors and, a year later, New Jersey was divided between Lord Berkeley and Sir George Carteret. New Amsterdam was granted to the Duke of York on the condition he capture it from the Dutch, which he did. William Penn received Pennsylvania in 1681, and the Hudson Bay Company was founded in 1670 to exploit the furs of northern Canada.

Even so, the crown steadily increased royal control over the colonies. Navigation Acts were passed to force colonial trade into strictly British channels and increase the profit from the colonies. In 1675 the Lords of Trade were established to supervise colonial affairs and were replaced in 1696 by the more efficient Board of Trade, which included customs and vice-admiralty jurisdictions. Finally, by the end of the seventeenth century, the royal navy had established a more or less permanent Caribbean Squadron. Growing royal power, however, was still for imperial purposes only, and was rarely exercised in the internal affairs of the various colonies.

Mercantilists and ministers regarded colonies in the West Indies, Africa, India and the American south as the heart of the empire, largely because of the tropical and oriental products they sent home. Nonetheless, in spite of merchantilist prejudices, the economic and political importance of colonies north of the Chesapeake Bay grew steadily after 1700. Of the northern colonies, Pennsylvania exemplified the patterns of growth, prosperity, and freedom that were ultimately to wreck the old empire. Established as a haven for persecuted Quakers, Pennsylvania also extended toleration to other religious minorities. Mennonites, Moravian Brethren, Swedenborgians, and others from the gathered churches of the continent joined the Quakers in the colony. Equally welcome were the Calvinist dissenters from England, Roman Catholics, and Jews. Nationalities other than English migrated to Pennsylvania. In the years after 1730 Scots-Irish settled broad tracts of land in the Susquehanna Valley, while Germans went to Bethlehem, Germantown, and Lancaster County, still known as Pennsylvania Dutch country. This unlimited migration reinforced the necessity for toleration and enabled the province to boast a quarter million inhabitants by the Revolution.

Pennsylvania's prosperity equalled the growth in population. Philadelphia became one of the largest cities in the British empire, enjoying an extensive commerce in grain, lumber, and livestock with the West Indies, whose sugar and molasses and dye woods were then sent to England and northern Europe. It was a prosperous preindustrial commerce, although it did not fit into the theoretical patterns established by mercantilists. The Pennsylvania economy was too close an approximation of England itself and was regarded in London as a potential competitor. Dark suspicions were entertained in London concerning the origin of the sugar, dye, wood, and molasses that Pennsylvania ships brought to England. Did these products come from Jamaica and Honduras, as they were supposed to, or had they been bought from the French and Spanish in violation of the Navigation Acts? Too often it was the latter, the Board of Trade thought, and there was a tightening up of the customs service, designed to correct these regrettable lapses in commercial activities.

Pennsylvania government generally followed the lines established in the English Bill of Rights of 1689. Religious toleration was enlarged, and Quakers, English nonconformists, and German sectarians were allowed to vote and hold office. Electoral districts were far more equitably drawn than in England, although Philadelphia and the near countries were favored, and the franchise was substantially more extensive. Finally, the lower house of the Pennsylvania assembly was considerably more powerful than the House of Commons in England. It did not have to contend with a resident king, the pervasive influence of the Lords, an established church, or a royal bureaucracy. Both council and governor had less real authority than the assembly because both taxes and authorization for expenditure had to be initiated in the lower house. Popular control over government was immensely greater than in England, a crucial distinction between colony and mother country.

The British were the most successful of the early modern imperial states, however that term was measured. While the British empire did not produce the mountains of silver that financed the Spanish fling at political and religious domination, it showed even greater profits through trade, agriculture, and industry. Nor were British colonies political and military liabilities, like the ones of France and the Netherlands. Finally, if the British were no better than the Spanish in planting their culture abroad, they certainly were not worse at it. It was not for nothing that the British empire was the wonder and envy of all Europe.

VI

Although the colonial experience of the European states varied, there were several unifying factors that cut across political lines. The most significant, certainly, was the technological superiority that Europeans enjoyed over non-Western peoples, which steadily increased until European empires were invulnerable to native revolt, although not to the uprisings of ungrateful colonials. Europeans treatment of non-Western peoples was another constant of colonial expansion; it was horrible in the fifteenth century and never rallied from its barbaric precedents. Finally, colonials, in spite of the best efforts of their governments at home, generally enjoyed more freedom and a higher standard of living than their fellow subjects who stayed in Europe.

European receptivity to non-Western customs, in an age of religious reform was quite limited, and Europeans' first impulse was to loot. Non-Western peoples were to be exploited, and slavery, or at least due subordination, was the natives' proper estate. Atrocities were quite common. Vasco da Gama cut off the ears, noses, and hands of about 800 Muslims and suggested that the ruler of Calicut make curry out of them. Arabs, Indians, and Indonesians regarded Europeans as dirty and degraded gangsters, whose word meant nothing and whose conduct was pathological.

Asians fared well compared to American Indians. Even in Canada, where the French needed the Indians to supply furs and Jesuit missionaries tried their best to understand and protect them, contact with Europeans debauched the Indian and extinguished his tribal life. Brandy and furs did it.

". . . the fur traders make them [Indians] quite drunk on purpose, in order to deprive these poor barbarians of their reason, so that the traders can deceive them more easily and obtain almost for nothing their furs . . . . Lewdness, adulteries, incests and several crimes which decency keeps me from mentioning are the usual disorders through the trade in brandy, of which some traders make use to abuse the Indian women who yield themselves readily in their drunkenness to all kinds of indecency."[3]

This tale of woodland wickedness was repeated too often to be utterly inaccurate, and what we know of the morality of commerce confirms it.

The Spanish, like the French, endeavored to find some use for the native Americans, and the use they found was slavery. The Indians were rounded up and entrusted to the care of a Spaniard, who was to work them, feed them, and see they became Christians and gave up sin. But the Indians of the Caribbean did not adjust well to slavery, and they retaliated by dying. The Spanish had no intention of doing the labor themselves and replaced the departed Indians with black slaves imported from Africa. They stood up better under the regimen and soon became the basic labor source for Caribbean plantations.

Treatment of the black slaves who replaced the Indians was none to gentle. Brutality began with the slave trade. Blacks were stuffed head to toe into the dirty and airless holds of the ships. It was common for one-third to die on the voyage over since the slavers gave them little food and water and paid no attention to sanitation. Indeed, one of the reasons the British and Dutch did so well in the slave trade was their efficient brutality. The Portuguese, even the Spanish, were too soft to compete.

A further characteristic of Europeans abroad was a greater wealth and freedom than their relations at home enjoyed. In part, this was the result of an abundance of land that contained fewer seigneurial or ecclesiastical encum-

[3] Chrestien Le Clercq, *Nouvelle Relation de la Gaspesie* (Toronto, 1910), 254–255.

brances. Farms in America were bigger and taxes were less. In part, also, wealth came from the large assortment of cash crops from the colonies that commanded premium prices at home. Sugar, tobacco, and indigo were the most profitable, but lumber, pitch, fish, furs, and grains also contributed to colonial affluence. Colonials also enjoyed a relative paucity of nobles, a class noted for its ability to consume and its reluctance to work. The framework of seigneurial privilege might be transported to the new world, but nobles enjoyed fewer privileges abroad than at home. Thus, colonials lived in a society where wealth determined class structure and social mobility was greater.

Finally, colonies tended to enjoy more self-government than was common in Europe. Direction from home, although theoretically substantial was, in fact, quite sporadic, and governmental decisions were quite responsive to local needs and pressures. Moreover, colonial officials tended to come more and more from the local aristocracies and, by the eighteenth century, this practice was permanent. City governments *audiencias,* superior councils, and colonial legislatures, all came to dominate imported officials, and represented colonial interests against the king. There was some complaint about this from ministers at home, but nothing was done. Colonies were politically autonomous long before they became independent in fact.

VII

European colonial expansion attracted the careful attention of merchants, pamphlet polemicists, promoters both lay and clerical, and government lawyers and bureaucrats. They all advanced numerous explanations and justifications for their own particular scheme or swindle. Priests, political theorists, and other practitioners of politics in the abstract sought intellectual justification for the things their kings did. Kings themselves, anxious to appear in an appropriate and constitutional guise, issued elaborate rationales for their imperial policies. The habits of theology had spread to state-craft as officials sought to explain and organize the arts and mysteries of imperialism.

These collections of thoughts, ideas, impressions, prejudices, mistakes, axioms, and epigrams were called mercantilism. They were not a coherent system of economics and politics but a mixture of notions both true and false, many of which were mutually contradictory. But, the mercantilist literature was believed anyway, partly because most of it seemed reasonable, partly because no real alternatives appeared, but mainly because mercantilists were devoted royalists, who stressed the need for royal centralization of political and economic power. Kings responded to this support against their towns, estates, and nobles by subsidizing mercantilist pamphlets, organizing mercantilist companies, passing mercantilist laws, and giving solemn credence to mercantilist canons and doctrines.

The origins of European mercantilism are to be found in the economic policies of the medieval city. Royal officials, trained in law, theology, or war, were unprepared to enact the complicated commercial regulation thought necessary for proper exploitation of the new empires. Their search for precedents and guidance led directly to the laws and practices of towns. Urban governments and guilds were constantly preoccupied with the prosperity of their citizens, and passed all manner of rules to insure it. Trade in the town was confined to citizens as were crafts, such as carpentry or shoemaking. Tariffs, quotas, currency restrictions, and money-changing regulations were all designed to aid the home market and manufacturers. Prices were controlled, quality and quantity of manufactured goods were regulated, export products were encouraged, and trade secrets were jealously guarded. By the seventeenth century, urban regulation had been subordinated to royal power, but the same spirit of competition and exclusion had been adopted by the king's ministers. The road to prosperity and power was to be the same for kings as for merchants.

The doctrines of mercantilism, distilled from urban precedent, imperial experience, and persuasive pamphlets were actually quite simple and bore a remarkable resemblance to the childish propaganda that flows from American Chambers of Commerce. Foremost among them was the notion that growth was good and more growth was better. This applied to population, money, trade, industry, colonies, navies, and merchant fleets. Merchantilists were ardent expansionists. Although the term Gross National Product had not been devised, mercantilists were on cozy terms with the concept, and they claimed their prescriptions would produce sustained and inevitable economic growth. Mercantilists also placed great faith in the new science of statistics, which first emerged in the last years of the sixteenth century. Exact figures were hard to come by, but mercantilists were untiring in their efforts to obtain them and discover new areas of human endeavor that were applicable to quantitative measurement. Further, mercantilists tended to see the world as an arena for constant economic warfare. The prosperity of one state would be at the expense of another, as Sir Francis Bacon commented: ". . . the increase of any Estate must be upon the Foreigner . . . (for whatsoever is somewhere gotten is somewhere else lost . . . .)." Wildly inaccurate during the boom years of the sixteenth century, this comment was a shrewd observation in the depression years after 1600. Thus, a major object of statecraft was to beggar one's neighbor, to seize his trade, to ruin his industries, and to conquer his colonies. Finally, mercantilists believed in a substantial amount of government regulation to achieve the aims aforesaid. Government programs and laws would foster industry, manipulate and control overseas commerce, produce a favorable balance of trade, and strengthen royal authority. These good things would not occur on their own. The king must make them happen.

The most obvious monument of mercantilist ideals was the immense number of laws and regulations concerning trade and industry. Mercantilist trade regulations were first issued by the Portuguese in the fifteenth century in an attempt to centralize African commerce in Lisbon, thus assuring that the king would get his cut. The Spanish adopted this system with the *Casa de la Contratación* (1503). The *Casa* had a legal monoply on American commerce, and it had three functions: make certain the king received his fifth of the silver, provide maximum profit for Spanish merchants sending goods abroad, and exclude foreigners from Spanish colonial commerce. In this last the *Casa* failed completely because by the end of the sixteenth century, foreign goods accounted for more than half of the *legal* trade with Spanish America and all of the smuggling.

By the seventeenth century, Europeans had invented a new scheme for exploiting colonial trade. This was to joint-stock company, such as the various East India Companies, the Hudson Bay Company, or the numerous French companies that failed to develop Canada. The commercial companies had certain advantages. They could provide a larger capital investment than individual merchants, a market for colonial products, and they confined trade to approved routes and enhanced royal control. In spite of this, however, the companies usually failed. The capital they raised was never enough to carry the immense and continuing expenses of colonization and defense. Profits from colonial trade (and these existed) were simply devoured by military and administrative expenses. Moreover, the colonials were stubbornly unwilling to labor ceaselessly for the merchants and directors back home. In general, the companies were too small and poor to accomplish what the king himself could not.

These sad facts made little impression on contemporaries, however. New companies were chartered all the time. The French, in particular, had a touching and simple faith in commercial companies. It was never rewarded. The Holy Scripture, which mentions the faith that moved mountains, wisely avoided comment on a faith that made money.

Mercantilists also called for laws to regulate trade. These rules were collectively called Navigation Acts, and all countries had them. Despite certain differences in detail, the Navigation Acts included the following principles: (1) development of a merchant marine by excluding, insofar as possible, foreign sailors and ships (usually Dutch) from colonial and internal trade; (2) establishment of a national monopoly on colonial trade; (3) a colonial monopoly of the home market; and (4) the colonies paying for the system by customs dues. If these principles were followed, mercantilists were convinced that the road was open to increased wealth, trade, and power.

The most clearly articulated system of Navigation Acts was the British, which took their classic form after the restoration of Charles II. In 1660, a Navigation Act stated that all English colonial trade must be in English ships with English masters and crews. Moreover, certain English colonial products could go only to England and nowhere else. These "enumerated commodities" were few at first. In 1660 they included sugar, tobacco, cotton, indigo, ginger, specklewood, and dye woods. The list was later inlarged. In 1673, coconuts and cacao were enumerated; in 1704, rice, molasses and rum; naval stores were added a year later, and copper and furs were enumerated in 1721. In 1663, an Act for the Encouragement of Trade added a new aspect to the mercantilist system. All European products destined for the colonies must be unloaded in England and then shipped overseas. Thus England became the "Staple," or trade center for all European goods sent to the colonies. English merchants and the customs revenue could only prosper under such an arrangement, and the accursed foreigners would be hurt. From the mercantilist viewpoint, the Staple was perfect.

Although there were thousands of amendments, interpretations, and legal opinions were added to the Navigation Acts, the Staple, Enumeration, and national shipping remained the basic principles of trade regulation. The problem was enforcement. Charles II established commissions to supervise trade and colonial affairs as soon as he returned from exile. Their mission was to stem "the immoderate desire" of continental states ". . . to engross the whole traffic of the universe."[4] But the commissions did not work very well, nor did the Lords of Trade who followed them in 1675. This could not continue, and the Navigation Act of 1696 reorganized the administration of colonial trade. Customs and vice-admiralty officials in the colonies were given stronger backing by being allowed forcible entry to seize goods traded in defiance of the law, and a Board of Trade was established in London to direct the entire system. The new law did not eliminate trade outside the legal patterns, but growing British prosperity made strict enforcement unnecessary, and none was attempted until the Sugar Act of 1764.

The second basic element of mercantilism was government encouragement of domestic industries. Every state passed laws and concocted hundreds of schemes both sensible and outlandish to support industry. Bounties and rewards were promised to enterprising merchants and, now and then, some were actually paid. Privileges were granted new manufacturers, and tariffs were raised against foreign competition. The modern patent system arose from mercantilist solicitude for industry and invention. Government support, though frequently unintelligent, was certainly genuine.

The scope of royal regulation was clearest in France, where a strong bureaucratic government was animated by classic mercantilist principles. In 1601, as soon as he had pacified the country, Henry IV set up a Commission of Commerce, which held hundreds of meetings and considered all sorts of schemes. Its most ambitious project was to increase the French silk industry. The Commission invested large sums in a scheme to plant 400,000 mulberry trees, supply silkworm eggs, and print a pamphlet telling peasants how to care for both. The Great Mulberry Mirage ran into immediate difficulties, financial, human, and botanical. Even so, silk production in southern France grew several times over its previous level, so the king's money was not totally wasted.

Under Jean-Baptiste Colbert, finance and colonial minis-

[4] Lord Clarendon, quoted in C. M. Andrews. *The Colonial Period in American History*, IV, 54.

ter under Louis XIV from 1661 to 1683, efforts to stimulate industry were redoubled. Colbert was fairly successful in dealing with tariffs. In 1664 he suppressed many internal duties, making central France the largest free trade area in Western Europe. Colbert produced the first single external tariff for the entire realm. He also subsidized canal construction. The largest and most successful of these projects was the Canal du Languedoc, which joined the Atlantic to the Mediterranean. There were also failures. Colbert was never able to abolish many river, bridge, and road tolls, nor was he able to extend free trade to all France. He could not get a uniform system of weights and measures. These reforms awaited the Revolution.

Colbert's most persistent efforts were toward stimulation of French manufacturing. He had an aristocratic bias and thought luxury products for the nobility were more profitable than cheaper goods for common people. Thus, he concentrated his efforts on quality as much as on quantity and was rarely concerned about high productivity. Colbert was particularly interested in French silk, lace, furs, glass, china, rugs, and tapestries. He gave numerous privileges to the glass industry, including tax exemptions. His efforts built up French glassworks and cut deeply into a traditional Venetian industry. The crown also established the Gobelins Tapestry works, which received enormous subsidies, lost vast sums of money, and produced magnificent works of art. In silk and lace, Colbert extended privileges previously granted.

All of this regulation required a large bureaucracy and continuous administrative attention, as it does today. Colbert sent out thousands of orders, exhortations, opinions, advice, criticisms, and complaints to merchants, artisans, and officials. He understood merchants well, commenting that they ". . . always consult only their own individual interests, without examining what would be for the public good and the advantage of commerce in general."[5] The crown must lead the way and, if necessary, compel.

Along with advice went inspectors to see that French

[5] Cole, *Colbert and a Century of French Mercantilism*, 2 vols., I, 334.

manufacturing attained the level of quality that Colbert
thought essential. The inspectors and bureaucrats were a
plague upon the land, then as now. Industrialists had to buy
them off to keep them from enforcing rigid and stupid regulations. On rare occasions, graft did not work, and Colbert's
rules were enforced. Goods that did not meet specifications
were destroyed at enormous cost in time, work, materials,
and markets because merchants could not produce what
their customers demanded. The officials and inspectors were
sent out with a noble and impossible purpose: to persuade
businessmen to see a general good beyond their ledgers. Contemporary English and Dutch experience suggests that Colbert would have done better abandoning his crusade against
human nature and simply leaving everyone alone. But that
asks more than a mercantilist could give.

VIII

During the Old Regime, colonial enterprise bore a close relationship to power and prosperity at home. Many of the
products most wanted in Europe originated overseas, and
such goods as sugar, silk, tobacco, spices, and indigo brought
high profits to both king and merchant. The value of these
goods was so great that the colonies were able to trade with
Europe for manufactured products on a fairly equal basis.
Colony and mother country alike maintained a symbiotic relationship, each able to supply the other's needs. Under
these conditions, a state without colonies or colonial trade
was substantially poorer than her neighbors. Such economic
advantages were not always translated into military power,
as the rise of Prussia was to show, but British commercial
and colonial supremacy in the last century of the Old Regime
was quite clearly a major factor in her military and economic preeminence, and contemporaries grasped that equation
with their accustomed ease.

By the third quarter of the eighteenth century, however,
Europeans were not as convinced as their fathers had been
of the value of colonial enterprise. Support for imperial ad-

venture waned everywhere. In part, this disillusionment reflected total British victory in the Great War for Empire
(1739–1763), which placed all colonial powers in the unfortunate position of seeing the profits of empire go to the British while the expenses remained at home. In part, also, the
disenchantment with far places coincided with a growing
rambunctiousness among colonials, who demanded more autonomy and revolted to get it. It also reflected a continuous
decline in the price of colonial products and a reduction in
the profits of growing them. The costs of empire—economic,
military, and intellectual—were becoming greater than the
profits, even for the British. Thus, European imperial expansion, begun with such huge hopes for gain and glory, having
played such a great part in the affairs of kings and common-
ers, faded out in losses, rebellion, disillusionment, and disinterest.

BIBLIOGRAPHY

C. M. Andrews, *The Colonial Period in American History* (4 vols.), is a massive and outstanding study of the formation and early development of English colonies in North America. The first three volumes deal with the foundation of the colonies, while the fourth describes English mercantilism and the Navigation Acts. Indispensible for the interested student. Highly recommended, particularly Volume 4.

Charles Gibson, *Spain in America*, is an excellent, short study of Spanish colonialism in the New World. It avoids the narrative approach and deals with topics such as the church, royal government, trade, and plantations. This is a truly outstanding synthesis of a large topic, is easy to read, and is highly recommended.

J. H. Parry, *The Spanish Seaborn Empire*, is another, excellent study of Spanish colonialism (hard cover).

D. P. Mannix and M. Cowley, *Black Cargoes*, is a study of the slave trade, which was one of the most lucrative commercial ventures of the Old Regime. An excellent book.

C. W. Cole, *Colbert and a Century of French Mercantilism* (2 vols.), is a long examination of mercantilism in France. Here, the state played a consistent role in terms of capital investment and commercial and industrial investment. Cole examines this phenomenon in detail (hard cover).

C. R. Boxer, *The Dutch Seaborn Empire: 1600–1800,* is the best single study of the Netherlands overseas. The student interested in Dutch colonialism and imperialism ought to begin here (hard cover).

George Masselman, *The Cradle of Colonialism,* is a long analysis of the formation of the Dutch East India Company and the role it played in the establishment of Dutch control in Indonesia. Excellent on the role of Jan Coen, the real founder of the Dutch East India colonies. Also throws light on the Portugese failure in the Far East (hard cover).

J. H. Parry, *The Establishment of the European Hegemony,* is a short survey of European imperialism and colonialism from Henry the Navigator to 1715. It deals with each country, and contains chapters on the technology of colonialism and overseas trade. Although this book is not too easy to read, the student interested in overseas expansion ought to begin here.

CHAPTER FOUR

HARD TIMES:
THE GREAT DEPRESSION: 1590–1660

"There are no merchants left of
estate, quality or credit, as there
were in former times . . ."

Viceroy of Catalunya to Philip IV, (1628)

Like all kings, Henry II of France was desperately short
of money. He had all the usual expenses, along with a demanding mistress, Diane de Poitiers, for whom he was
building the stupendous chateau at Chenonceaux. To pay his
bills, Henry resorted to borrowing and, when ordinary loans
failed, he consolidated his debts in 1555 into a huge fund,
called the Big Deal. The Big Deal tapped the money market
of Lyon, and it paid 16 percent a year. People rushed to invest. The king's debts increased marvelously. There seemed
to be no end to the river of cash—until September, 1557,
when Philip II, king of Spain and the richest monarch in
Christendom, bankrupted. Confidence collapsed, but Henry
II, with regal bravado, announced he would never default on
the Big Deal since his debts were a sacred royal trust. While
not entirely convincing, that bald lie did keep the king afloat
for another season until December, when Henry, too, suspended payment on his debts.

The great fiscal crisis of 1557 affected all of Europe and
was the first major break in nearly a century of continuous
economic growth. Depression did not come at once. After a
kind of shudder, the European economy continued its up-
ward movement. People forgot that kings could go bankrupt.
New speculations began, kings drifted back to the money
markets, trade expanded, silver flowed into Europe from the

New World, and everything seemed all right again. But, prosperity rested on too narrow a foundation. Primitive technology, inefficient agriculture, a vicious price inflation, and the waste of war and persecution all inhibited European economic growth. There were new crises, like the one in 1557 and new shocks, even more severe and destructive. By the end of the century the golden years were over, and Europe was headed into the most profound and prolonged depression since the Black Death.

I

During the sixteenth century, when money was easy and trade was good, prosperity seemed permanent and hard times banished forever. Alas, they were not. The European economy suffered from serious structural shortcomings that made a new depression almost inevitable. These shortcomings included considerable waste and malinvestment of scarce resources in nearly continuous wars and religious persecutions. Constant inflation and a progressive credit collapse after 1574 were also fundamental economic problems and were reminiscent of an earlier economic collapse after 1340 during the fourteenth-century general crisis.

The most basic structural deficiency was a primitive agriculture that bound most Europeans to the land in an endless war against poverty, famine, and malnutrition. Harvest yields of six bushels of grain for each bushel of seed were exceptional; three or four were far more common. Livestock were scrawny, and many were slaughtered in the fall because winter feed was inadequate. One-third to one-half of the land lay fallow each year as primitive crop rotation systems tried to compensate for the lack of legumes and fertilizer. Agricultural implements were simple and inefficient, and poor storage methods ruined part of the modest harvest that was collected. Prosperity did stimulate some clearing of waste, and opened the Western market to Baltic grain, but there was little increase in agricultural efficiency or improvement in agricultural technology. These things were untouched. Most people never even thought about them.

Industry and commerce in the sixteenth century seemed to show a much brighter prospect, at least on the surface. Here, there was genuine growth: more ships, more cargoes, more mines, more looms, more foundries, and more shops. There was even some technological improvement, particularly in metallurgy and shipbuilding. But the industrial and commercial expansion was still rather small and rested on too narrow a market. There was no general increase in the depth of the market. Luxury goods, and many ordinary products as well, remained well beyond the reach of most people.

In addition to primitive agricultural and industrial technology, there was the steep and general inflation that lasted the entire sixteenth century. The causes of the price inflation are clear enough to modern historians and economists, although they escaped contemporaries almost completely. During the period from 1475 to 1620, Europeans found two new sources of coined wealth; mines in Bohemia and specie from America. They added about 1 billion ducats to the economy, an incredible sum for a society in which a family could live comfortably on 25 ducats a year. There was, however, no corresponding increase in industrial production, commerce, or productivity. The modest growth in these areas simply fell far short of the steady and spectacular increase in cash.

Therefore, prices rose. They moved up slowly at first, in the last decades of the fifteenth century but, by 1520, the price rise was steeper and more rapid. Inflation was most severe in the Iberian peninsula, where the prices of everyday goods rose 400 percent between 1500 and 1640. Elsewhere the rise was more moderate, averaging between 150 and 300 percent. Wages rose, too, but not as fast and not as much. This produced a steady erosion in the real wages of workers, in spite of formal increases wrung from reluctant masters. In all of Europe, the lower classes suffered a general decline in their living standard. In England, the drop in buying power between 1475 and 1640 was about two-thirds, and there were similar losses everywhere.

Income erosion affected persons more exalted than workers and journeymen. Princes, nobles, and bishops suffered the same affliction. The cost of magnificence, status, war, government, and politics went up alarmingly, just at a time when overseas trade had made new and expensive products available. Country nobles who had converted their manorial dues into money payments suffered the most, and many were forced to sell out. Kings borrowed money and issued paper, bishops hunted for plural benefices to exploit, and the secular aristocracy bought government offices that allowed them to benefit from rising royal incomes. It was hardly accidental that everywhere in the sixteenth century there was a general and inexorable rise in the number and variety of royal officials. The aristocracy were more successful in their search for more money to spend than were workers, which is only what we might expect.

The related phenomena of rising prices and increasing amounts of money had a dual impact on the finances of kings. In formal terms, their incomes rose to unheard-of heights, and they appeared rich. But the money bought so much less, particularly expensive items such as armies and navies, that many monarchs were actually poorer than ever. Kings scrambled desperately for money. "I believe that lack of funds will ruin the state . . .," wrote Jean-Baptiste Colbert to Cardinal Mazarin in 1652, a year of severe depression, and that complaint echoed the continuous wails of bankrupt monarchs a century earlier during a time of prosperity. Kings were as needy as ever, in spite of the relative abundance of cash. To cover expenses they increased taxes as much as they could or dared and, when this was not enough, they borrowed.

Early in the century royal borrowing was relatively modest. The interest was usually paid and the privileges given creditors were worth the risk, even if no one pretended the principal could ever be repaid in cash. By the 1550s, under the pressures of war, inflation, and religious reform, this all

changed. Royal borrowing increased rapidly, and kings issued paper to cover their debts. By 1557, monarchs had
acquired an immense debt, far heavier than they could manage. Philip II had borrowed over 5 million ducats in Antwerp, largely from great German bankers like the Fuggers
or the Welsers. In Castile his debts reached beyond 40 million ducats. Henry II of France had skimmed 12 million
livres just from the merchants and bankers of Lyons, along
with a great deal elsewhere, and his resources were far
smaller than Philip's. The merchants and bankers who had
lent these princely sums found their own resources strained.
The crash came in the fall of 1557. First Philip II and then
Henry slid into bankruptcy. They stopped payment on their
debts, and issued paper to cover the default.

The financial crisis had severe repercussions. The Fuggers
and Welsers were badly hit, and the latter, at least, never
really recovered. Smaller German bankers who depended on
the giants were forced into semiliquidation. Many banking
houses in Lyons went out of business, and those that did not
cut their investments in trade and industry. Commerce between Seville and America was sharply depressed and did
not recover for five years. The city of Antwerp was compromised and, borrowing on its bourse, never again reached the
precrisis levels.

Bad as it was, though, the crisis passed. Silver shipments
from America held up, losses were absorbed, trade picked up
again, especially in the Mediterranean, and royal expenses
grew as smartly as they ever had. Prosperity returned, even
in France which was slipping into civil war. Let the good
times roll, say the Cajuns, and European monarchs fell in
with this spirit by borrowing a lot more money. They borrowed too much. By 1572, Philip II was again in trouble and
was pressing his bankers for even more to tide him over the
immediate emergency. There was only so much the creditors
could give and, in September, 1575, the Habsburg monarch
went under again. This time he ruined a large number of
Spanish bankers and began a general run on Italian banks
that lasted until 1584. In the wake of Philip's default, 24

Italian banks closed, with a net loss of over 4 million ducats. There was the usual depression in American trade, and the international trade fair at Medina del Campo closed down, only opening three years later when Spanish private and royal credit was somewhat restored.

The Spanish catastrophe had its repercussions in France, now firmly mired in the religious slaughter of St. Bartholomew's Day. The Lyons money market suffered a sharp slump in 1574 and never really recovered. Although general failure was avoided, individual banks continued to collapse regularly. The fairs at Besançon, in Franche-Comté, did even worse. They folded altogether in 1579.

In spite of everything, the losses, the uncertain future, the continuing wars, and the rising costs of trade and manufacturing, Philip II was able to borrow more money. But his credit rested on a thin foundation. American silver and Genoese bankers were all that held Philip II up. That was not enough, even though taxes were increased and the revenue from America reached its highest level. In 1596, the Spanish crown again suspended payment on its debts.

This time, the ill effects of royal financial failure were permanent. The trade fair at Medina del Campo closed down for good, and the commerce in woolens that used to support it went to the French, English, and Dutch. The number of ships trading with America fell by two-thirds after 1596 and never recovered. Among Philip's creditors, only the Genoese survived, and they went under in the Spanish bankruptcy of 1608. The financial and credit center of Europe moved from the Mediterranean to Amsterdam. Spanish industry was as depressed as trade, and Italian manufacturing also felt the credit squeeze. After 1596, the entire western Mediterranean basin moved swiftly into a severe and prolonged depression.

Repeated royal bankruptices had a disastrous impact on the activities of merchant-bankers and on the amounts of cash and credit available for investment in commercial and industrial ventures. Kings used their greater political powers to sop up the large capital accumulations that might otherwise have gone into commercial and industrial investment. Bankers and merchants, therefore, became a species of tax collector, functioning as private agencies to funnel investment capital to the king. Eventually, the king's needs outran the bankers' ability to supply fresh funds. Whenever that happened the king bankrupted and left the merchants to absorb the loss. Over the course of half a century, kings simply devoured their merchants and bankers.

For most of the sixteenth century, the adverse factors in the European economy were not strong enough to throw the balance from general prosperity to depression. Commercial growth, increases in industrial production, new sources of food and a somewhat expanded agriculture all combined to sustain general economic growth everywhere until the 1580s, and in northern Europe until 1620. Eventually, however, the accumulated burdens of technological limitations, inflation and extensive credit disorders polished prosperity off.

II

When prosperity cracked and faded, it did so first and most severely in the Mediterranean Basin, long the richest area of Europe. As early as the 1580s, there were definite signs of decline and, by 1600, the real depression had come. The economic crisis in the Mediterranean Basin was composed of several elements, all transcending national and imperial boundaries. Plague, famine, regressive tax policies, capital flight, declining trade and industry, price inflation, and technological backwardness affected Turkey and Italy as well as Spain. These general conditions were joined by a host of local, individual catastrophes, many of which were surmounted during the prosperity of the previous century but now, in hard times, they simply added to the general woe. These included the expulsion of the Moriscos from Valencia, growing piracy in the Adriatic Sea, decline of the silk industry at Messina, and the end of the trade fairs at Medina del Campo. The Mediterranean depression, therefore, was a mosaic of disasters, some general, some particular, and all combined so that only a few places escaped the general ruin.

Inflation, capital flight, and currency manipulations were common in southern Europe after 1600 and followed the patterns set in the previous century. The Turkish silver asper, traditionally stable, scarce, and sound, enjoyed a high value until the end of the sixteenth century. Then, as Spanish silver moved east to pay for Oriental goods, the asper became more abundant and suffered a severe loss of purchasing power. After 1580, the asper fell 350 percent, and the Ottoman government accelerated the process by debasing the coin. By 1620, the asper was no longer acceptable for international payments, and the Ottoman government was forced to mint the silver para as its replacement. Within a few years it, too, was debased.

In Spain, there was a similar story of currency manipulation. Debasement began in earnest under Philip III (1598–1621), when the crown tampered with the value of the copper coinage, and only ended in 1680 with a general currency revaluation that was a severe jolt to what remained of Spanish economic life.

Along with the currency manipulations and royal bankruptcies went a substantial capital flight from the Mediterranean states. In part, this was a transfer of funds to northern Europe, particularly to the still prosperous Dutch Republic. In part, also, capital flight meant a sharp increase in investment in office, land, church, and titles of nobility. These forms of investment were not unprofitable; by 1600 they offered a higher return in Spain or Italy than did trade. Moreover, noble rank and official position were the essential elements of social status, a crucially important value in an aristocratic and hierarchical society. But such investments, while reasonable and attractive, only deepened the depression in trade and industry.

Financial problems in southern Europe were accompanied by a depression in the real economy. Agriculture, trade, and industry failed to keep pace with northern competition.

Spanish wool production declined steadily after 1580, the victim of high costs and soil erosion on grazing lands. By 1600, the Mediterranean basin had become a consistent importer of foodstuffs. Commerce also dropped off. By 1600, most of the goods sent to America by legal channels of trade were Dutch. In Venice, long the major center of Eastern trade, goods entering the customs house dropped decade by decade after 1600, and the rich spice trade was lost forever. Spanish and Italian shipping, even in the Mediterranean, cost more than the Dutch, was technologically backward, and suffered from insufficient investment capital.

Industry in southern Europe also declined. Italian woolen manufacturing, the industrial staple of the peninsula since 1100, dropped continuously during the seventeenth century, particularly in such established industrial centers as Milan. Part of the loss was because of the Dutch, and part was the result of industrial decentralization, as shops moved from the larger cities to small provincial centers. The significance of such a trend was unmistakable. Instead of producing for an international market, Italian manufacturers were making cloth for local consumption.

If the decline in Italian industrial production was relatively moderate, in Spain it was catastrophic. Spanish textiles, iron, and leather products virtually vanished from the market, and Spain became an importer of manufactured goods as well as food. Spanish mercantilists proposed various remedies for this industrial depression, but none worked. Indeed, so disorganized had Spain become that few remedies were even tried.

Economic and fiscal factors of the depression were compounded by intellectual ones. The paranoia of counter-Reformation Catholicism about heresy and freedom of thought shut Italy and Spain off from the intellectual currents of the rest of Europe at a time of great progress in science and technology. In the seventeenth century Dutch shipbuilding and textile manufacturing employed new and sophisticated techniques unknown in Spain. The Spanish were also outstripped by the English and Swedish in the manufacture of guns. Dutch civil engineers used techniques in drainage and water control that the Spanish had never heard of. Such knowledge was shut out of Spain and, to a lesser extent, Italy, because both kings and prelates felt any contact with Protestant learning was dangerous.

An additional factor in technological backwardness was the attitude of urban craft guilds, which assumed a growing defensive position after 1590. Possessing considerable local power, and anxious to preserve their members' livings in a time of depression, Spanish and Italian guilds fought any changes in technique on the grounds that it would force craftsemen out of work. Featherbedding became a way of life, as guilds restricted industrial technology and forced the production of goods that few wanted at a price even fewer would pay.

The cultural and social factors in the depression were vividly illustrated in the expulsion of the Moriscos from Spain. Ordered to convert from Islam to Christianity by Ferdinand and Isabella in 1502, the Moriscos had complied, but with reluctance, and were suspected by everyone of secretly retaining the old faith. High taxes and religious persecution drove the Moriscos of Castile to revolt in 1569–1571, which only confirmed the prevailing hatreds. Between 1609 and 1611 about 300,000 Moriscos were driven out, about 85 percent from Aragon and Valencia. In these two provinces they formed the bulk of the peasantry and petty artisans, and their departure produced an immediate and devastating economic collapse on top of already depressed conditions.

Political revolution compounded economic and social problems. In Spain, the gap between Castilian resources and ambitions grew so alarmingly that the government tried to increase taxation in Catalonia and Portugal. Both provinces revolted in 1640, with Portugal eventually winning independence in 1668. Three other revolts shook the Habsburg imperium—in Palermo in 1647, in Naples a year later, and in Messina in 1671–1674. Similar conditions caused all three revolts: general economic stagnation, unemployment, high bread prices, and the taunting memory of better times.

The final blow to the Mediterranean economy came from nature. Soil erosion and overgrazing in Spain and southern Italy restricted sheep pasturage and the output of wool and had begun to encroach upon the arable land as well. From 1599 to 1601, an outbreak of plague and a series of bad harvests struck Spain, causing widespread mortality and hastening the process of urban depopulation. In 1630 and again in 1657, Italy and Spain suffered from visits of the plague. As a result, the larger industrial towns—Milan, Burgos, and Medina del Campo—showed sharp population losses, which were not made up until the next century.

In the Mediterranean basin, the depression was so severe, so prolonged, and had so many adverse effects on all levels of government that it may be called a general crisis of state and society, reminiscent of the disasters of the fourteenth century. Previously powerful Mediterranean states suffered a reversal in every aspect of public life, and their peoples lost the sense of openness, confidence, and the impulses toward expansion so evident during the Renaissance and Reformation.

III

The depression in northern and central Europe began a generation later than in the south. Economic collapse coincided with the outbreak of war in 1618–1620: in Germany between the Habsburg Emperors and their Protestant subjects in Bohemia to open the Thirty Years' War; in the Low Countries between Spain and the Netherlands at the end of the Ten Years Truce of 1609, and in France between the king and the Huguenots. Universal war was more than the northern European economy could stand. The sharpest statistical indication of depression was the dramatic break in sound tolls—duties charged by Denmark on ships entering and leaving the Baltic Seas. These taxes dropped by two-thirds in the years after 1620 and only slowly recovered afterward.

The great depression in France began in the ordinary

way, with a collapse of royal credit and a break in international trade. In 1619, the crown bankrupted, having spent all the money saved by Sully in the regin of Henry IV. War, both civil and foreign, exacerbated the fiscal problems. This combination threw the fragile French economy into a sustained depression, marked by numerous peasant revolts against seigneurial and royal authority. As in southern Europe, economic difficulties were reflected in political and social turbulence. The slump reached its nadir in the 1650s, with stagnant trade, depressed agricultural prices, regressive royal taxation, and endless war.

A certain recovery came after 1660. France entered a decade of peace, and the mercantilist minister, Jean-Baptiste Colbert, struggled to create prosperity. Colbert's ideas included government support of industry, high tariffs, aid to shipping, lower taxes on agriculture, and a considerable government investment in social capital, such as roads, canals, and bridges. These efforts had some success, and French trade and industry showed genuine growth after 1660.

After Colbert's death, however, the crown reduced its aid to industry and turned once again to war and religious persecution. The war years, from 1685 to 1715, were a time of profound depression. The textile industry of Languedoc faded badly because of the renewed persecution of Huguenots, and overseas trade was nearly shut off by the British and Dutch navies. Royal finances fell into incredible disorder, and the few private lenders charged usurious rates. What money there was went into hiding or the purchase of nobility or royal office. Once again, poverty and persecution were accompanied by uprisings; the revolt of the Camisards in 1703 was so serious the government was forced to negotiate with the rebels. In spite of abundant royal folly, however, this second depression was not all the fault of the government. In 1691–1694 and again in 1709–1710 there were tremendous famines. The last was the worst natural disaster in the nation's history, and one million people perished from starvation, exposure, and disease.

French recovery from the seventeenth century depression,

therefore, waited until 1720. Nonetheless, eighteenth century France enjoyed a sustained prosperity, marked by a large population rise, sharp increases in trade, and a general growth in agricultural output. In spite of prosperity, France did not experience an industrial revolution on the British model. French manufacturing, while it expanded, did not undergo any substantial technological change. Thus, French economic history diverged sharply from the British in the century after 1675, and was also quite different from patterns in the Mediterranean basin and central Europe, where recovery was much slower and less pervasive.

IV

Not every European state experienced a general economic collapse in the first half of the seventeenth century. England and Holland did not experience a genuine economic retreat with less trade, demographic decline, fewer manufactured goods, and a reduction in agricultural productivity. Instead, they benefited from a shift of trade and industry from the Mediterranean basin northwards. The British and Dutch cornered the market on banking and credit, overseas trade, and basic industries at a time when most states were becoming progressively poorer. Although the total amount of wealth was smaller in 1640 than it had been half a century earlier, it was much more highly concentrated, confined to a remarkable degree to the northwestern corner of Europe.

Although the British did not enjoy the enormous prosperity of the Dutch, England escaped the awful economic carnage that occurred in Spain, Germany, and Turkey. Continuous war in the early seventeenth century kept up the demand for British cannon and textiles, and English shipping had a small but profitable share of the trade in sugar, slaves, tobacco, and fish. English coal and iron production grew after 1600. Agricultural productivity did also, partly because of continuing enclosures of the land and draining of fens and marshes. Nonetheless, this modest prosperity had some soft spots, which showed up most clearly where the English were directly competing with the Dutch. British carrying trade remained markedly inferior to the Dutch, who even captured a large share of the English coasting trade. In the Far East, the English were expelled from the Spice Islands by the Dutch in 1620 and were forced back on the less-profitable Indian trade. It was the same with manufacturing. The Cockayne project, 1614–1622, an attempt to prohibit export of undyed wool to the Netherlands, thus encouraging domestic dyeing, was a disastrous failure and damaged the British textile industry.

Reflecting on their economic position, contemporary English merchants saw numerous opportunities and loudly lamented that the Dutch were everywhere ahead of them. Dutch ". . . riches and multitude of shipping is the envy of the present . . . and yet the means whereby they have advanced themselves are . . . in great measure imitable . . . by us of the Kingdom of England," wrote the Restoration merchant Josiah Child. Along with envy and imitation went growing hostility. Oliver Cromwell warned that the Dutch wished to drive British Baltic trade from the seas and implied that war would be needed to stop the Dutch. The trade was worth it, and the wars were fought.

Dutch prosperity in the midst of universal distress was genuine and marvelous, and contemporaries sought explanations for it in every area of activity from divine intervention to criminal conspiracy. Actually, the reasons were both simpler and more complex, partly the result of fortunate circumstances, partly also coming from the industry and audacity of the Dutch themselves.

The Dutch alone possessed a government that gave first place to trade and profit and opposed war and religious conformity. "Above all things, war, and chiefly by sea, is most prejudicial and peace very beneficial for Holland," wrote a Dutch merchant and politician, Pieter de La Court, and he spoke the simple truth. Even for the Dutch, even fighting the decaying Spanish monarchy, war ate up the profits of peace, spectacular successes like Piet Heyn's capture of an entire

Spanish fleet notwithstanding. After the middle of the century, war with France and England would be even less rewarding, and the Dutch government consequently made great efforts to preserve peace.

In the seventeenth century, the booming Dutch economy rested on three pillars: a diverse and technologically sophisticated industry, universal domination of the carrying trade, and control of European banking, credit, and insurance. Dutch industry was the most varied and profitable in Europe and grew spectacularly on the ruins of industry elsewhere. Leyden became the center of the light and cheap "New Draperies," which were rapidly replacing the "Old Draperies" of Flanders and Italy. Amsterdam became the center for sugar refining and brewing, and the Dutch dominated printing, paper making, and the book trade well into the eighteenth century. Glass, pottery, tiles, and silk were all prosperous Dutch industries, migrating there from Italy and France. Dutch manufactures were largely finishing trades, where the profits were larger, the skills needed were greater and the technology was more sophisticated.

The most important Dutch industry, of course, was shipbuilding, which was a major concern of most of the towns along the Zuider Zee. The great shipyards at Zaandam near Amsterdam turned Baltic timbers into dozens of ships a year. These were mostly a new type, called *fluit*, invented at Hoorn about 1597 by Jan Linschoten. The *fluit* was the most advanced ship of the age, an immense improvement over conventional galleons because it was easier to handle and carried far more cargo with one-third the crew. The technological superiority of Dutch shipping amply reinforced their overwhelming numbers. In the early seventeenth century the Dutch owned between one-half and two-thirds of all European ships. They sent over 1000 ships a year to the North Sea fishing fleet, another 1500 or 2000 into the Baltic, another 2000 or so to Spain and the Mediterranean, as well as hundreds to Africa, the Far East, and America. The Dutch controlled every trade that existed. They were the only Eu-

ropean nation allowed to trade with Japan and, in 1619, a
Dutch ship arrived at the new colony of Virginia with its
first load of slaves.

Dutch superiority also extended to banking, credit, marine
insurance, and business methods generally. Amsterdam became the banking capital of Europe after the collapse of
Antwerp and the failures of Italian and Spanish banking
houses. The Bank of Amsterdam was founded in 1609, and
the Loan Bank in 1614, and they attracted liquid funds from
everywhere. The exchange bank quickly became the strongest financial institution in Europe, surviving the panic during the French invasion of 1672, and increasing its capital in
the long years of war that closed the seventeenth century.
Asmsterdam also possessed a bourse that was both a commodity exchange and a stock market. Marine insurance was
also available in the Netherlands, at better rates and from
more reliable underwriters than anywhere else. The Dutch
had rationalized business methods beyond anything seen outside of the now-decayed Italian city-states, and this provided
the base for large and continuing invisible exports.

The vigor of the expanding Dutch economy could also be
seen in the export of capital, business expertise, and engi-
neering skills. Dutch engineers were employed to drain
marshes all over Europe—in Poland, Tuscany, Rome, France,
Germany, and England. Only Spain escaped the Dutchman's
improving hand. The Dutch also played the dominant role in
developing the economies of the Baltic kingdoms. Louis de
Geer and Elias Trip, Amsterdam merchants, exploited the
resources of Sweden, using Dutch capital and technology
and business skills. They mined iron and copper; built saw-
mills, warehouses, and retail stores; marketed Swedish
products; and dominated Swedish public finances after 1618.
At the same time, the Marselis and Irgens families were
managing a similar empire in Denmark.

The most dramatic example of Dutch economic dominance, however, was the incredible Tulip Mania of
1634–1636. Imported from Turkey, tulips slowly became an
aristocratic status symbol and increased sharply in value.

Naturally, the Dutch controlled trade in this important commodity, and organized a market to sell rare bulbs. Tulips so captured aristocratic imagination that their price rose phenomenally, and the rarest specimens were selling for thousands of gold guilden each. In 1636, a single bulb went for:

two lasts of wheat
four lasts of rye
four fat oxen
eight fat pigs
twelve fat sheep
two barrels of wine
four barrels of beer
two barrels of butter
1000 pounds of cheese
one bed
one suit of clothes
one silver drinking cup

The crash came in November, 1636, and many people lost heavily, especially those caught with bulbs. But prosperity continued, and no one was discouraged from investing in Dutch banks, trade, or industry. Not until the sharp English competition after 1660 and the French war of 1672 did the Dutch lose their economic preeminence. And, even then, there was no absolute decline in trade or banking; instead the English, and later the French, grew so fast that the Dutch were simply left behind.

V

The seventeenth century depression marked the boundary between the medieval and modern configurations of European society and economy. Before 1600, the Mediterranean basin was the richest area of Europe and had been since the Egyptians. Wealth had been accompanied by technological superiority and a greater knowledge of science. In the sixteenth century, everyone bought Italian cannon and studied at Italian universities. Southern Europe also possessed the social and political attributes of wealth. Mediterranean society was more urban, more literate, more industrialized, and more polished. Governments were better organized, and several states—Venice, Turkey, Aragon, Castile, and Portugal —came equipped with empires. By comparison, northern Europeans were crude and the society backward, and they were called barbarians by the sophisticated Renaissance Italians.

In the late sixteenth century this all began to change. English and Dutch towns grew rapidly, while those in Italy and Spain declined. Scientific and technological knowledge steadily expanded in the north, and Cambridge replaced Padua as the most important university in Europe. Trade routes shifted from the Mediterranean to the Atlantic, to the great benefit of northern Europeans. English, Dutch, and French manufacturing eclipsed Italian and Spanish, particularly in the basic industries of textiles and metallurgy. Banking and credit institutions flourished in Holland but no longer in the south. Religious toleration crept into northern Europe, and intellectual freedom accompanied it. Northern governments gradually became more efficient and energetic than those of the Mediterranean basin. By the middle of the seventeenth century, even Englishmen were speaking sadly of the past glories of Italy, and condemning the sloth, poverty, and backwardness of Spain.

The great depression hit sooner in the Mediterranean basin, hit it harder, was much more pervasive, and remained far longer. Recovery in the Mediterranean area was not well under way until 1750, and, even then, remained slow and uneven. In some areas of the economy, such as American trade, the Mediterranean spice trade, or the Italian woolen industry, the losses were not made up at all. Collapse was permanent.

Outside of the Mediterranean, in general, the economic retreat, though genuine and severe, was temporary. The old economy was restored. Losses in trade, industry, population, and agricultural output were made up after 1660. Northern and central Europe were richer and more industrialized, and their traditional sources of wealth were on a firmer footing in 1730 than they had been a century or so earlier. Europe emerged from the depression, therefore, with the economic map familiar today—an industrialized and wealthy north and a backward, agricultural, and impoverished south. In the eighteenth century, northern Europe increased its economic superiority. The shift in patterns of economic dominance has been permanent.

BIBLIOGRAPHY

Serious historical scholarship on the seventeenth-century depression has just begun. Much of the bibliography is in the form of articles, and most of it is not in English. The three items listed below, therefore, are the best and most readily available of a rather skimpy historical literature.

Trevor Aston, *Crisis in Europe: 1560–1660,* is a collection of essays, half on England and half on continental history, dealing with various aspects of the seventeenth-century depression. They are all taken from the English journal, *Past and Present.* The lead article is a coherent Marxist interpretation of the depression by E. J. Hobsbawn, who initiated study of the crisis. His work is immense, but his conclusions are not entirely convincing, particularly about the origins of the depression. This is, in general, a difficult book, but essential for the student interested in the seventeenth-century depression.

Violet Barbour, *Capitalism in Amsterdam,* is a study of the economy of the leading Dutch commercial and industrial city. It contains a lot of detail presented in a rather confused manner.

J. H. Elliott, *The Revolt of the Catalans,* is a long, detailed, and superb book on one small part of the general depression. It deals with the history of Catalonia from the 1590s until the outbreak of revolution in 1640. It is fascinating reading. Highly recommended (hard cover).

THE WORLD RECONSIDERED: THE DEVELOPMENT OF MODERN SCIENCE

"I profess to learn and to
teach anatomy, not from books,
but from dissections, not from
the positions of philosophers
but from the fabric of nature."

William Harvey, *De Motu Cordis*

Men once believed that the seas were full of monsters ready to devour sailors who ventured too far from land. Mermaids would sing to sailors and entice them to their doom. Many thought that the southern seas were boiling and would destroy ships. The land was populated with strange animals, such as unicorns and the basilisk, a winged serpent whose very glance killed men. The earth itself stood in the center of the universe, and everything on it was composed of four basic elements: air, earth, fire, and water. In 1600, many still believed that the earth was flat, and almost none could be found to deny it was God's will that kept the stars in the heavens.

Some of these myths were merely fairy tales, and others were based on logic and learning. Some myths were believed by common folk, and others were taught in universities, as psychiatry is today. But these differences were only superficial. What mattered were attitudes and habits of thought. For centuries, as soon as Europeans had cast off one myth they substituted another, no less false or fanciful. Before the advent of modern science, with its experimental and mathematical methodology, there was no test for truth other than logic and revelation. These tests were as likely to give a coherent wrong answer as a right one. Patient scientific endeavor changed that, and, in the process, enabled Western man to develop the technology of modernity.

The development of modern science was a distinct although gradual break with the intellectual past, and also divided European civilization from the rest of the world. It changed the way men thought and set them searching for verified facts as the way to solve problems. Philosophy became sharply divided from science. The scientific revolution was one of the transcendent factors of western civilization. It outweighs ". . . everything since the rise of Christianity and reduces the Renaissance and Reformation to the rank of mere episodes. . . ."[1] That large judgment is almost certainly an understatement.

I

The astronomer and physicist, Galileo Galilei (1964–1642) did not work in isolation. He taught at the University of Padua and later gathered a group of assistants and students. At his death they did not all disperse nor abandon scientific studies. Two of them, Viviani (1622–1703) and Evangelista Torricelli (1608–1647), remained in Florence and, in 1657, established the *Accademia del Cimento,* the first formal scientific society in Europe. The purpose of the *Accademia* was to stimulate scientific research, publish the results, and bring scientists together to discuss their projects. This seemed like a good idea, which the English copied in 1662 when Charles II granted a charter to the Royal Society. In France, too, an academy was established, developing from informal meetings of scientists and mathematicians and receiving recognition and support from Louis XIV in 1666. Such societies filled the role played in medieval Europe by universities, now in deep decline, inhospitable to science, and sunk in traditional law and theology.

Academies were not the only factor clumping scientists to-

[1] Herbert Butterfield, *The Origins of Modern Science,* p. 7.

gether in the seventeenth century. There was also the coincidence of birth and nationality, which was reflected in centers of research. Scientists gathered in four areas in the seventeenth century, not far from the birthplaces of most of them. These were Holland, where there was no formal academy, southern England, Paris, and northern Italy, particularly the major towns of Florence, Padua, and Bologna. Three of these clusters were in northwestern Europe, and there was constant and general contact among them. Thus, René Descartes (1596–1650), the French mathematician-philosopher, worked in Holland, claiming there was more freedom there, while Christian Huygens (1629–1695), the Dutch physicist, spent much of his time in Paris.

The academies and the clusters of scientists illustrated two of the basic social factors responsible for the development of modern science: convergence (groups of scientists who compared their work) and impetus (the building of one scientific discovery upon another). These two factors were obviously interrelated; both impetus and convergence were clearly apparent in the functioning of the scientific centers in northern Italy and northwestern Europe. Scientists born outside of these general areas traveled toward them. Gottfried Leibniz (1646–1716) came from Germany to Paris, the anatomist Andreas Vesalius (1514–1564) came from Belgium to Padua, and Nicolaus Copernicus (1473–1546), the astronomer, came from Poland to study at Padua, Bologna, and Rome. In an age of poor communications, imperfect scientific vocabularies, inexact mathematical notation, widely varying skills in instrumentation, and the constant threat of religious persecution, such personal and professional contact was absolutely necessary. No one, working alone, could break through the medieval ideas of nature. The body of scientific information only grew with communication, with impetus, and with convergence.

These factors were first observed in Renaissance Italy, the mecca for philosophers, humanists, and artists of all Europe. By the 1580s, however, as the Counter-Reformation reached full stride, Italian science, letters, and philosophy came under attack from the church. In Italy, the Roman Catholic Church existed in all its wealth, power, and prestige and was imbued with the growing paranoia about heterodoxy and intellectual freedom. Galileo was arrested by the Inquisition in 1633 for having supported Copernican views and spent the rest of his life under house arrest. The papacy succeeded in persuading the Republic of Venice to censor the University of Padua, and the *Accademia del Cimento* in Florence ended in 1667 when its Medici patron became a cardinal. With the collapse of the *Accademia,* one of its members, Antonio Oliva, was arrested by the Inquisition, and he killed himself to escape torture for heresy. Clerical persecution was too great for the small cluster of scientists to survive, and they were snuffed out in the name of God.

In northwestern Europe it was different. The established churches in England and Holland were relatively weak and had too limp a hold on political power or the people's affections to impose any notions of scientific, or even theological, orthodoxy. In both states there was a modest toleration and religious persecution, although it existed, was sporadic and ineffectual. Moreover, technological improvements were more numerous in the north, and the instrumentation for experiments was correspondingly better. Finally, governments were at least marginally interested in science because it was good for business. Improvements in draining technique and navigation were essential to Dutch prosperity, and the government gave some encouragement to men with technical and scientific expertise. In northern Europe, convergence and impetus tended to mean an increase in the number of scientists and technicians, a greater range of subjects studied, an increase in the number of books published, and a general expansion in the amount of scientific knowledge. And, at least in England, this was a significant factor in the coming of industrialization.

II

During the Renaissance, Western man thought of his world in much the same way as his ancestors had for centuries. Christian theologies of nature, grafted on Greek and Roman foundations, were generally accepted as correct. The traditional natural concepts and ideas were logical, coherent, reasonable, and in accord with what could be seen and verified by observation. They had the additional merit of being relatively consistent with most of the mathematics inherited from antiquity. Finally, they seemed to glorify God and His handiwork, which was a good and pious thing for men to do. There was no reason to abandon the old ideas.

The most elaborate of the inherited concepts of nature involved the heavens. Celestial bodies were seen revolving around the earth, and what was observed was incorporated into an elaborate theory of astronomy. The earth itself stood still at the center of the universe and was infinitely heavy and solid. Everything else moved in allotted curved paths through the sky around the earth. This earth-centered (geocentric) theory had been inherited from the Hellenistic philosopher Claudius Ptolemy, who had synthesized the work of several of his predecessors. Ptolemy's work had survived into the Middle Ages through Islamic intermediaries and was readily accepted by Christians. It accounted for most of the phenomena that could be observed with the unaided eye and had a satisfactory, indeed, excellent level of predictability. What deviations there were could be assigned to the awesome and mysterious power of God. By and large, geocentric astronomy worked just fine and answered all the questions about the heavens that medieval philosophers cared to ask.

Allied to Ptolemaic astronomy as a kind of physics, inspired by Aristotle. It, too, had a high level of predictability and was reasonable, coherent, and explained the observed data. Aristotelian philosophers argued that no object moved without a mover and, when the mover ceased his pressure, the object returned to its natural state—rest. Certainly, an apple on a table did not move on its own. Neither did the earth, which was so big, so solid, and so heavy that nothing could move it. The Prime Mover, who had set the heavens in motion, had given things the power to move toward the center of the universe that, of course, was the earth. Heavy things like iron naturally fell faster than light things such as a feather, as any fool could plainly see. It all made a lot of sense.

Though subsequently proved wrong, these ideas were far from unscientific. They rested firmly on observed reality and were supported by a rigorous system of logical analysis. Symbols or myth, the bulwarks of medieval art and sculpture were absent from Aristotelian or Ptolemaic science. These were based on nature, not magic. Much of this exactness derived from medieval scientists, such as Jean Buridan, Roger Bacon, Nicolas d'Oresme, or Grosseteste, who based their philosophy on careful observation of nature. To this must be added the intellectual precision of medieval theologians, particularly the Scholastics. Thus, the scientific revolution did not occur out of nothing but grew logically and directly from the traditions and habits of medieval thought.

None of the medieval concepts survived the assault made upon them by higher mathematics, disciplined investigation, numerous experiments, new scientific instruments, and the insights of genius during the seventeenth century. As the traditional axioms were discarded, they became not merely false but ridiculous. No sane man could believe in them, and many wondered how their ancestors, so wise in other things, could have been taken in by such transparent nonsense. But Ptolemaic astronomy and Aristotelian physics were not transparent and, for a society with a primitive technology and modest mathematics, they were not nonsense. To a peasant looking over his fields the earth appeared flat and, for all his purposes, it was flat. The sun seemed to circle the earth, not just once but every day. Common sense and long experience combined to assure everyone that nothing moved without a mover; when the oxen stopped pulling the plow the plow stopped also. The medieval scientific concepts about the natural world may have been wrong, but they conformed to experience and observation to an exceptional degree, and they still do.

In the last years of the Renaissance, however, theological attempts to explain and order nature began to break down. Ancient texts recently recovered included treatises on mathe-

matics and science as well as philosophy, and much of the
new material did not fit into the existing theologies. The insights and computations of previously forgotten Greek philosophers pointed up embarrassing inconsistencies in the accepted Ptolemaic astronomy. New investigation showed
areas where the revered ancient masters, such as Aristotle,
had not said the last word. The erosion of medieval scientific
doctrine was fairly slow for several decades after 1500,
hampered by the tumult of the Reformation, the persistent
opposition of all churches, the lack of a clearly scientific
method, and insufficient mathematics. But medieval science,
in spite of its prestige and orthodoxy, was slowly being
abandoned.

III

The first dramatic repudiation of inherited scientific doctrine occurred with the publication of *The Revolution of
Heavenly Bodies* by Nicolas Copernicus. Copernicus did not
publish until on his deathbed, fearing the ridicule and hostility that must come from espousing heretical doctrine during
religious troubles. In spite of delays in announcing his
views, however, Copernicus had held them for a long time.
In 1500 he had been teaching mathematics in Rome and had
come into contact with the ancient Greek theories that held
the earth was revolving on its axis around the sun. Using his
mathematical knowledge, Copernicus uncovered numerous
errors and inconsistencies in the Ptolemaic theory, and he
swung to the concept that the earth actually circled the sun,
in spite of all appearances to the contrary. Copernicus had
not emancipated himself from the preconceptions of philosophy, however. He did not make the astronomical observations necessary to prove that the earth was the satellite. Instead, he argued from mathematics, logic, and reason, just
as Ptolemy himself had done. Furthermore, Copernicus
argued that the earth moved in a circular orbit around the
sun because the circle was the most perfect geometric form,
and anything less would be contrary to the glory of God. In

spite of this traditional approach, Copernicus' book drew mainly scorn. Philosophers and theologians, including Martin Luther, dismissed his work and continued to believe as before.

Nonetheless, Nicolas Copernicus had made a serious dent in the Ptolemaic astronomy, which was now shown to need constant, numerous, and significant readjustments. Other mathematicians and philosophers examined these discrepancies, but without new observations and data no one could prove the case for either theory. As the experiments were made, however, they went beyond merely providing additional data to solve a theological argument. Experimentation widened the scope of discussion immensely, offering the distressing possibility that both theories might be wrong. Much more, the experiments in astronomy initiated a change in the methodology of science. Logic and reason, the tools of medieval scientist-theologians, were proving inadequate as things both logical and reasonable enough were shown to be untrue. Logic and reason were made subordinate to experimentation, to precise and continuous measurement, and to observation. After Copernicus, astronomy became heavily experimental, as scientists concentrated on accumulating reams of data and making computations from that. Copernicus had been a mathematician-philosopher who had happened to be right. Essentially, this was accidental; Copernicus' mathematics and logical deductions could have as easily led to the opposite conclusion, as for most men it did. Reliance on experiment ended all that.

The accumulation of data began with the work of Tycho Brahe (1546–1601), a Danish astronomer. Brahe designed and constructed the most advanced scientific equipment of his time which enabled astronomers to pinpoint star location and make accurate star altitude measurements. Using his new instruments, Brahe made mountains of measurements, which tended to discredit both the Copernican and Ptolemaic views, the latter much more severely. Brahe thus built his own theory, a kind of compromise between the two systems, stating that the planets moved around the sun, while the sun it-self circled the earth.

If Brahe's theories fell through at the first push, his meas-urements were quite accurate and complete. Johan Kepler (1571–1630), his sometime assistant, showed what could be done with them, using the new mathematics of logarithms recently perfected by John Napier (1550–1617). Kepler worked for years over Brahe's data, to which he added his own. In the end, he discovered the three essential laws gov-erning the solar system. Kepler discarded the circular orbits of Copernicus and proved that the planets moved in elliptical orbits with the sun at one focus of the ellipse. He also showed that planets traveled faster when closer to the sun and slower when farther away. The third law was more technical. Kepler proved that the times needed by the planets to complete their orbits were proportional, when squared, to their cubed distance from the sun. This was difficult to un-derstand, and it still is. It marked a major benchmark in the journey of science from something understood by all educat-ed men to a group of disciplines that only specialists could grasp, and then only in part.

While Kepler was struggling toward his three laws of planetary motion, Galileo Galilei was also observing the heav-ens. Using a telescope of his own invention, Galileo peered at the planet Jupiter and saw four of its moons. He saw indi-vidual stars in the Milky Way and the rings of Saturn. It all convinced him of the Copernican theory, and he said so. He presented his views in a superb book, *Dialogue on the Two Principal Systems of the Universe* (1632), and obliterated the Ptolemaic theories. The Roman Catholic Church was out-raged. The Inquisition had stated in 1616 that ". . . the view that the Earth is not the center of the universe . . . is philo-sophically false." Galileo was brought to trial and forced to recant his horrible heresy. He also had to give up astronomy.

Galileo and Kepler had destroyed the Ptolemaic theories utterly and proved that the Copernican system, as lately cor-rected, was right. But the basic laws that governed the uni-

verse still eluded precise and mathematical definition, in spite
of the vast amount of data that had been acquired. Sir Isaac
Newton (1642–1727) fit it all together. In 1687 he published
his *Principia Mathematica,* after considerable prodding
from his colleagues. Newton stated that gravity varied according to distance and to mass, which was the amount of
matter an object contained. The greater the mass, the greater the gravitational pull. The amount of gravitational force
exerted by a body varied inversely as the squared distance
between their centers. Newton also described inertia, the
force that kept bodies moving continuously on the same line.
Thus, the solar system was the balance between inertia and
gravity and, by extension, this applied to star systems as
well.

Newton's work not only contained new and startling scientific insights, which completed the work of Kepler and
Galileo, it also presented laws of such grandeur and general
validity that his synthesis passed into philosophy. In simple
and general terms, although not in technical detail, the heavens were comprehensible again. Philosophers came to com-
pare the stars and planets to a giant and stable clock, running in absolute and placid obedience to Newton's laws. God
was no longer needed, at least He was no longer continually
on call. He was seen as the primeval engineer who had put
the system together in the beginning and given it motion.
Now, He was retired.

Astronomy, therefore, had been completely divorced from
theology. It had become a self-sufficient, scientific discipline
with its own laws, methodology, insights, and conclusions. It
was the first science to be stated in its own terms, outside
the framework of religious explanation or philosophical
speculation. Even the clerics agreed.

IV

During the seventeenth century, work in the physical sciences included more than astronomy. There were numerous
experiments in light, mechanics, heat, sound, magnetism,

and gases and liquids, far more indeed than in astronomy it-self. But physics and mechanics attracted far less attention than astronomy although the progress made, at least in technological terms, was much more significant. There were several reasons for this. Aristotelian physics had never become a basic part of theological speculation, and so it was not heresy to upset old ideas. Nor had medieval physics been very complete, and most experiments and theories of seventeenth century scientists dealt with phenomena previously unknown or unexplained. Medieval philosophers themselves had disagreed sharply about various components of Aristotle's work, and so heterodox explanations were already in the public domain. Finally, the work of physicists rapidly became heavily technical and very hard to understand, so few could follow or cared to debate the results that experiments produced.

As important as the insights of scientists was the development of adequate instruments, without which there could be no experiments. So closely were these connected that they frequently revolved around the equipment, and success in one meant success in both. Nowhere was this relationship sharper than in experiments with air pressure and vacuums, which destroyed the old axiom that nature abhorred a vacuum. A German nobleman, Otto von Guericke (1602–1686), conceived the experiment but could not perform it until he had built a vacuum pump and two perfectly round metal hemispheres. Having constructed his equipment, von Guericke performed a spectacular experiment before the Imperial Diet at Ratisbon in 1654. He bolted the copper hemispheres together, pumped much of the air out, and hitched two teams of horses to the spheres. The horses did their best, stimulated by the whip, but they couldn't pull the hemispheres apart, proving the immense power of air pressure and the fact that air had weight and volume. The same relationship between instruments and experiments could be seen elsewhere, with astronomy and the telescope, with the clock and studies of motion.

Galileo was the real founder of modern physics, and his

achievements here were even more substantial than in astronomy. He was interested in several things: the motion of a pendulum, laws concerning falling bodies, the path of projectiles, theories about sound, and the weight of air. Galileo's work was both mathematical and experimental, although the most famous experiment of all, dropping unequal weights from the Leaning Tower of Pisa to see them hit the ground together, never took place. Experiments to discover the laws of falling bodies took place on an inclined plane. After considerable effort, part of which was devoted to using a pendulum to measure elapsed time, Galileo discovered that objects fell at a uniform, accelerating velocity, which he expressed mathematically. From this, Galileo calculated the arc of a projectile, such as a cannonball, to be a parabola. Most of this research, which was the basis of the science of dynamics, was published in his last book, *Dialogue on Two New Sciences*, published in Holland in 1638, after his ordeal with the Inquisition and after he had become blind.

Scientists throughout the century kept busy following Galileo's leads. His assistant, Evangelista Torricelli, invented the barometer and provided irresistible proof of Galileo's contention that air had mass and weight. The English physicist, Robert Boyle (1627–1691), elaborated on the experiments of Torricelli and formulated Boyle's Law, which stated that air can be compressed by pressure, and when the pressure is removed, it returns to its former dimensions. Boyle also conducted experiments that supported and improved upon Galileo's theories about sound, while the Dutch scientist Christian Huygens followed Galileo's theories about pendulums and invented a pendulum clock, by far the most accurate timepiece in Europe.

The area where scientists went farthest beyond Galileo was in optics. Although Galileo had worked with both microscopes and telescopes, he had not really investigated the properties of light, other than to try to determine its velocity, which was far too great for him to measure. Kepler was concerned with light and arrived at a basic law of photometry: that light intensity varies as the square of the distance from the source. He found this formula in a truly inspiring manner. He more or less guessed it since his experimental proof was primitive and inadequate. Nonetheless, he was still right.

Kepler's work, both its success and its limitations, led directly to the optical research of Sir Isaac Newton. Newton became interested in optics because of the chromatic aberration or color distortion around the edges of the lens of his refracting telescope. Newton experimented with prisms and arrived at some enlightening results. Isolating the various colors produced by the prism, he found that the colors were of unequal length, and that the laws of refraction applied to each color separately. White light was thus made up of the various colors of the spectrum, and the colors of things resulted from various colors being reflected in different degrees. Newton published these experiments and conclusions from time to time, and included them all in *Opticks* (1704). He also gave up trying to correct refracting telescopes and built a reflecting one instead.

In spite of vast and astounding progress in physics and mechanics, there were few general laws that brought a sense of order to man's view of his world. The feats of astronomy were not duplicated. Terrestrial mechanics never assumed the guise of certainty that caressed astronomers. No one thought of the world as a giant clock. Moreover, physics had become technical, so dependent on precise instrumentation and higher mathematics and so contrary to common sense that most people never thought of it at all but consigned it to the experts. There were few popular handbooks on physics like Voltaire's little work explaining Newton to the ladies.

V

The stupendous progress in astronomy and physics rested on equally large changes in mathematics, which made explanations and computations about motion, mass, and gravity possible. In 1500, Europeans were still assimilating algebra and geometry inherited from the Greeks and Arabs.

This was relatively simple mathematics, and its notation
was primitive and variable. In spite of this, however, mathematics was the most advanced science Renaissance Europeans knew, and the most highly esteemed.

Mathematics was a traditional discipline, of course,
taught in medieval universities and occasionally incorporated into theological speculations—although not doctrine. Under these conditions, progress in mathematics followed traditional lines. Algebra, geometry, and notation were the first
areas of improvement. The initial major leap was the invention of logarithms by the Scottish nobleman, John Napier.
Napier's two books included his tables of logarithms and
rules for their use. Logarithms made the extraction of roots
a simple matter of division and enabled Kepler to calculate
his three laws of planetary motion. So useful were they that
mathematicians began compiling logarithm tables for ever
larger numbers, and a Dutch book of 1628 covered all numbers up to 100,000, enough to take care of most ordinary
needs.

While work in geometry had been continuous since the
Renaissance, René Descartes, the French philosopher-mathe-
matician, made some serious and original contributions. In
his book, *Geometry* (1637), Descartes presented, in a rather
sketchy fashion, the principles of analytical geometry. This
was reinforced by a more complete exposition of analytical
geometry by Pierre Fermat (1601–1665), a leader in the
Paris group of scientists that evolved into the French Academy of Sciences. At the same time, a young French prodigy,
Blaise Pascal (1623–1662), produced a book on conic geometry at the age of 16. Pascal was also a founder of probability
theory. Asked by a gambler why some dice combinations
were more frequent than others, Pascal corresponded with
Fermat on the problem and produced some tentative theories. His work fulfilled a widely felt social need.

The most complicated mathematics of the period was the
work of Isaac Newton and Gottfried Leibniz. This was the
elaboration of the principles of integral and differential calculus, complicated and difficult material as every student

knows. Newton thought mathematical quantities resulted from motion: ". . . lines are described . . . by the continued motion of points. . . ." This added a new dimension to geometry. Always reluctant to publish, Newton held his work back, some of which was not printed until his death. Thus Leibniz, working in the same direction, came up with similar theories, somewhat after Newton but before Newton's work was known. Though basically the same, Leibniz' papers contained a clear, precise, and superior notation, which has since been retained.

These new discoveries in mathematics were far beyond the capacity of everyone to understand, and they surpassed the capacities of many philosophers as well. In medieval Europe, mathematics had been the ally of philosophy and the guide to logic. Now, it was becoming part of science. Its very exactness and precision, so important to the abstract speculations of theology, have become an impediment to describing human affairs and conditions. The change in the uses of mathematics was a large part of the growing separation of science and philosophy in Western culture. Recent attempts by logicians to revive the medieval alliance between mathematics and philosophy have been unconvincing.

VI

Although controversies about the heavens were genuinely spectacular, they had far less impact on the daily life of most Europeans than more homely discoveries in biology and medicine. These raised almost no fuss at all, largely because biology had not been incorporated into theology, having previously been considered tainted, the province of witches and Jews. Thus, biologists outraged only doctors, then a far less influential segment of society than priests. But these quiet discoveries counted for something just the same. Official medicine during the Renaissance had been atrocious, and the ministrations of witches and other non-Euclidean quacks were not much better. In 1550, faith healing was still the high road to recovery. The discoveries of anatomists, surgeons, and biologists during the Old Regime began to change this, providing the basis for medical cures and vastly increasing man's knowledge of the life around him.

Eighteenth-century Londoners sang a ditty about one of their most famous physicians, a certain John Lettsom. It was not encouraging.

> *When any sick to me apply*
> *I physicks, bleeds and sweats 'em*
> *If, after that, they choose to die.*
> *Why, verily, I Lettsom.*

In spite of pessimism that peeps through such passages, and such practices as fire-axe amputation, medicine had made considerable progress by the eighteenth century, although much of this improvement was made by comparison to its previous low and barbarous condition. Gains in medical practice occurred primarily in three areas : improved instruments and treatment, new medications superior to bat wings and pulverized lice, and more detailed study of particular diseases. But these changes did not come easy. As a rule, both doctors and patients were against them.

Improved medical instruments changed diagnosis radically, introducing quantitative data into the tricky business of deciding what ailed the patient. The thermometer was a good example. Probably invented by Galileo, it was first used extensively in clinical practice by his friend, Sanctorius Sanctorius (1561–1636). Previously, a doctor could only tell for sure if a patient had a fever when he approached delirium. It was the same with the pulse. Prior to the pulsimeter, again introduced by Sanctorius, doctors had no idea what a normal pulse was and were reduced to saying that a patient with no pulse at all was quite sick. These two instruments alone added immensely to the exact statements that could be made about various diseases.

Doctors also improved their treatment, which they badly needed to do. The great French surgeon, Ambroise Paré

(1510–1590), commented that the ". . . operations of Chirurgery are learn't by the eye and by the touch . . . ," and his years as a military surgeon demonstrated the wisdom of that view. In his first campaign in Italy in 1537, Paré immensely improved the method for treating gunshot wounds. It was customary to pour boiling oil in the wounds but Paré, running out of oil, used a poultice instead. The following morning Paré's patients were recovering and were not feverish, while many of the others were in great pain with infected wounds. Paré also began treating burns with soda and salt and invented the tourniquet for use during amputation. Perhaps Paré's greatest insight, which he shared with the English physician Thomas Sydenham (1624–1689), was that many of the old medications and treatments were harmful to the patient and ought to be abandoned. The doctor would do well if he did not damage his patient more than the disease did, and most people would get well faster if doctors did less for them. Both Paré and Sydenham frequently prescribed rest and a good diet, and both were regarded as the greatest physicians of their age.

Doctors also improved their ability to recognize varieties of disease, clearly an important matter. Effective medicine rests ". . . upon getting as genuine and natural a description, or history, of all diseases as can be procured . . . ," wrote Thomas Sydenham, stating a view widely held by everyone. Beginning with a poem on syphilis in 1530 by Girolamo Fracastoro (1478–1553), there appeared a steady stream of books on particular illnesses. Some were excellent, most were less than that, but they all had the merits of being based on observation of the facts, more or less. Gradually, physicians came to distinguish between diseases, even ones they could not cure.

Although medical knowledge grew enormously in the century and a half since Luther, it remained disorganized, scattered in hundreds of separate books and pamphlets in various languages written over 15 decades. Much of the new knowledge was not taught in the medical schools. More important still, there was no theoretical base for medicine. Sydenham flirted with the germ theory of disease, but he was far from specific and no one followed the hint. Nor was there much attempt to explain mental illness beyond the pernicious intervention of devils. Medicine remained an almost completely empirical profession, and treatment involved mainly trial and error, particularly error.

A final barrier to improving medical knowledge and care was the easy way people entered the profession. Medical schools were not much good, but they gave better training than that received by a barber's apprentice, who practiced a crude therapy indeed. The sixteenth century charter of the Royal College of Physicians stated that ". . . a great multitude of ignorant persons . . . as smiths, weavers and women boldly and accustomably took upon them great cures, to the high displeasure of God . . . and the grievous hurt, damage and destruction of many of the King's leige people." Well, during the eighteenth century, they still did. But the damage was not quite so great, and the slow increase in biological knowledge meant that medicine would get better yet.

The study of biology in the years after 1550 lay primarily in three areas: anatomy and physiology, the description and classification of plants and animals (taxonomy), and investigations with the microscope. The progress in anatomy was particularly dramatic and involved in a sharp break with inherited doctrine. During the Renaissance, Europeans still accepted the notions found in Galen, the biologists' Aristotle. Galen taught that the four elements—heat, cold, wetness and dryness (air, earth, fire, and water)—found their counterpart in the body in the form of humors—blood, phlegm, and black and yellow bile. Health was the proper balance of these substances, illness the opposite. Blood was thought to be formed in the liver, and various parts of the body produced incorporeal "vital spirits," also necessary to health. This elaborate and quite reasonable theory was sharply attacked in the sixteenth century. Andreas Vesalius, a professor at the medical school at Padua, published a monumental study, *On the Structure of the Human Body* in 1543, and the revolution in anatomy began the same year as the one in astronomy. Vesalius took his doctrine from nature, from numerous and careful dissections, and his book contained elaborate and accurate plates. Vesalius' work was a masterpiece, and also a revolution.

The method of study by dissections that Vesalius used continued at Padua after his death. The English physician, William Harvey (1578–1657), studied at Padua, absorbed the methods used there, and described the circulation of the blood in his great treatise, *On the Movement of the Heart and the Blood*. Harvey showed that arteries carried blood from the heart to the rest of the body, and veins carried it back. He did not understand the capillary system, which was only described in 1660 by Marcello Malpighi (1628–1694). Nonetheless, Harvey's work destroyed the physiology of Galen and opened new avenues of medical treatment.

Along with growing knowledge about man, scientists added to an understanding of plants and animals. Botany grew out of the aristocratic practice of maintaining gardens of rare and useful plants, more as a status symbol than anything else. The curators of these gardens wished to classify their plants, and, finding no satisfactory system at hand, made up their own. These early botanists, Clusius (1525–1609), Lobelius (1538–1616), and Kasper Bauhin (1560–1624) made many mistakes in their classifications, but they worked directly from the plants and were right far more often than they were wrong. Zoology, however, was not so far advanced, since it lacked aristocratic patronage and depended solely upon scientific curiosity. Nonetheless, there was some work done. The English biologist, John Ray (1628–1705), who had written a book on plants, also published a classification of animals as well, dividing them into species and families and recognizing that fossils were the remains of extinct forms.

Botany and zoology involved large species, which everyone could see, whether or not he knew what they were. The microscope opened a new world that no one had known about before. Crude microscopes existed around 1610, and both Galileo and Harvey used them, although sparingly. The first extensive microscopic investigations were made by Marcello Malpighi and Jan Swammerdam (1637–1682). Malpighi examined silk worms and chicken embryos and first explained how lungs worked. Swammerdam's research with microorganisms led him to reject the hallowed and ancient notion of spontaneous generation. The premier microscope investigator of his age was the Dutch civil servant, Anton van Leeuwenhoek (1632–1723), who was entirely self-taught and who constructed his instruments himself. He looked through the microscope because he enjoyed it, and his research was vast and disorganized. As a result of immense, random viewing, Leeuwenhoek discovered both bacteria and protozoa and could tell them apart. He did not attempt to fit all this into any coherent theory. Leeuwenhoek was no philosopher and, basically, he did not care how his discoveries affected current doctrine. He left that to others.

By the early years of the eighteenth century, Europeans probably knew as much biology as astronomy, mathematics, or physics. But the biological knowledge was not organized into any theoretical framework, and scientists were unaware of the implications of what they did know. Not until Linnaeus was there any attempt to integrate Leeuwenhoek's discoveries into a consistent theory of taxonomy. Little effort was made to incorporate biological knowledge into public sanitation or medicine. Indeed, scientists were sometimes hostile to the implication of their own work. John Ray's insights on fossils and extinct species were incompatible with both Biblical and popular conceptions about the Creation and the age of the world. For biology, the struggle between science and orthodoxy was just beginning.

VII

"We were entirely mistaken . . . ," wrote Blaise Pascal in 1656 in his *Provincial Letters*. "It was only yesterday that I was undeceived. Until that time I had labored under the impression that the disputes in the Sorbonne were vastly important, and deeply affected the interests of religion." Pascal intended to ridicule his Jesuit opponents and, in a light and agreeable manner, make a serious case for his own doctrine. The great mathematician and philosopher believed that the interests of religion were peculiarly important, the central question for all mankind. Once everyone had thought that. Now religion was losing its overriding importance in the minds of many Europeans. The insights of science were replacing the insights of revelation, and Pascal's mathematics seemed more important than his theology. The doctrines for which Pascal pled so eloquently would soon die of disuse. The new science was not, of course, incompatible with a religious view of life, but it was fatal to theological speculations that attempted to explain the natural world in terms of awe and mystery, logically organized.

Although the great doctrinal struggles were ending, the intellectual habits supporting systematic religion lingered on. Knowledge was still imperfectly separated from belief and faith, and all learning, of whatever origin, was regarded as a unity, a whole. Men still thought it possible to combine all knowledge into a single, coherent system of thought. The division of learning into sciences and humanities had only begun. This unity of thought did not survive the extraordinary expansion of science after 1600. Knowledge was increasingly divided into compartments, each with different methods of inquiry, separate areas of study, and large and complicated bodies of data. There was more to know, and people who knew different things drifted apart into different fields of study. Questions that scientists asked had become separated from those about which philosophers might speculate.

The most serious problem faced by theologians and philosophers was the collapse of credibility in large speculative systems. Traditionally charged with explaining everything in a precise and logical manner consistent with revelation, theologians had advanced theories now and again since the Stone Age. These theories sank in the seventeenth century, victims of some inconvenient data and the extraordinary complexity of the natural world. As a result, speculative thinkers of all sorts suffered a substantial loss of intellectual territory. The advance of experimental science began to remove the natural world from the realm of theology or philosophy.

The intellectual ground unwillingly abandoned by theologians did not lie fallow. Men still wanted to know the meaning, order, and purpose of the world, and there were philosophers who endeavored to bring the insights and methods of science to bear upon the traditional questions of philosophy and theology. The first to attempt this in any large way was Francis Bacon (1561–1626), who was Lord Chancellor of England until he was convicted of taking a bribe. Bacon harbored a monumental and unreasonable contempt for theology, stating that ". . . this kind of degenerate learning did chiefly reign amoung the Scholastics, who, having . . . small variety of reading . . . and knowing little history, either of nature or time, did, out of no great quantity of matter . . . spin out unto us these laborous webs of learning . . ." (*Advancement of Learning,* Book I). Traditional theories about the universe were worthless, and no new theory ought to be accepted unless it corresponded rigorously to empirically and experimentally verified data. Observation and experiment was needed but, instead, philosophers just chopped logic. Their vast speculations might be stitched together with meticulous precision, but they were not grounded in experiment and so were based on false premises.

Bacon's theories had serious drawbacks when examined in detail, however. His idea of inductive, scientific reasoning was awkward and clumsy and, in his antagonism to theory, he equated any attempt at synthesis with nonsense. Yet Bacon's own scientific speculations were not distinguished, and resembled the philosophy he detested far more than the experiment he admired. But his ideas took root and were the basis for the foundation of the Royal Society in 1662.

Bacon's insistence that philosophy should be based on experiment was matched by René Descartes' demand that it follow mathematics. Brought up in a humanist tradition, Descartes suffered an adult conversion to mathematics, much as Luther had embraced justification by faith. Descartes came suddenly to believe that the universe could be expressed in mathematical, symbolic terms, and he set out to do it. The methods of mathematicians were the best because they were the most exact and began with the simplest notions and axioms, proceeding only then to the more complex. Descartes did the same thing. He reduced everything to one single statement, which was unqualifiedly true: "I think; therefore I am." From this small start, Descartes built an entire vision of the universe by rigorous application of deductive logic based on mathematical models. His universe had two characteristics. It was utterly mechanistic, including man who was treated as a machine, and it demanded a sharp, irreconcilable division between mind and body.

The Cartesian system, because of its mathematical rigor and simplicity, proved to be incompatible with both observed reality about man and experimental science. The deductive method of logical analysis excluded exceptions and complexity, and this assumption of radical simplicity was its downfall. The "fabric of nature" simply did not conform to the precise and total simplicity Descartes had imagined. His notions, which passed the theological test of logic, failed in the school of experiment. Bacon, in spite of his intellectual disorder, had the keener insight into the nature of things.

A third philosopher whose work was greatly influenced by scientific methods and discoveries was the English physician, John Locke (1632–1704), who spent most of his life as a politician. These absorbing pursuits did not obliterate his interest in philosophy and, in 1690, Locke published his *Essay Concerning Human Understanding*. Locke denied the existence of innate ideas, ideas born in the mind. Instead, man got all he knew from sense perceptions. All thoughts, ideas, impressions, and reflections began with seeing, hearing, touching, and so on, with physical and intellectual contact with the environment. Experience was the book of knowledge. The mind then organized experience into general patterns and theories and reflected upon these and refined them as new experiences and new knowledge indicated.

Locke's views thus reflected the empirical and experimental traditions of Bacon, rather than the tight and simplistic logic of Descartes. Indeed, Locke depended only marginally on logic. Instead, it was the first serious attempt to explain how we know what we know in terms of exclusively natural and material phenomena, in terms of what was observed to occur.

In Newton's time, the sharp boundary now drawn between philosophy and science did not yet exist. Men worked in both fields and were not embarrassed to hold philosophical doctrines that contradicted the science they knew, nor were they ashamed to use different methods in different places. Thus, Pascal was both a religious mystic and a mathematician and was best known for the former. The mathematician Leibniz believed in something called monads, with God as the Great Monad, and worked all his life to find a formula of reconcilation between Catholics and Protestants. Descartes was a Platonist, believing in the reality of ideals; the physicist Robert Boyle tried to find a place for God in the science he knew; while Johann Kepler was an astrologer and a number mystic. These pursuits were not seen as personal aberrations or as lapses from scientific rigor. On the contrary, they were highly respectable and well received. A man of learning was traditionally expected to have general interests and to be well versed in philosophy and theology. Seventeenth century scientists were too close to this tradition to be exempt from it or to ignore it themselves. Few were willing to accept the consequences of their work: that science and philosophy occupied separate domains and dealt with separate topics. "The proper method for inquiring after the properties of things is to deduce them from experiments," wrote Sir Isaac Newton. That was still a vision of the future.

VIII

In 1733, Voltaire wrote a small book, *Letters Concerning the English Nation,* and included seven chapters on science, so justly celebrated in the nation of Newton. He exaggerated in one of them to say that "nobody before Chancellor Bacon had understood experimental philosophy . . . ," a statement not completely true, but not so far off that in Bacon's time experiment was either common or frequent. Writing in a later chapter, Voltaire commented that ". . . hardly any read Newton . . . for it takes considerable knowledge to understand him."

In this offhand way, Voltaire, who did not miss much, illuminated two of the basic facts about science, both in his own time and ours. Since the time of Brahe and Versalius, science had become more experimental and also overwhelmingly technical. Enthroning experiment as the fundamental method of testing hypotheses and guesses is the very nature of science. Logical consistency was not discarded, of course, but it was no longer the ultimate test of truth. That depended on the facts, which scientists arranged into a growing body of knowledge that became more difficult to understand. Once, every educated man knew the rudiments of scinetific knowledge and some of the fine points as well, but the discoveries and insights of the seventeenth century put an end to that. By 1700, some of the bare scientific laws might be generally comprehensible, but the data and computations that supported them were not. Even the laws were difficult, as indicated by the Newtonian notion that gravitational pull between two bodies varied inversely according to the squared distance between their centers.

Thus, as scientific experiments became more numerous and sophisticated, there occurred a strange paradox. The natural world became more ordered and comprehensible; at least it appeared to be governed by predictable natural laws that could be understood rather than by divine mystery that could not. But very few persons could understand the laws, and the promises of theory were denied in fact. Western man had become less able to explain what he knew, which at least had been possible in the days of the Aristotelian science. The dedicated efforts of scientists have meant that we all have vastly more accurate ideas about the nature of things, but we understand very little of it. Perhaps it is the same for the scientists themselves.

BIBLIOGRAPHY

Books on the development of scientific thought and theories are usually difficult to read and understand because the ideas they describe are difficult. The student needs a pretty good knowledge of mathematics, at least trigonometry and preferably calculus, to grasp the more technical books. Therefore, only a short bibliography is presented. None of these books is easy to read, but they are, at least, clear and within the range of the interested student.

A. R. Hall, *The Scientific Revolution: 1500–1800,* is an exceptionally good book, as clear as texts on science are going to get. The interested student ought to start with this one. Highly recommended.

T. R. Pledge, *Science Since 1500,* a difficult book, with a good deal of technical information. It is particularly good on clusters of scientists and the transmission of scientific knowledge in the seventeenth century.

H. Butterfield, *The Origins of Modern Science: 1300–1800,* is a good good survey, and omits most of the technical data. It is interesting also in that it connects modern science to the medieval intellectual climate.

A. Wolf, *A History of Science Technology and Philisophy in the Sixteenth and Seventeenth Centuries* (2 vols.), is an exhaustive survey of invention and discovery in every field of scientific and technological work. It is especially valuable for its discussion of technology and its numerous pictures and diagrams. It is hard to read and useful mainly to collect data.

J. Bronowski and B. Mazlish, *The Western Intellectual Tradition from Leonardo to Hegel,* is a general survey of intellectual history and includes a good deal of information on science.

E. A. Burtt, *The Metaphysical Foundations of Modern Science,* is a classic and also a very difficult book for the beginning student.

CHAPTER
SIX

THE AGE OF ENLIGHTENMENT

"These are the days of shaking,
and this shaking is universal."

Jeremiah Whittaker, sermon, 1643

"The more things change, the more they stay the same,"
runs the French proverb and, by and large, this is true. But
not this time; the Enlightenment, while it bore a resemblance to thoughts past, marked a sharp and surprising departure from the way men had once thought. The Enlightenment was the intellectual divide between a medieval and
modern climate of opinion, between a religious and secular
view of the world. It contained elements of both visions, but
novel ideas predominated. The break with the past, while not
total, was loud and enthusiastic and accompanied by scorn
for ideas that everyone once believed.

So rapid a change in the prevailing opinions magnified
disagreement. Sides were sharply drawn between those who
attacked Christianity and those defending it, between those
supporting existing social arrangements and others who
condemned them. The Enlightenment was a time of contro-
versay and noise, of shouting and insults, of hordes of petty
polemicists, and of popularization rather than creation. The
climate of opinion was more significant than the notions of
particular philosophers. In the midst of universal ferment,
only the high culture, art, music, drama, and architecture,
with its continued dependence on aristocratic patronage, remained the same. Elsewhere, the critics—dealers in new notions, prophets of a new Utopia, and men who shocked and
alarmed—set the tone of eighteenth century thought and debate.

I

In December, 1680, Halley's Comet passed over Europe in its usual manner and aroused discussion everywhere. It revived the old superstition that comets were the portent of political catastrophes, natural calamities, and the death of princes. Men freely predicted the worst, from the end of the world to less general but still startling disasters. Such pronouncements were received solemnly and with real concern. They were the traditional reaction to comets. Nothing appeared to have changed.

This time, however, there were different opinions on the subject. Edmund Halley (1656–1742), the British astronomer, saw the comet as a natural phenomenon, and published a sober treatise calculating its orbit and predicting future appearances of this wayward star. In France, Pierre Bayle (1647–1706), the Huguenot philosopher, wrote a powerful book, *Divers Thoughts on the Comet* . . . , which assailed the superstition about comets, denounced superstituion in general, and belabored the miracles of the Christian faith. From this beginning, the infection spread to everything. Within a decade of the comet, both Bayle and John Locke had written imposing pleas for religious toleration. Locke proposed a new knowledge theory in his *Essay Concerning Human Understanding* (1690) and defended liberal politics in his *Two Treatises on Civil Government* (1690). Sir Isaac Newton published his *Principia Mathematica,* completing the journey of astronomy from being part of the Faith into a secular science. In only one decade, the intellectual landscape of Europe changed with a speed and abruptness previously unknown.

Established ideas had been challenged before, of course, both singly and in battalions, but this time the notions of the heretics received almost instant applause. The ideas of Newton, Locke, and Bayle became the new orthodoxy as soon as people heard them. Traditional ideas, such as approval of religious persecution, the efficacy of superstition and magic, the divine right of kings, or the earth as the center of the

universe—each hallowed by long usage and universal acceptance—suddenly lost all standing among men of letters and
were mentioned with scorn and derision. The speed with
which the climate of opinion shifted from the old to the new
was as startling as the ideas that now came into fashion.

The fact is, of course, that religious toleration, scepticism
toward superstition and miracles, ideas of limited monarchy,
anticlericalism, and a scientific view of the heavens had all
been seething and stewing underground before they commanded wide and astounding acceptance. People had been
preaching religious toleration since 1560 to a very small audience. There were anticlericals even in the height of the
Reformation madness, but not many. Galileo thought along
the same lines as Newton, although he was less successful in
convincing others. Superstition had been denounced before
Bayle discovered it. The Great Remonstrance (1621) and
the Petition of Right (1628) elaborated the rights of Englishmen and the powers of Parliament, but the king ignored
them. Nonetheless, circulation of subversive ideas continued.
Eventually, their time came. The ideas that no one believed
became the new orthodoxy and dominated the new climate of
opinion.

Although Locke, Bayle, and Newton disagreed with their
predecessors about the answers to questions of political theory, religion, and science, they were still agonizing and argu-
ing over the same problems. The proper relationship between kings and their subjects had interested Thomas
Aquinas as well as John Locke, and both men sought to define
the duties of the monarchy. Both the scholastics and Enlightenment philosophers placed great emphasis on the doctrine of
natural law, and they differed only in detail on what it
meant. Theologians and philosophers each searched ardently
for the absolute—absolute truth, absolute values, absolute
virtue, absolute proofs—and neither found them because
they don't exist. Locke and Bayle were as concerned about
human virtue as any confessor or Jesuit. Newton and Leibniz thought understanding God was a particularly crucial
human endeavor. And, finally, the philosophers used logic

and reason precisely as did their theologian opponents; they bent and shaped it to prove what they already knew to be true. Nonetheless, Enlightenment thought contained an unspoken presupposition: that old problems might be solved in a new way with new answers. Old bottles were to be refilled with a new and better brew.

II

"Born to lament, to labor and to die . . . ," wrote the poet Matthew Prior about the condition of man. Theologians dwelt darkly on this theme, elaborating on original sin and men's evil nature. The world was a vale of tears, all within it was vanity, and the evils that beset us were God's will and thus incurable. But was this so? Simply because priests said it meant nothing since they and their churches were a blot on society. Many Enlightenment philosophers took issue with the priests and theologicans, and argued that man was basically good and had only been corrupted by society. They claimed that Nature was kind and beneficent, that both man and society might improve and progress indefinitely. Alexander Pope incorporated such views in his epic poem *Essay on Man*, declaring:

> *All discord, harmony not understood*
> *All partial evil, universal Good*
> *And, spite of Pride, in erring Reason's spite,*
> *One truth is clear, whatever is is right.*

Such doctrines acquired the name "optimism," and nothing could have been in greater contrast to the dour and gloomy opinions of the previous century.

Yet so soothing an idea, which dominated the early Enlightenment, collapsed overnight. In 1755, an earthquake and tidal wave destroyed Lisbon. The kind and bountiful Nature of song and theory had just reached out and obliterated a great Christian city. Why? In an effort to explain the catastrophe, Voltaire (1694–1778), the leading spirit of the

Enlightenment, looked again at the philosophy of optimism, and the problems of evil, sin, and unmerited disaster. In a long poem, *The Disaster of Lisbon,* Voltaire expressed his disillusionment with optimism and argued that evil and disaster had been accounted for no better by Enlightenment philosophers than by theologians. He followed this poem with his best book, *Candide,* a short satirical novel that described a series of unparalleled disasters that befell the hero and his companions, most of which were undeserved and could hardly have occurred in the best of all possible worlds. Voltaire's concluding advice was reminiscent of Job—let us stay home and cultivate our own gardens.

For a while, it appeared as if Voltaire and the Lisbon earthquake had obliterated all ideas of optimism, progress, and moral improvement. But these ideas were seductive ones, and they reappeared toward the end of the century under a new name. Now called the doctrine of progress, ideas of constant moral betterment found a home in the philosophy of the Marquis de Condorcet (1743–1794), a pathologically cheerful aristocrat who finished his book while hiding from the police and perished in prison while awaiting the guillotine. Condorcet argued that the regular operation of natural laws applied to human affairs as well, and he perceived a progression of ages in human history, each marked by greater virtue and enlightenment. The French Revolution was the last age, and the principles of peace, virtue, and justice were about to triumph. The tyrants and priests could no longer prevent it. Under the circumstances, Condorcet's arguments were not too convincing.

If Condorcet's hymn of faith in human perfectability failed to win converts, it was not merely because of the Revolution. In the two decades before 1789 the Enlightenment climate of opinion had begun to change, away from dependence on the harsh rigor of science and reason toward the more human terrain of emotions. Virtue and justice were still the goals, but the immutable and impersonal laws of science might not lead there. Virtue must come from within. It must be inculcated through education, said the Swiss Philosopher Jean-Jacques Rousseau (1712–1778) in *Emile*. A natural education, far from the corruption and artificiality of society, would produce a truly moral man. The novelist Bernardin de Saint-Pierre carried this theme forward in his romantic books, notably *Paul et Virginie*. In this early soap opera, two children were abandoned on a West India isle and grew up living with nature rather than with society. They were profoundly virtuous, the product of a beneficent nature and their own innate goodness. This touching tale mirrored the new mood precisely. People were tired of logic. Feelings were more important.

These various inquiries into the human condition were prompted by a general search for a new system of ethics and morality. Moral strictures had traditionally come from God, but that was hard to admit in a secular age with its emphasis on science and man. One of these, or both, must be the foundation of moral virtue, and the moral laws must be as absolute and unshakable as when they were derived from God. No one took this more seriously than Benjamin Franklin, a rising young man from Philadelphia. In his *Autobiography*, Franklin described his plan to reach moral perfection. He listed 13 salient virtues, and emphasized each one until he mastered it. Alas, it did not work. ". . . I soon found I had undertaken a task of more difficulty than I had imagined," Franklin wrote, "While my care was employ'd in guarding against one fault, I was often surprised by another. . . ." His contemporaries lacked his sturdy realism, and they kept searching for the origins of virtue in all the disciplines they knew. They, too, failed. The religious explanations of virtue and morality remained intact.

III

The age that venerated virtue held the same opinions about reason and science. They were the essential tools to unlock the secrets of man and nature, to discover the truth that everyone still believed existed. There would be no more arguments about the soul, angels, heaven, or the nature of

God himself; such things were the domain of belief, and reason could shed no light at all. Instead, reasoned inquiry would be limited to areas where there was evidence, to secular or scientific problems that could be solved. Philosophers no longer regarded reason as a substantive thing, as Plato or Aquinas had, around which a whole speculative system might be built. It was to be a tool, subordinate to facts, that must be gathered and arranged according to the scientific method. Research and experimentation, the patient observation of man and nature, and a careful reasoning from this sure foundation would lead to truth about everything far more quickly and certainly than the vague and grandiose nonsense of theologians. Or, at least, that is what people said now.

And yet, in spite of the prestige given to scientists and their marvelous method, the Enlightenment did not see a general continuation of the great discoveries of the previous century. What occurred, instead, was a mass of detailed experimental work. The researches of the Bernouilli family were typical. Three generations of Bernouillis worked on higher mathematics, popularizing calculus, working out problems in analytical trigonometry, infinite series, and mechanics. Important work, certainly, but it was along lines already well established. It was the same with the Karl Linnaeus (1707–1778), the Swedish biologist, who made a general classification of plants and animals. Linnaeus incorporated much previous work into his *Systema Naturae* (1735), which went through repeated editions and enlargements. Linnaeus based his classifications on external appearance, as Aristotle had, rather than on internal structure. A further error in Linnaeus' work was the idea that species remained constant, thus eliminating any concept of evolution. In spite of this, however, the Linnaean categories survived and became the basis for modern taxonomy.

Only in chemistry did eighteenth century scientists move well beyond the theoretical framework they inherited. In 1775, an English Unitarian minister, Joseph Priestley, published experiments proving he had isolated and identified

oxygen. Four years later, the Dutch scientist Jan Ingen-
housz proved that plants exhaled oxygen. Then in 1781 the
French chemists Claude Berthollet and Antoine Lavoisier established oxygen, hydrogen, and carbon as the basic elements of organic substances. In 1789, Antoine Lavoisier
theorized that oxygen was the vital element in both combus-
tion and breathing, and his book, *Elementary treatise of
Chemistry*, made basic contributions to both organic and in-
organic chemistry. Chemistry had hardly existed when the
Enlightenment began; now it was a science exact enough to
rival physics.

Although the French Revolution disrupted or destroyed
most lines of Enlightenment thought, scientific investigation
was hardly affected. The number of scientists continued to
increase, and their successes gave an increasingly scientific
cast to Western thought. Patient measurement, constant experiment, and endless investigation and questioning—these
attributes of science do not succumb to mere political upheaval or war.

For Enlightenment philosophers, reason was as important
as science in the long campaign for human betterment. The
use made of reason in the eighteenth century was in critical
analysis of society, law, religion, and of everything previously thought immutable and ordained by God. For example,
reason became the flail of miracles. "A miracle is the violation of mathematical, divine, immutable, eternal laws . . . ,"
Voltaire argued in his *Philosophical Dictionary* (1764), "a
contradiction in terms: a law cannot at the same time be immutable and violated." Those things the priest boasts of never happened, or, if they did, there was quite a simple explanation that had escaped contemporaries or was omitted by
pious chroniclers. It was the function of reason to point this
out, not to rationalize and defend "miraculous" events, as
was the habit of theologians.

The same mode of critical thought applied to secular customs, many of which were unreasonable and indefensible.
In the *Persian Letters* (1721), Baron de Montesquieu
(1689–1755), whose legal training, surprisingly, had not de-

stroyed his capacity to think, wrote a trenchant satire on contemporary French government and society. The magistrate is made to say that he sold his law library to buy a judicial office and does not regret this sale for a judge does not need to know any law at all. The French mistake honor for virtue and fight duels over nothing. They mistake virginity for virtue and care more for their bride's purity than for her character or personality. They make marital sex a legal duty, and sue each other in court for nonperformance or malfeasance. They sell public offices to fools and complain when government is inefficient and tyrannical. They practice legal torture, even though judges know torture produces far more lies than truth. Can reason sustain such customs?

Used as a tool of criticism, reason had its limitations and might lead to unreasonable ends. It could be pushed to radical scepticism and complete doubt. Pierre Bayle, the first of the Enlightenment philosophers, explored this cul-de-sac with his demand that each doctrinal and philosophical assertion be based on facts and hard evidence. All too often, there was no evidence, at least none that could be trusted or checked; frequently, the evidence on one side of an issue was as good as evidence for the other side. The process of destroying myth, of establishing truth, and of finding virtue, Bayle discovered, was endless and impossible.

The trouble with radical doubt, of course, was that it demolished everything, including the doubter's capacity to distinguish between what was probably true and what was probably false. This was useless and self-destructive, and the exiled Huguenot pastor Elie Benoist proved it in his *Collection of Historical, Philosophical and Theological Remarks* . . . (1712). How do you know, asked Benoist, that Pierre Bayle is really the author of the famous *Historical and Critical Dictionary* (1697)? Bayle can amass evidence, of course, in the form of sworn witnesses and solemn depositions, but these depositions may well be lies and the witnesses perjured or perhaps mistaken. Such things have happened before, given the nature of man. There was no absolute proof of Bayle's authorship, Benoist concluded, only partial and approximate proof. What applied to this case applied to them all. We must partly take things on faith. We can only ask that the evidence be as sound as possible. To demand more is useless.

Benoist's temperate treatise failed to cool philosophers' dreary ardor for the absolute. Nothing could do that. But, it did point to one of the main themes of Enlightenment rationalism—that ideas and knowledge should be useful. The cult of useful knowledge reached its apex in the *Encyclopedia*, a stupendous collection of 21 folio volumes with 13 volumes of plates (1751–1780). It was edited by Denis Diderot and Jean le Rond d'Alembert, both widely known philosophers and publicists who subscribed to the rational, secular, and scientific bent of their age. The articles of the *Encyclopedia* were quite uneven. Articles dealing with such things as mechanics, agricultural technology, handicrafts, and architecture were excellent. Perhaps these were humble things, but the happiness of countless human beings depended on them. Certainly they were more important, more likely to contribute to human virtue and happiness than theology. Usefulness was a salient value, more mundane perhaps, but almost as important as truth.

IV

"Every sect, of whatever opinion it may be, is a rallying point for doubt and error . . .," wrote Voltaire in his *Philosophical Dictionary*, and he expressed a general Enlightenment opinion. Beginning with Bayle, Enlightenment philosophers had mounted a general assault on both the Christian church and Christian faith, pronouncing them major impediments to progress and virtue. The philosophers' immediate demand, and perhaps the one most distasteful to clerics, was for religious toleration. Bayle and Locke began the campaign. In *A Letter Concerning Toleration* (1689), John Locke argued that religion was a private matter, an affair of the heart between a man and his God. It was no business of the king. Moreover, in view of the weakness of human thought, religious differences were inevitable, and one opinion had as good a chance as another to be the truth. Heresy might send one to hell—theologians could argue that—but it should not send a man to the hulks or gallows. Pierre Bayle said much the same thing under far more trying circumstances. A victim of Louis XIV's persecution of the Huguenots, Bayle produced a bitter tirade against intolerance. He described persecution as an offense against both God and man, as a sin as well as crime.

The demand for toleration broadened rapidly into a general assault upon the church. Critics repeated the old charges that the clergy were corrupt and lived spaciously off the pennies of the poor. They had abandoned apostolic poverty and received when they should have given. Now, it was said that the church itself was a fraud and a crime, apart from the casual sins of any individual clerics. Bayle, in his *Historical and Critical Dictionary,* discussed church history and argued that the massacres, atrocities, and inquisitions were caused by the clergy who urged their flocks on to these monstrous crimes. Pietro Giannone took up the same theme in his *Civil History of the Kingdom of Naples* (1723). He concentrated on the efforts of bishops and abbots to seize temporal power and to establish a theocracy. The church was the main barrier to human progress, therefore, as well as being an affront to reason and decency. It was unworthy of a Christian people.

The growing popularity of these ideas was sharply tested in Toulouse in 1762. Jean Calas, a Huguenot merchant, was barbarously executed after being convicted on the trumped-up charge that he murdered his son to prevent his conversion to Catholicism. The evidence was flimsy; it was fairly obvious that the son, who was seriously depressed, had committed suicide. The whole case was so clearly the product of religious fanaticism that the Calas affair became a general scandal. Voltaire himself denounced the persecution and demanded rehabilitation of Calas and the release of his imprisoned family. Continued outcry embarrassed officials in Toulouse and, ultimately, the Calas family emerged from jail and the conviction was reversed. It was the first time that had ever happened. Incredibly, in a Christian country, religious persecution could become unpopular.

While most Enlightenment commentary on religion dealt with persecutions and the general silliness or improbability of various dogmas, there was also an attempt to find an acceptable substitute for Christianity. Voltaire, for instance, turned to Deism. "I was absorbed in the contemplation of nature . . . ," he wrote in the *Philosophical Dictionary*, "A man must be blind not to be impressed by this Spectacle, he must be stupid not to recognize its author, he must be mad not to adore Him." There certainly is a God, whom we ought to worship, but beyond that we know little about Him. Such a view comforted men who had lost their faith in revelation, miracles and dogma, but still wished to pray and worship.

The general assault upon Christianity left an indelible mark on Western culture. Ridiculed and doubted, the Christian faith moved steadily away from the center of intellectual life toward its periphery. Christianity had once informed and sustained the entire culture, but now it was becoming the private possession of a few. Enlightenment criticism of religion was a major step in the secularization of western thought. From having been interpreters of the general culture, priests and theologians came to echo the Psalmist: "How shall we sing the Lord's song in a strange land?"

V

In political theory, as in everything else, the Enlightenment involved a sharp shift from the orthodoxy of the seventeenth century. It began with John Locke, whose *Two Treatises on Civil Government* were written to refute divine right absolutism and support the ideas of limited government and political liberty that triumphed in the English Glorious Revolution. Locke presented the myth that government began when men abandoned a primordial "state of nature" and delegated authority to one man or a Parliament for private convenience and the general good. Thus, ultimate sover-

eignty resided in the people. Such views entailed two consequences. The people, who were the ultimate rulers anyway,
could retrieve their lent power from the king if he should
abuse it, and there were certain natural rights, defined as
life, liberty and property, that the government could not
abridge. People were not placed on earth for the glory of the
king.

These were intriguing ideas, and they became standard
Enlightenment doctrine. They formed the basis of the political theories of Jean-Jacques Rousseau. In his *Social Contract* (1762), Rousseau began with the large assertion that
"Man is born free; he is everywhere in chains. . . ." The
state of nature had been glorious, while the present governments were all tyrannical and unjust, having usurped man's
natural rights and freedoms. The only free government
would be one responsive to the "general will," a vague phenomenon that was like a consensus reached in a Quaker
meeting. In such a system, Rousseau claimed, government
would be legitimate and men would be virtuous. That double
promise was too much for contemporaries to resist. Rousseau's doctrines were repeated endlessly by revolutionaries
who had no idea what they meant.

The proper form of government could also be ascertained
by examining the law. The monumental effort of this genre
was the immense and labored volume by Montesquieu, *The
Spirit of the Laws* (1748). Montesquieu tried to derive the
natural laws of political development, to see which climate,
which peoples, and which institutions inclined normally to
despotism and which to liberty. No one doubted that these
formulas existed. The laws of nature were universal, and
Montesquieu's ponderous prose convinced everyone he had
found them. One observation seemed particularly pertinent.
Montesquieu observed that the liberties of England were the
result of a division and separation of powers between the
legislative, executive, and judicial branches of government.
This concept, incorrect regarding England, became exceed-
ingly popular and was incorporated into the constitutions of
France and America.

The natural laws of government could also be understood by observing the imperfect world of the Old Regime. The laws actually in effect were peculiarly unenlightened, which everyone agreed was the result of centuries of obscurantist and clerical rule. The natural liberty and equality of man and his inheritance from the state of nature could hardly be found anywhere. All of this was clearly pointed out by a Milanese aristocrat, the marquis Cesare de Beccaria (1738–1794). A morose and unprepossessing gentleman, Beccaria nonetheless wrote a significant book, *On Crimes and Punishments* (1764). Beccaria's experiences with visiting and managing Milanese prisons convinced him that the ferocious punishments, then common failed to deter crimes. Judicial torture was barbarous and seldom succeeded in convincing criminals to tell the truth. The aim of punishment should be the rehabilitation of the criminal, thus protecting society. Criminal law should be reordered on a rational basis, to serve society and adhere to the natural rights of man.

"In order for a punishment not to be, in every instance, an act of violence of one or of many against a private citizen, it must be essentially public, prompt, necessary, the least possible in the given circumstances, proportionate to the crime, dictated by the laws."

Becarria closed his book with that maxim, which instantly became a part of Enlightenment political philosophy.

The proper aim of government could be found in an appeal to history as well as arguments from law and philosophy. David Hume traced the development of British constitutional liberty in his *History of England* (1754–1761). He wished to know how the English enjoyed liberty while other peoples were ruled by despots unfettered by law. The answers were to be found in the peculiar history of England, particularly in the constitutional struggles of the seventeenth century. Equally instructive was the story of enlightenment lost. In *The Decline and Fall of the Roman Empire* (1776–1788), Edward Gibbon chronicled the catastrophic collapse of the greatest civilization man had ever known. The villain was Christianity, with its intolerance, its emphasis on salvation rather than citizenship, and its obscurantist hostility to all that was best about classical culture. Acquaintance with this dismal tale might warn us of present dangers and help preserve what liberties we have.

These doctrines of natural rights and political liberty did not remain the exclusive possession of philosophers and their public. As the century wore on, political struggles were articulated in terms of natural rights and Enlightenment philosophy. The demand for parliamentary reform rocked England between the Peace of Paris and the French Revolution. The inalienable rights of man were written into the American constitution and Declaration of Independence. Dutch and Belgian revolutionaries quoted liberally from contemporary political philosophy, and even the backward Poles cast their struggle for national reform in terms of natural rights. In the course of a century John Locke's views on political liberty, legal equality, and the rights of man had been transformed from philosophical speculation into revolutionary slogans brought into battle.

VI

The Enlightenment, which attacked orthodox opinion in every quarter, had orthodoxies of its own, which were vigorously defended, and its own heresies, all attacked roundly. The most obnoxious heresies, the ones most consistently denounced, were atheism, the evils of private property, and the hideous possibility that social progress rested not on virtue but man's incurably perverse nature. These vile doctrines were assaulted by both polemic and philosophical treatise. Ultimately, however, Enlightenment philosophers failed to produce a definitive defense of property or a rebuttal against atheism or the social utility of evil, and so fell back on repeated assertions that such throughts were repugnant to decent men. Yet these heresies showed a sturdy capacity to survive in a hostile climate of opinion.

"Theology is only ignorance of natural causes reduced to a system . . . a long tissue of chimeras and contradictions . . . ," wrote the atheist Baron d'Holbach in 1772. Voltaire and his friends could not argue with that; they had said as much and more themselves. But they were horrified at the conclusions d'Holbach drew from his statements. D'Holbach went far beyond the conventional Deism of the Enlightenment. He denied the existence of God.

Atheism attracted public attention only toward the middle of the century. In 1748, Julien Offray de La Mettrie published a small book, *Man: A Machine,* in which he denied the existence of the soul and argued that man was only a physiological mechanism. This notion made a great uproar, and La Mettrie had to leave the country. His ideas survived, however, amply supported by Baron Paul d'Holbach, who maintained a salon where atheists and anticlericals gathered to insult God. D'Holbach himself contributed to the ferment with a long and mediocre book, *System of Nature* (1770), republished and condensed in 1772 as *Common Sense.* D'Holbach said nothing new about atheism, which is a simple religion, but he did keep the faith alive and provide a center for respectable blasphemy.

There were atheists in the streets as well as the parlors. A printer named Boulanger published dozens of atheist and antireligious tracts, running them off in his shop as fast as the hacks could turn them out. For a while Boulanger did very well in his enterprise. His pamphlets were denounced by the authorities, they seemed daring and clever, they possessed radical chic. Eventually, however, the public became bored with polemics denouncing monks and throwing mud at God. Enthusiasm for atheism waned.

The basic objection most Enlightenment philosophers had for atheism was not its scepticism or its hostility to church and clergy. Instead, philosophers worried about its impact on society. Almost everyone except the atheists believed that the common man needed a belief in God to remain virtuous and obedient to social superiors and moral laws. Without religious faith, most men would give in at once to their numerous evil desires, and sin without stint or limit until it hospitalized or killed them. This was an unsavory prospect, and the good of all demanded that everyone believe God lived. "If God did not exist, it would be necessary to invent him," Voltaire wrote and, as usual, he struck the proper note. So sharp a philosopher as David Hume agreed, and Hume's *Dialogues on Natural Religion* lay unpublished in his desk until after his death.

Almost as disreputable as atheism, perhaps even worse, were the alarming ideas of Bernard Mandeville (1670–1733), a Dutch physician living in exile in London. Mandeville attacked head-on a favorite Enlightenment idea—that private virtues added up to public benefits and ought to be encouraged for the general good. In 1705 Mandeville published the *Fable of the Bees,* a short poem to which he added long appendices and explanations. The message was clear and simple.

> *Millions endeavouring to supply*
> *Each other's Lust and Vanity . . .*
> *As Sharpers, Parasites, Pimps, Players*
> *Pick-Pockets, Coiners, Quacks, South-Sayers . . .*
> *Fraud, Luxury and Pride must live*
> *While we the Benefits receive . . .*
> *So Vice is beneficial found.*

Vice is beneficial; my God, what could be more subversive? A society trying to find a firm secular base for virtue did not relish being told that private vices led to public good. And it was no good trying to shout the monster down. He was a tough debater and stoutly defended his criminal thesis. Not everyone was convinced by Mandeville that man's rottenness had social value, but his ideas were never quite dismissed. There were enough realists and cynics to keep them afloat.

Equally abominable in theory, although expressing a more abstract and distant danger, were ideas of communism. In an age of criticism, when everything was questioned, there were even critics of private property. In 1775, Morelly published *Nature's Code,* in which he outlined the laws and precepts for a Communist society. Morelly argued that original sin was fatally increased by the personal possession of property, the abolition of which would ". . . cut off at the root the vices and all the evils of society." Although they sympathized with the goal, most philosophers were not taken in by the simple delusion that poverty made men virtuous. In fact, most philosophers did not take communism too seriously. They may have harbored illusions about man giving up his vices, but they knew he would never surrender his property.

All of these heresies offended the conscience of the age. Yet, they emerged clearly enough from the general tendencies of Enlightenment thought, from religious scepticism, and from the passionate search for virtue. The heretics simply carried Enlightenment premises to their logical conclusions. Most philosophers, however, were not interested in hearing that particular fact. It is, after all, the function of philosophers to defend revealed and orthodox faith as much as it is to attack false doctrines.

VII

These were optimistic men, the Enlightenment philosophers, who felt the joy and challenge of standing at the edge of a new and better world. They wrote and argued with the untroubled gusto of men who thought their labors would help make a more perfect society. When the occasion demanded it, they even sanctioned revolt with the same clear conscience, appealing their case from vicious kings or recalcitrant nobles to the good opinion of mankind and the gratitude of posterity. They were confident of the result.

The revolutions that the philosophers worked best, of course, were the ones of the mind. Enlightenment philosophers eroded the moral foundations of Old Regime society, government, and religion. They had appealed beyond tradition to reason and destroyed much of the sense of legitimacy that once supported the existing order. Conditions and ideas once regarded as normal became an affront to God and reason. The old ways and the old verities became incredible and unworthy of belief.

In all of this, the Enlightenment philosophers were enormously convincing. Their ideas triumphed. The democratic ideals and the pervasive secularism of modern culture, the adoration of science and the cult of utility, the habits of criticism, and the facile assumption that every problem has a solution have all been inherited from the Enlightenment. We may no longer give these notions unreserved belief, but we have not discarded them either. They still inform and guide our thought.

BIBLIOGRAPHY

1. Primary Sources

There are dozens of Enlightenment philosophical tracts and polemics published in paperback and regularly assigned to students. Listed here are some of the more important ones and some of the entertaining ones.

Pierre Bayle, *Historical and Critical Dictionary: Selections,* is one of the basic Enlightenment texts from which many *philosophes* got their material. The footnotes are more important than the text in this book, so concentrate on them. Highly recommended.

John Locke, *Two Treatises on Civil Government,* are an influential attack on absolutism and a defense of political liberty. Like all political theory, they are a bit dry and stuffy.

John Locke, *Essay Concerning Human Understanding* (2 vols.), is the basic Enlightenment statement on psychology and knowledge theory. Obviously, it is a difficult book.

Voltaire, *Philosophical Letters,* is a series of short comments on England, where there is liberty and, by implication, on France also, where Voltaire thought there was none.

Voltaire, *Candide,* a superb and amusing book, in which Voltaire destroyed the notion of Optimism—that all was for the best in the best of all possible worlds. Highly recommended.

Charles Hendel, ed., *Jean-Jacques Rousseau: Moralist,* contains comments on many of Rousseau's most influential writings.

Cesare de Beccaria, *On Crimes and Punishments,* is a short, eloquent and impressive account of the shortcomings of European prisons and penal codes.

Bernard de Mandeville, *The Fable of the Bees,* is an attack on Enlightments ideas of virtue.

Frank Manuel, ed., *The Enlightenment,* is a group of short selections from various *philosophies.*

Lester Crocker, *The Age of Enlightenment,* is another, and longer, document collection.

2. Commentaries on the Enlightenment

Paul Hazard, *The European Mind,* is a major study of the early Enlightenment, up to about 1720. It is filled with information and is difficult to read. It presents the thesis that by 1720 all the standard

Enlightenment ideas were in place and, thereafter, it is a matter of popularization rather than creation.

Paul Hazard, *European Thought in the Eighteenth Century,* is the sequal to the above. It, too, is a brilliant book.

Ernest Cassirer, *The Philosophy of the Enlightenment,* is an examination of the Enlightenment from the point of view of academic philosophy. Extremely difficult.

Carl Becker, *The Heavenly City of the Eighteenth Century Philosophers,* is a genial, charming, and short treatise that argues that Enlightenment philosophers asked the same questions as the Scholastics, were concerned with the same issues, and took many of the same things on faith. It is generally convincing. Highly recommended.

R. O. Rockwood, ed. *Carl Becker's Heavenly City Revisited,* is a series of articles on the Becker thesis.

CHRONOLOGICAL CHART:

Dates	Great Britain	France
1640–1688		
1648		Treaties of Westphalia
1659		Treaty of the Isle of Pheasants
1660	Restoration of the monarchy	
1664	War with Holland	
1667–1668	War of Devolution	War of Devolution
1670		
1672–1678	Dutch War	Dutch War
1676		
1677–1681		
1681		
1681–1682		
1683		
1685	Accession of James II In England	Revocation of the Edict of Nantes
1685–1687		
1687		
1689–1698	War of the League of Augsburg	War of the League of Augsburg
1689	Glorious Revolution	
1696		
1697		
1699		
1698–1699		
1760–1721		
1700		
1701–1713	War of the Spanish Succession	War of the Spanish Succession
1708		
1713–1714	Treaties of Utrecht and Rastadt	Treaties of Utrecht and Rastadt

EUROPE, 1648–1795

Netherlands	Austria	Spain
Treaties of Westphalia	Treaties of Westphalia	
		Treaty of the Isle of Pheasants
War with Great Britain	Truce of Vasvar	
War of Devolution		War of Devolution
Dutch War	Dutch War	Dutch War
	Beginning of the Long War with Turkey	
	Siege of Vienna	
	Battle of Mohacs	
War of the League of Augsburg	War of the League of Augsburg	War of the League of Augsburg
	Battle of Zenta	
	Treaty of Karlowitz	
		Death of Carlos II
War of the Spanish Succession	War of the Spanish Succession	War of the Spanish Succession
Treaties of Utrecht and Rastadt	Treaties of Utrecht and Rastadt	Treaties of Utrecht and Rastadt

CHRONOLOGICAL CHART:

Dates	Great Britain	France
1714	Accession of George I, the Protestant Contender	
1715		Death of Louis XIV Accession of Louis XV
1719–1720	South Sea Bubble	John Law
1721		
1740		
1740–1748	War of the Austrian Succession	War of the Austrian Succession
1748	Treaty of Aix-la-Chapelle	Treaty of Aix-la-Chapelle
1754	Renewal of Colonial Conflict in America	Renewal of colonial conflict in America
1756–1763	Seven Years' War	Seven Years' War
1760	Accession of George III	
1762		
1763	Peace of Paris	Peace of Paris
1772		
1774		Death of Louis XV
1775	American Revolution	
1780		
1786		
1787–1789		Beginnings of the French Revolution
1787–1792		
1790		
1791		
1793		
1794		
1795		

EUROPE, 1648–1795

Netherlands	Austria	Spain
	Accession of Maria Theresa	
War of the Austrain Succession	War of the Austrian Succession	War of the Austrian Succession
Treaty of Aix-la-Chapelle	Treaty of Aix-la-Chapelle	Treaty of Aix-la-Chapelle
	Seven Years' War	Seven Years' War
	Treaty of Hubertusburg	Peace of Paris
	First Partition of Poland	
	Death of Maria Theresa and Acession of Joseph II	
	Death of Joseph II	
	Third Partition of Poland	

CHRONOLOGICAL CHART:

Dates	Prussia	Russia
1640–1688	Reign of Great Elector	
1648	Treaties of Westphalia	
1659		
1660		
1664		
1667–1668		
1670		
1672–1678		
1676		
1677–1681		Russo-Turkish War
1681		
1681–1682		
1683		
1685		
1685–1687		
1687		
1689–1698		
1689		
1696		Capture of Azov
1697		
1699		Treaty of Karlowitz
1698–1699		Peter the Great begins modernization of Russian army and government
1700–1721		Great Northern War
1700		Battle of Narva
1701–1713		
1708		Battle of Poltava
1713–1714		
1714		

EUROPE, 1648–1795

Turkey	Poland	Sweden
		Treaties of Westphalia
Truce of Vasvar		
Conquered Island of Crete		
Treaty of Zuravno Russo-Turkish War	Treaty of Zuravno	
War with Austria and Poland begins Siege of Vienna	Siege of Vienna lifted by Polish king Jan Sobieski	
	Venetian Conquest of Peloponnesian Peninsula Battle of Mohacs	
Battle of Zenta	Treaty of Karlowitz	
	Great Northern War	Great Northern War Battle of Narva
		Battle of Poltava

CHRONOLOGICAL CHART:

Dates	Prussia	Russia
1715		
1719–1720		
1721		Treaty of Nystadt
1740	Accession of Frederick the Great	
1740–1748	War of the Austrian Succession	
1748	Treaty of Aix-la-Chapelle	
1754		
1756–1763	Seven Years' War	Seven Years' War
1760		
1762		Accession of Catherine the Great
1763	Treaty of Hubertsburg	Treaty of Hubertsburg
1772	First Partition of Poland	First Partition of Poland
1774		
1775		
1780		
1786	Death of Frederick the Great	
1787–1789		
1787–1792		
1790		
1791		
1793	Second Partition of Poland	Second Partition of Poland
1794		
1795	Third Partition of Poland	Third Partition of Poland

EUROPE, 1648–1795

Turkey	Poland	Sweden
		Treaty of Nystadt
	First Partition of Poland	
	Reform constitution proclaimed	
	Second Partition of of Poland	
	Nationalist Uprising	
	Third Partition of Poland	

CHAPTER SEVEN

STATE BUILDING AND STATE CRAFT: 1648–1789

"It is none of your business to
meddle in the affairs of my state . . ."

Louis XIII to the Parlement of Paris

"Believe me, you Polish Cavaliers, . . .
if your glorious republic continue
to be managed in such a manner . . .
the day will arrive, and the day is
perhaps not far off, when this glorious
republic will get torn to shreds
hither and thither, be stuffed into
the pockets of covetous neighbors,
Bradenburg, Austria, Muscovy, and
find itself reduced to zero and
abolished from the face of the
world. . . ."

Jan Kasimir to the Polish nobles (1668)

In 1589, the Italian political theorist Giovanni Botero published an influential book, *On the Reason of State*. Princes read it with excitement and approval because Botero advanced the theory that the interests of the state took clear precedence over the medieval privileges of towns, nobles, church, or provinces. Botero envisioned a rationalized monarchy freed from inherited restraints both sacred and secular. The revitalized monarchies would be governed only by their needs and goals and would be responsible to no one.

Botero's book brought to the surface of debate ideas that had been stewing and simmering for some time. Belief in the virtues of the older constitutional monarchies of the Renaissance and later Middle Ages had been in decline before Botero's public condemnation. The late medieval states had been constructed on theories of the divisibility of public power between the king and the magnates. The king was supposed to rule within a complex web of mutually contracted feudal obligations, not trespassing on the privileges of his subjects. Thus, the "state" was but one element in a network of government that included all the nobles, towns, and churches in the realm.

This system had not worked too well for a long time. During the Reformation, kings had been unable to keep the peace against the unhealthy and antisocial religious zeal of their subjects. Monarchs had not dispensed justice, nor had they protected the rights and liberties of their vassals. Continuing disasters in public affairs demanded changes in the way people thought about their government.

Botero's ideas about the supremacy of state power over the subjects were given a religious articulation appropriate for a Counter-Reformation audience and emerged as divine-right absolutism. It was a simple doctrine, claiming only that all power belonged rightfully to the king because he received it from God. This assertion was buttressed by numerous Scriptural, historical, and theological authorities, which added a rich pattern of variations to the main theme. During the seventeenth century, with its need for stable government and the general belief that religion was a necessary part of secular legitimacy, divine-right absolutism was both satisfying and convincing.

Although divine-right absolutism was the majority doctrine, it did not stand alone. In England and Holland there developed a system of parliamentary institutions, although the monarchs made tremendous efforts to prevent it. Along with the parliaments went political doctrines to support their pretentions to power. Here, the medieval ideas of contract and consent did not die, and to these ideas were added a miscellany of theories about the rights of man, the constitution of a commonwealth, and other radical or unpopular ideas. In spite of their unfashionable insistence on the limits

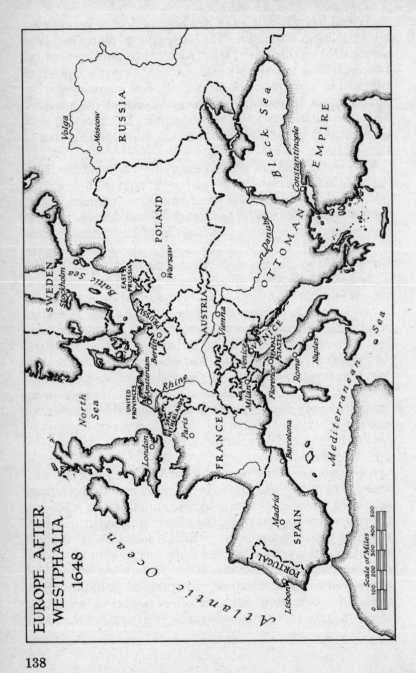

EUROPE AFTER
WESTPHALIA
1648

Atlantic Ocean

North Sea

London

Paris

FRANCE

UNITED PROVINCES
Amsterdam
Rhine
SP. NETHERLANDS

Barcelona

Madrid

SPAIN

PORTUGAL
Lisbon

Mediterranean Sea

SWEDEN
Stockholm

Baltic Sea

Berlin
PRUSSIA

EAST PRUSSIA

POLAND
Warsaw

AUSTRIA
Vienna

MILAN
Milan
Venice
VENICE
Florence
PAPAL STATES
Rome

Naples

Volga

Moscow

RUSSIA

Black Sea

Danube

OTTOMAN EMPIRE

Constantinople

Scale of Miles
0 100 200 300 400 500

138

of royal authority, however, ideas of parliamentary power were convincing enough in two states to justify revolutions against the king.

There was a third political possibility in the aftermath of the religious wars. This was the path of feudal decentralization, a continuation of the medieval patterns of government that had already failed. In Poland, Spain, and the Ottoman Empire, theories of divine-right absolution failed to persuade powerful feudal and provincial magnates to surrender real power to the crown. In Poland, ideals of feudal liberties held sway and, in Turkey, tribal and religious concepts of unlimited royal power were never organized into a coherent doctrine of state authority that applied to all the peoples of the empire. In an age when even the strongest governments depended heavily on the consent of the governed, failures in political theory were reflected in the decline of the state.

I

The rise of absolute monarchies was indistinguishable from the growth of royal armies. With reliable armies, kings could defeat their own subjects, a major consideration in an era of religious wars and aristocratic conspiracies. Thus, monarchs put the bulk of their resources into the military— five-sixths of the royal income in the case of Spain—and made the condition of the army the primary concern of the state.

During the Old Regime, the king's troops might be his own subjects or mercenaries. In general, mercenaries were more reliable and, in the years before 1660 when armies were relatively small, they were composed mainly of them. Even after armies had become too large to be recruited entirely from abroad, most monarchs continued to use mercenaries as specialists while relying on native peasantry and convicts for cannon fodder. Naval captains, navigators, artillery and engineer officers, drill masters, and generals were frequently foreigners. In Russia they invariably were.

The king's struggle to build a loyal army was successful first in France, where Henry IV combined his own forces with the forces of the Duke of Lesdiguières into a fairly large and efficient army. To support this army, Henry placed his closest friend and advisor, the Duke of Sully, in charge of the royal arsenal and instructed him to acquire and maintain weapons. Sully was an able man who did his job well, and, in 1610, when Henry IV was assassinated, royal power dominated France.

At Henry's death, government fell into the hands of his widow, Marie de Medici, a fat, suspicious, and stupid woman, who dismissed Sully and let the royal army fall apart. Royal power went down with it and, by 1618, the French crown was again fighting its subjects and not doing too well. Not until after 1630 was a new prime minister, Cardinal Richelieu, able to rebuild a loyal army, mostly from mercenaries. His success was demonstrated dramatically during the revolution of The Fronde (1648–1652), an unsuccessful assault on the growing power and coherence of the state. France's leading general, the Prince of Condé, defected to the Spanish, but his army refused to go with him. A century earlier it certainly would have.

Under Louis XIV, who was immensely interested in military affairs, the French army became an efficient instrument of royal policy. Louis' war minister, Louvois, worked for three decades to recruit, organize, equip, and train the royal army. He established a table of ranks and promulgated a promotion policy that was actually used in the few cases where family influence was not decisive. He insisted on uniforms and housed many of the troops in barracks where they could be watched instead of having them billeted in private homes. He ordered noble officers to live with their regiments, and his discipline was so severe that some actually did. He organized a supply service, hospitals, and stocked military maps. He wrote drill regulations and insisted that the troops march until they learned how to do it right. There were frequent audits and inspections designed to make certain that the regiments were up to strength and the officers were not stealing the ration money. Permanent garrisons were established at frontier fortresses and, where forts did not exist, Marshal Vauban, the chief of engineers, had them built.

These were massive reforms, but remnants of the old system remained. Louvois was unable to end the practice of buying commissions. Colonels still raised their own regiments and captains their own companies, and there was a great deal of fraud in the process. The troops continued to be recruited by jail delivery and kidnapping. Military punishments remained barbarous, seldom stopping before actual murder, but this could not prevent a desertion rate that ran over one-third. Even so, France possessed the best army in seventeenth century Europe, not only the biggest but also the best equipped and organized. Only in command was it frequently deficient.

What the French did the Prussians did also, and did better, although on a smaller scale, Frederick William, the Great Elector (1640–1688), also built an effective and loyal army. He eliminated mercenaries almost entirely and found both his officers and soldiers in Prussia. As in France they were housed, fed, equipped, and commanded by the king. As in France, they were used in domestic revolt as well as foreign conquest. But the Great Elector went a step farther than the Sun King. He made the Prussian army the basic, unifying institution for the entire state.

Armies did not exist alone, of course, since the state had to be governed, not occupied. Absolute monarchs developed massive civil bureaucracies to cope with the arts and intricacies of taxation, justice, police, and general regulation appropriate to the public good and royal glory. Again, France led the way. Here, the bureaucracy was the largest, the most expensive, the most pervasive, the most powerful and, occasionally, the most efficient in Christendom. It was also the most envied, and its better features were copied in the other bureaucratic monarchies.

The central figure in the French civil bureaucracy was the provincial intendant, who ruled a province in the king's name. Appointed by the crown and responsible to it, the in-

tendant possessed wide powers of police, justice, and taxation. He could evoke cases from the regular courts and judge
them himself or arbitrarily arrest almost anyone in his ju-
risdiction. He apportioned the direct tax burden in his
district and supervised the collection. He built roads, established hospitals and workhouses, fed the destitute, encouraged farmers, and checked the local authority of nobles and
towns. Toward the end of the seventeenth century the intendant acquired subordinates—subdelegates—who enforced
his orders in the remote and wretched towns he himself seldom visited. In the past, officials this powerful had escaped
from royal control. This time they did not and were thus the
vital link between royal orders and provincial obedience.

Above the intendants were the ministers, appointed by the
king and in intimate contact with him. During the course of
the seventeenth century, the ministers had come to exercise
definite functions, one in charge of finances, another for foreign affairs, a third for the army, and so they functioned
with relative efficiency. They also developed ministerial bureaucracies to deal with the increasing loads of paper as the
king extended his purview into more and more areas of the
nation's life. Louis XIV watched his ministers closely and
checked on their activities because he had no intention of allowing them to usurp the king's authority for themselves.
His successors were not so careful.

In an age of general illiteracy, and one that still retained a
respect for pomp and symbol and ceremony, kings had to
show themselves as absolute monarchs as well as give orders
to ministers. Visual propaganda was far more important
than the written word. In this endeavor, Louis XIV excelled.
Versailles was a vast and spendid stage, the biggest, most
expensive, most sumptuous royal palace Europeans had ever
seen or heard of. In it, Louis was treated like a sort of god.
Everything depended upon the Sun King. A complicated etiquette emphasized his grandeur. His menial servants were
dukes and princes. He was flattered and imitated to such an
extent that when he had an anal fistula removed several

courtiers had the same dangerous surgery performed on them. Surely, such a powerful monarch was God's vice-regent on earth. Every sacred and secular symbol known at the time shouted that he was.

But the glittering facade of Versaille masked failures as well as shouting success. The ranks of officials and clerks concealed two serious failures in French administration, both of which were prominent in the coming of the Revolution. No French monarch or minister ever solved for long the problem of insufficient finances, nor were they free from the opposition of royal officials who owned their offices. These evils were recognized by everyone, and there were numerous programs to reform them. All failed. Over the years things just got worse.

French finances were a complicated mess. Taxation was regressive, falling most heavily upon the peasants who were least able to pay. The privileged nobility and bourgeoisie escaped most levies and evaded others. The social costs of such taxation were enormous, and the revenues were inadequate. Equally serious was the failure of the crown to account for its income. There was no budget, no central treasury, and no uniform system of accounts or payments. No one knew how much the king made, only that it was never enough. Nor did anyone know what the king had spent or borrowed, only that it was too much. It was not a good system, and nothing was done about it.

A second administrative problem was venality—ownership of office by the men who held them. Whole groups of offices fell under this curse, particularly the judiciary. Venality had grown from two roots: the need of the king to reward his servants and his equally pressing need to extract money from those who could pay. By the end of the sixteenth century, venality had become an irrevocable custom, and royal legislation thereafter only concerned extending it to other offices and extracting more money from the purchasers. As a result, the government lost control over a large number of its officials and found itself inventing new positions, such as intendants, to carry out orders that venal officials refused to obey. This whole problem was made more galling by the fact that the orders that venal officials evaded were generally orders that concentrated power in the king's hands and aided the process of state building.

There were also failures in policy. The power of the state was often used too narrowly for the glory of the king or the interests of the dynasty, while the glory and the interest of the nation were forgotten. Prosperity, except in tax revenues, was not high on Louis' scale of values. Nor did the Sun King use his authority to attack social, legal, and political privilege. Manorialism remained, venality of office was extended, France had no uniform legal system, the courts were expensive and corrupt, and the privileges of guilds, towns, and provinces were confirmed. The increased power of the state was used to reinforce privilege and, in general, the nobility and gentry were richer and more secure after Louis XIV than before him. Finally, the Sun King engaged in a squalid and degraded persecution of his Protestant subjects, which failed to make France Catholic and damaged the economy. Thus, absolutism in France presents a paradoxical picture. Royal power and glory were mixed with substantial remnants of independent authority. The government was strengthened and enlarged, only to be overthrown a century later because of the very problems of privilege, bigotry, and lack of political liberty that it sustained.

In Russia, also, the crown succeeded in imposing the authority of the government on a reluctant people. Until Peter the Great (1689–1725), Russia had no army or government in the Western sense, relying instead on feudal levies, the weakness of her neighbors, the church, and the gentry. Peter began to change all that with incredible brutality and speed. He had been brought up in some contact with Western ways and was eager to learn more. He was particularly anxious to absorb the military techniques that Westerners in Moscow described for him. In 1698, Peter made a tour of Western Europe, visiting arsenals, shipyards, and shops and working as a carpenter himself. The trip was cut short by a revolt of the Streltzy, a feudal guard whose leaders could see well enough where Peter's Western ideas were leading. The revolt was crushed by Peter's German mercenaries. Peter rushed home, took a barbaric revenge on the Streltzy and began a rapid and hodgepodge Westernization of everything around him.

Driven by the pressures of the Great Northern War (1701–1721), Peter the Great tried to do everything at once. He organized, trained, and equipped a new army and, when that was destroyed by the Swedes at Narva in 1700, did it all over again. To support this army Peter and his advisors invented hundreds of new taxes. Taxes were placed on vodka, water, beards, births, marriages, graves, and coffins— anything likely to produce a profit. These revenues were collected by a bewildering welter of agencies and bureaus. Only after 1712, when Peter imported over 150 foreign administrators, was any order brought out of bureaucratic chaos. Even then, they only made a start. To enforce obedience to his new government, Peter the Great established the first Russian secret police, a social and political institution that has become a permanent feature in Russian life.

Peter reformed provincial and local government as well. Between 1705 and 1711 he established provincial districts, each ruled by a governor responsible to the czar. Municipal government was taken away from the old military governors and given to the urban bourgeoisie because of the ". . . waywardness and excessive stealing of our military governors. . . ." Equally important, however, was the hope that bourgeois management of the cities would add to the czar's taxes.

All this, radical though it was, had a smaller impact on Russian life than the social revolution forced through by Peter the Great. He ordered nobles to trim their beards, to wear European clothes, to use tobacco, and to send their sons to European schools. He personally clipped some beards himself. These measures were neither silly nor superficial, nor without effect, for they drove a wedge between the Europeanized court aristocracy and the rest of Russian society, a division that lasted until the Great War in 1914.

Peter changed the status of both the nobility and peasantry. The latter he repressed into serfdom, owing labor to their lords and sons to the army. The nobility were forced to do state service. Since there were not enough lords for all the new slots in the army, bureaucracy, and diplomatic service, Peter the Great created thousands of new nobles. The nobility in Russia was not an independent caste, as in Western Europe; it was a status dependent on the good graces of the czar. Such an arrangement was a formidable weapon in the royal drive for control of the state.

Although Peter's reforms accomplished their immediate objectives, military victory and the beginnings of "Westernization," they were chaotic, incomplete and, in some cases, impermanent. State service for the nobility had to be abandoned since the crown could not demand this from the class on which it depended for support. The Russian army was still mainly a mob, in spite of the veneer of Western officers who commanded it. The administrative system Peter left his successors needed constant revision. But the main battle was won. Russia was on the way to being a bureaucratic and absolutist state on the Western model, a process that is continuing today.

The process of political centralization that transformed Russia and France also occurred elsewhere, notably in Austria and Prussia. Here, too, a more modern army was accompanied by a growing bureaucracy. State building encountered less resistance in Prussia than in Austria. Austrian nobles were richer and more powerful than their Prussian colleagues, and the Austrian government was diverted from the task of centralization by the constant threat from Turkey. Within a century of the accession of Frederick-William, the Great Elector, in 1640 the Prussian civil service was the most efficient in Europe, while Austrian administrative reform was concentrated after 1750. The result was the same in both states, however. The dramatic increase in military

THE LOW COUNTRIES IN THE EARLY MODERN PERIOD

- – – – – – – – Boundaries of the Spanish Netherlands in 1560
- The Netherlands in 1609
- French conquests of Louis XIV
- The Spanish Netherlands in 1609

ENGLAND

North Sea

HOLLAND

Amsterdam
Utrecht

The Brill

Antwerp
Bruges
Ghent
FLANDERS
Brussels
BRABANT
Oudenarde   xWaterloo
Ramillies x
Lille
Fleurus x
Malplaquet x
BISHOPRIC OF LIÈGE
GERMANY
Rhine
LUXEMBOURG

FRANCE

Paris

Scale of Miles
0   25   50   75   100

strength and internal political coherence meant Great Power status. For kings, this was a worthy goal. The subjects, of course, were not consulted.

II

"I will govern according to the common weal, but not according to the common will," replied James I to his House of Commons in 1621. He spoke for kings everywhere. In the seventeenth century monarchs viewed parliaments as a stumbling block on the path toward political centralization. In most countries, royal armies and bureaucracies destroyed the power and often the existence of representative institutions. In England and Holland, the kings failed. Here, parliaments survived because of victory in civil war and revolution.

Politics in England and Holland, therefore, followed different patterns from patterns elsewhere. The political battles were fought, as it were, on two fronts. There was the inexorable increase in the power of the central government, common to all the Great Powers. But there was also a struggle for control of that power, fought between kings and the representative institutions that defeated them. Contemporaries, astounded at the deviation from absolutism, concentrated their attention on the latter. Yet it was the increase of power at the center that began the struggles between crown and parliament because centralization enormously enlarged the rewards of victory.

In the Netherlands, the institutions and patterns of government were an inheritance from the wars with Spain. At the center of the state were the *stadhouder* and the states-general. The *stadhouder* was a prince from the House of Orange, who held the supreme military command, and some of the powers, though not the title of king. The powers of the *stadhouder* naturally expanded in war and dropped off in peace. Opposing the *stadhouder* were the representatives of the seven provinces—the states-general. Descendant of a medieval parliament, the states-general was particularly sensitive to the wishes of the nobility and urban patriciate. The deputies saw the preservation of provincial liberties and privileges as their major function and carried over into their relations with the *stadhouder* their distrust of Philip II of Spain. Below the states-general came the towns and states-provincial. They had borne the brunt of the war and now expected the rewards of victory. They had fought to preserve local autonomy, and were sharply hostile to any steady siphoning of local powers to the center. Finally, towering above all the cities and provinces and, occasionally above the state itself, was Amsterdam, the economic and psychological center of the nation. Amsterdam so dominated the Netherlands that nothing could succeed without her support. Amsterdam's rulers took the lead in opposing the *stadhouder* and, paradoxically, because they were so powerful nationally, in reducing provincial and municipal autonomy. Thus, they established and owned the United East India Company and forced it on reluctant smaller towns, but kept its revenues and colonies out of the *stadhouder's* reach.

In the years after the truce with Spain in 1609, the endemic conflict between the *stadhouder* and Amsterdam became acute. The issues were both religious and political. Amsterdam, led by its advocate, Jan de Oldenbarneveldt, supported a liberalized Calvinism and states rights, while the *stadhouder,* Maurice, adhered to a rigid predestination in religion and royal power in politics. In 1618, Oldenbarneveldt led the province of Holland to the brink of secession. Maurice invaded Holland, executed Oldenbarneveldt, and established a considerable measure of royal control. He was assisted in this program by the outbreak of the Thirty Years' War (1618) and the renewal of war with Spain in 1619.

Maurice's brother, Frederick-Henry (1625–1647) continued the politics of royal absolutism. He prosecuted the war against Spain, gained control over foreign policy, and created a magnificent court. When William II succeeded his father, he continued to increase royal authority. He moved against the Estates of Holland and the city of Amsterdam but died in 1650 before he could complete his plans. Because his son, William III, was born posthumously, there was a vacancy in the stadholderate. Led by Jan de Witt, the Grand Pensionary of Holland, the estates party, with the firm backing of Amsterdam, seized control of the government and virtually eliminated the *stadhouder*. This lasted until 1672 when the French invaded the Netherlands and came very close to conquering it. In the military emergency the nation turned to the *stadhouder*, William III, and political power shifted rapidly from the states-general to the Prince. William sustained himself through domestic political manipulation and an alliance with England. The English connection was strengthened by marriage to Mary, daughter of James II and, after the Glorious Revolution, William and Mary became the joint rulers of England.

After William III's death in 1702, power flowed back to the States-General, and it was not until 1747 that the Netherlands had a new *stadhouder*, William IV. Although the powers of the *stadhouder* expanded after the middle of the eighteenth century, the old traditions of states rights, provincial privilege and municipal autonomy did not collapse. They were revived during the Dutch Revolution of 1780–1787, were responsible for the welcome given the revolutionary armies of France in 1795, and formed the basis for the liberal Dutch institution of 1815. The Dutch *stadhouders* never succeeded in conquering their country.

In England, the other "Protestant Republic," the pattern of politics was similar to the Dutch. The results, however, were more significant because the British drama of parliamentary government was played on a world stage. Instead of declining after 1700, Britain became the leading Great Power with the largest and most profitable colonial empire. She also became the first industrialized state. Great Britain took the lead in the wars against the French Revolution and Napoleon and, ultimately, won them. Finally, the British developed a coherent theory of civil liberties and, upon appropriate occasions, put this into practice. The powers of Parliament played an important role in all of these things.

When Elizabeth I died in 1603, genuinely mourned by her

subjects, she was succeeded by a Scotsman, James I
(1603–1625). James had good intentions, but he was pedan-
tic, self-righteous, and a prig. His politics were even worse
than his shabby personality. James was a believer in divine-
right absolutism and total adherence to the established
church. He tried to enforce conformity to the Anglican ritual and levy taxes on his own authority. This brought the
king into conflict with the growing numbers of Puritans
(Calvinists) and with Parliament. His four Parliaments all
opposed his taxes as "impositions" and his high church religion as "popery." In 1621, Parliament passed the Great Prot-
estation, which stated that

". . . the liberties, franchises, privileges, and jurisdictions
of Parliament are the ancient and undoubted birthright and
inheritance of the subjects of England. . . ."

James rejected the protest and arrested its authors.

Charles I succeeded his father in 1625, and he continued
his policies in both religion and government. In 1628, Parliament repeated its position in the Petition of Right, which
stated that no taxes should be raised without parliamentary
consent, there should be no martial law in peace, and no one
should be imprisoned except on a specific charge. Charles
agreed but went back on his word almost at once and, in
1629, arrested nine leaders of the House of Commons.
Thereafter, he attempted to rule without Parliament. He
continued to persecute Puritans and to levy impositions. For
a while, things went pretty well. But, in 1640, Charles ran
out of money and was forced to call Parliament to bail him
out.

Parliament met in 1640 in an ugly mood. Charles' chief
minister, Stafford, was executed and the Archbishop of Canterbury, Laud, went to the Tower of London. Charles was
forced to agree to the Petition of Right, and Parliament
passed a bill requiring a session every three years and for-
bidding the king to dismiss it. For about 18 months Charles
accepted Parliament's attacks on his powers but by June,

1642, he had had enough. The nation drifted into civil war. The peerage and the central shires went for the King, while London and the outlying counties were for Parliament. This combination ultimately proved the stronger, although for the first two years of war Charles and the Royalists did fairly well. By 1644, however, Oliver Cromwell had organized his New Model Army, with its strong Puritan discipline and sense of divine mission. In 1644 at Marston Moor and in 1645 at Naseby, Cromwell defeated the king. After Naseby, the Royalists gave up, and Charles himself surrendered. Cromwell then turned to deal with the Presbyterian Scots, who had fallen out with the Congregational New Model Army. After defeating them, he went to Ireland, and conducted several massacres of the Roman Catholic Irish. In England itself, Cromwell had the king executed for treason in 1649 and, in 1654, sent Parliament home, being no better able to get along with a legislature than Charles.

To replace the fallen monarchy, Cromwell established the Commonwealth. It was basically a dictatorship. England was divided into military districts, each run by a major general. They governed with considerable efficiency and Puritan fervor. Dancing was forbidden, along with such popular sports as drinking, bear baiting, and fornication. The press was rigidly censored, and only Calvinist services were permitted. Abroad, the Commonwealth waged successful war. The Netherlands was defeated, as was Spain, and Cromwell laid the foundations for British naval supremacy. But the Commonwealth was an unpopular government. Virtue is tiring, particularly in excessive amounts. As long as Cromwell lived no one dared complain, but when he died there developed considerable sentiment for a royal restoration. In 1660, General Monk led his army to London and invited Charles II to England. Charles entered London on May 29, 1660, and England was a monarchy again.

Charles II was a far different man from his father. He had learned from his exile, and the first thing he promised was to call Parliament and respect its powers. Charles' character was also an improvement on his predecessors. He was an affable and pleasant man, given to drink, women, games, and fun. He suspected England was, too, particularly after the unhealthy moral excesses of Puritanism. He was right. Charles was a generally popular ruler, and only the discredited Puritans complained about his gaudy and spacious private life.

In politics and religion Charles tried to follow a moderate line. He supported religious toleration, although opposition from the Restoration Parliament (1661–1679) prevented him from accomplishing it. Parliament insisted on several repressive and intolerant laws, known as the Clarendon Code, and Charles reluctantly went along with them. Charles also supported expansion of trade and colonies, and here he had Parliamentary support.

The general success of the Restoration, however, could not overcome one large deficit. It was the problem of succession. James, Duke of York, was next in line, and he was a stiff-necked, absolutist Roman Catholic. In Protestant, Parliamentary England, used to the agreeable and slightly debauched Charles II, these were not good qualities. Charles himself recognized this, and once commented that the future of the Stuart house depended on whether he or James died first. Charles did, on February 6, 1685, and was succeeded by his brother, James II.

James quickly fulfilled his subjects' worst fears. He paid little attention to Parliament and began to fill official positions with Catholics. Most Englishmen were not prepared to accept Catholics in government and resisted James' efforts at toleration as a blind for the establishment of a Catholic regime. In 1687, James had a son, thus insuring that his policies would be continued into the indefinite future. This was more than the Anglican church, many of the peers, and the merchants could stand. An invitation was issued to William of Orange, *stadhouder* of the Netherlands, to come to England and rescue Protestantism and Parliament. William came in November, 1688, and James II, utterly bereft of support, fled to France. There was a bit of rioting in London, but no major disorders. The Glorious Revolution was a general and peaceful success.

Parliament met in January, 1689, offered the crown jointly to William and his wife Mary, and passed the Declaration of Rights. The Declaration stated that the monarch could not make or suspend laws without Parliament's consent, nor could he tax or maintain a standing army unless Parliament agreed. Parliamentary elections were to be free, the king's judges could not set excessive bail, dispense with juries, or confiscate the people's arms. In the Declaration of Rights, Parliament went beyond its own prerogatives, important though these were, and added several general civil liberties as well. It was a crucial document, which became the basic statement of British government principles and was copied later in the American Bill of Rights, now under such sharp attack.

The reigns of William and Mary (1689–1702) and Anne (1702–1714) were dominated by war with France, not domestic politics. At home the general drift of power toward Parliament continued, and both monarchs were careful to see that their ministers and policies had the confidence of the Lords and Commons. Abroad, the war went well, at least most of the time. British naval superiority over France was established at Cap de La Hogue in 1693, while James' attempt to recapture his crown died in defeat at Boyne in 1690. When peace broke out in 1697, ending the War of the League of Augsburg, the British made few gains, but they were clearly stronger than France. In 1701, war with France began again—the War of the Spanish Succession—and this time the British were victorious everywhere. The Treaty of Utrecht in 1713 established England as the foremost Great Power in Europe.

Anne died on August 1, 1714, the victim of obesity, a general decline, and lots of liquor. She left neither children nor close relatives. In this new succession crisis, the leading contenders were James II's son and the Protestant Elector of Hanover, George. George won out, and the party that had opposed him, known as the Tories, began to intrigue with the exiled Stuart prince. They attempted to raise Scotland against George I, and the pretender "James III" actually landed. Government troops put the revolt down easily. The leading Tories were arrested, and the government, now secure, fell into the hands of their opponents, the Whigs.

English government in the eighteenth century was the product of two great political facts: the Glorious Revolution and the disinterest of George I and George II in domestic politics. The Glorious Revolution had established the powers of Parliament and the king could neither govern against its wishes nor sustain ministers who had no friends there. This arrangement assured Parliament a coordinate share in government, but it did not, nor was it designed to reduce legitimate royal power or make the king the servant of his subjects. Royal disinterest in politics, however, led to the domination of government by the ministry and Parliament. Thus, there was a slow drift of power away from the crown to the ministers and Parliament and also a slow drift of public opinion toward regarding this reduced royal role as legitimate.

All royal power did not vanish, of course. It was still possible for George III (1760–1820) to manipulate elections and bribe Members with offices, pensions, and favors. The king could still act as his own party manager and dominate his own ministry. George III did that, and he did it well in the years from 1770 to 1782. Such tactics, however, ran counter to the drift of political practice, thought, and expectation. They were still legitimate. But they were also unpopular.

In spite of the temporary exercise of royal power by George III, before he went permanently insane, executive authority and policy making fell to the ministry, or cabinet. The ministers guided bills through Parliament and, more and more, they also wrote them. They ran the government bureaus, although generally not very well. They awarded favors and peerages, commissions, and commands in the armed forces and did their best to keep a majority in Parliament. No one was better at this complicated and endless game than Robert Walpole, prime minister from 1721 to 1742.

In Parliament itself, the ministers followed well-established customs of political management. The Members tended to fall into two large groups, the Court Party, or the King's Friends, and the Country Party, or Those Who Were Not His Friends. The King's Friends included royal officials, placemen, and Members who were friendly to the ministry and its policies. The Country Party included men opposed to the government on principle and men opposed to the particular ministry. Since there were seldom fewer than 100 placemen in Commons, the ministry started with a considerable advantage in gaining its majority. Even so, the ministry could lose and, in the period between the fall of Pitt (1761) and the accession of Lord North (1770), it lost frequently.

Within these broad divisions, the Members attached themselves into loose factions or blocs, held together by family connections or personal interests. These interests and connections were usually led by a peer, who was frequently a minister. By controlling several electoral districts, the peer could manage the election of his relatives and friends, and then direct their votes and speeches in Parliament. He could reward his followers with pensions and places and coerce them with threats of defeat at the polls. Most of the factions were small, from three to a dozen men, but they were the cellular units of a parliamentary majority.

None of this delicate web of custom, interest, and connection could have worked unless both Houses were composed of men who came from the same social class. Most of the Members of Commons were related to peers, and many were younger sons. Those not related to the peerage by blood were wealthy merchants or country gentry, who also belonged to the social aristocracy. Both Commons and Lords agreed on the rules and nuances of the political game and had the same expectations and hopes from it. They were able to maneuver deftly within complicated political customs, dealing with issues far more by personal negotiation and informal understandings than by debate and resolutions. In a very real way, therefore, the elections were unimportant. Whoever was returned would be an aristocrat, accustomed to the system.

The election procedures reinforced aristocratic control and the complex arrangements of interest and connection. Each shire sent two Members to Commons, as did selected boroughs, precisely as they had since the fourteenth century. Electoral districts had last been assigned in the sixteenth century, and time had changed some of them. A few boroughs had no population at all and were called pocket boroughs because the owner had its seats in his pocket. The most famous pocket borough was Old Sarum, the Pitt family seat. Less-decayed boroughs had fallen to a handful of voters, 12 or 20, few enough so the local magnate could control each of the voters personally. These were called rotten boroughs, after the methods used in elections, and there were several dozen of them by midcentury.

Pocket and rotten boroughs did not exhaust the list of electoral anomalies. Each borough set its own electoral standards. Sometimes owners of certain properties could vote, elsewhere the freemen of the city had the franchise. Nowhere were there more than 7000 voters, and that was in London. The shires were as bad, with a few hundred voters being average. All in all, there were not more than 250,000 voters in all of England, and fewer than 10,000 of these could control the House of Commons.

In such a system, political parties and political issues meant relatively little. Issues were seldom discussed in Parliament. Party affiliation, whether Whig or Tory, meant much less than family connections and interests. Nonetheless, the system had its advantages. The quality of the Members, while not very high, was still better than the sleazy shysters and low political poltroons who infest American legislatures. Furthermore, the system was successful. England was prosperous, the government was stable, people enjoyed a degree of freedom unmatched in Europe, and foreign wars ended in victory. Critics found it hard to argue with all that.

III

When the philosopher Samuel Pufendorf described the decaying feudal anarchy and incoherence of the Holy Roman Empire, he found that the traditional Aristotelian categories of monarchy, aristocracy, and democracy did not describe it. Nor did it seem to have any element of sovereignty since its head, the emperor, did not rule and its members, the princes, defied him at will. In the end, Pufendorf called the Empire a monster, an organism alien to the laws of nature and nation. Such a judgment on the disintegrating Empire would have been impossible as late as 1630 but, by the middle of the seventeenth century, with the changes in political theory and administrative practice, Pufendorf's conclusion was not merely appropriate, it was mild.

Pufendorf's judgment applied to states other than the Empire, and Poland was one. During the seventeenth century Poland became the classic example of feudal anarchy in which the nobles counted for everything and the king nothing. Poland was a monarchy in name only. Kingship was elective, and the nobles who voted for the king took care to elect someone as weak and innocuous as possible. They almost invariably succeeded. Polish kings were generally undistinguished, and they had very little independent power to support their royal rank. By the eighteenth century the monarchy had become a bad and bankrupt joke. It was held by such figures as Stanislas Poniatowski (1764–1795), a discarded lover of Catherine the Great of Russia and made king as a consolation, or August the Strong (1697–1733), whose exploits were mainly sexual; he was reputed to have fathered 365 bastard children. "Power [is] one of the things most necessary to the grandeur of kings and the success of their government . . . ," Cardinal Richelieu commented, and these kings lacked it altogether.

The weakness of Polish kings lay in the absence of any royal army or bureaucracy. For government Poland relied on the moral authority of her kings and Diet, along with the voluntary consent of the governed. No coercion was possible and, in the more remote provinces, it was difficult for the king even to learn whether he had been obeyed or not. For defense, there was only the feudal levy. In an age of more sophisticated military technology and increasing use of highly trained military professionals, the Polish feudal levy was almost ludicrous in its futility. Neither the Polish government or army was Westernized, as was the case in her chief rivals, Prussia, Austria, and Russia.

Politics in the old regime reflected social patterns, and the "aristocratic republic" of Poland possessed an archaic social structure even for the seventeenth century. In Poland, the dominant class was the landed nobility, who numbered about 12 percent of the population, far more than anywhere else. Polish nobles were a diverse lot, ranging from the Potocki clan who owned estates the size of Connecticut to thousands of landless gentry, who owned nothing but their honor. The poor gentry became retainers for the rich, enabling the magnates to have private armies and become virtually independent of the crown. Beneath the lords were the peasants, so far beneath that Rousseau's description of them as "less than nothing" exaggerated their status. They were serfs, owned body and soul by their lords who regarded them as animals and treated them accordingly. The urban bourgeoisie were better off than the servile peasants, having personal freedom and a modest income, but their political power was insignificant. Except for Warsaw and Cracow, the towns were small miserable places where the inhabitants were as likely to speak German as Polish. Alienated from the peasants whom they did not know and from the nobility who despised them, the bourgeoisie lived in a narrow and constricted world, without power, influence, or wealth.

In such a society, only the nobility could wield any real power. The nobility was organized into the Diet, a sort of legislature that had the right to elect the king and pass on all legislation. Each noble could vote, and unanimity was required to pass a law. A single veto, and the bill or treaty failed. The Diet was thus able to frustrate any attempt to strengthen the crown far more easily than it could develop any coherent policy of its own. Moreover, politics within the Diet reflected the power of the great nobles, who were virtually sovereign themselves. Families such as the Potocki and Branicki had their own foreign and domestic policy; the Potocki, for example, were pro-French and wished to retain the aristocratic constitution that Poland had. Such magnates could also call foreign powers into Poland, and Russian intervention frequently followed calls from Polish nobles. The result of these political arrangements was evident by the end of the seventeenth century. Poland had become a classic power vacuum, and her disposition was one of the main elements of the Eastern Question.

The other Eastern state that failed to consolidate its administration or modernize its army was the Ottoman Empire. In the two centuries after the onset of the great depression, the decline of the Ottoman Empire was quite marked, although it did not succumb to total catastrophe in the Polish fashion. Turkish decadence was a startling and welcome reversal from previous strength and vigor that in two centuries, had carried the Ottoman Empire to control over the eastern Mediterranean, the Black Sea, and Hungary and the Balkans. After the fall of Constantinople in 1453, Europeans had shuddered over the Turkish menace and concocted hundreds of plans, schemes, and crusades to throw the Turks back. Nothing worked. The Ottoman hordes crushed the Hungarians at Mohacs in 1526, beseiged Vienna in 1529, and threatened to push into Poland and Bohemia. Although Vienna was the farthest Turkish advance into central Europe, no one felt secure or safe. Even during the Reformation, Protestant princes contributed troops and arms to Catholic Habsburg Emperors for the constant wars against the Turks. Now, in the years after 1600, the Turks seemed stricken by a mysterious languor, and the monarchs of Eastern Christendom were immensely relieved.

The causes of Turkish decline came from several sides,

some discernible to contemporaries, some not, some general afflictions, and others pertained only to the Ottoman Empire. Perhaps first among Turkish problems after 1570 was a sharp decline in the quality of leadership. Sultan Selim the Sot (1556–1574) spent most of his time drunk, and Mustapha (1617–1618, 1622–1623) and Ibrahim I (1644–1648) were both feebleminded. Under this indolent and incompetent direction, imperial officials, who were Christian slaves of the Sultan, abandoned the public interest, directed their efforts to self-aggrandizement, and gorged themselves with lands, slaves, money, offices, and powers. In Turkey, the sultan's household was also the imperial government, a situation that had not pertained in the West since the high Middle Ages. Under such conditions, incapacity at the top meant that the whole administration went slack, as the decline in the quality of the bureaucratic registers and documents in the seventeenth century showed.

The army was also affected. Within the Ottoman tradition, the sultan was a war leader, who supported his troops out of conquered lands and plunder. When the conquests stopped and the plunder fell off, the feudal cavalry turned into landed gentry, and the Janassaries, who were the sultan's personal Christian slaves, turned to political intrigue, *coups*, even crafts and manufacturing, to support themselves. Murad IV (1623–1640), a vigorous though brutal ruler, tried to reform the Janassaries by permitting them to marry and turning them into a professional infantry. But they never recovered their former ferocity and effectiveness.

The Ottoman Empire also suffered from economic weaknesses. The trade routes around Africa diminished commerce through Egypt, and the eastern Mediterranean slowly ceased to be the source of spices, silks, and other oriental products. The decline of Turkish trade was compounded by a severe monetary inflation. At the same time, of course, the Ottoman government was expanding its bureaucracy and trying to convert the feudal and slave hordes into a modern, professional army. Taxes were increased, and the feudal lords, who were abandoning their role as soldiers, demanded more dues from their peasants. As a result, brigandage increased alarmingly, as did graft and extortion. The military and administrative magnates who had once plundered the infidel now began to plunder the Empire itself, and no one could do anything about it.

Finally, the Ottoman Empire suffered from cultural sclerosis. The scientific and technological progress of seventeenth century Christendom passed Turkey by. Turkish armies, technologically superior to the infidel in 1500, fell far behind in the seventeenth century. Even more glaring technological deficiencies drove the Ottoman navy from the seas. There was no growth of philosophical schools in the empire, nor was there any increase in the general standard of education. The Ottoman Empire retained the structures and standards of its age of conquest, kept its system of government by household slaves, and continued the enormous gulf between Moslem and Christian. "The Turks . . . found it impossible to liberate themselves from Ottman traditions."[1]

A third great power sinking into irreversible decay in the seventeenth century was Spain, once the greatest and proudest power in the Western world. Like the Turks, the Spanish had enjoyed immoderate power, prosperity, and glory in the sixteenth century and then came upon hard times. Unlike the Ottoman Turks, the Spanish collapse was swift and complete, with no period of seeming recovery, no ephemeral successes. So total and absolute was the Spanish catastrophe that observers between 1600 and 1700 were moved to awe and sought explanations in the realm of religion and demonology as well as politics, diplomacy, and trade. A seventeenth century Spanish lawyer, after recounting the more mundate ills of his land, added a plaintive comment on divine disfavor:

"It seems as if one had wished to reduce these kingdoms to a republic of bewitched beings, living outside the natural order of things. . . ."[2]

---

[1] Paul Coles, *The Ottman Impact on Europe*, p. 172.
[2] Gonzales de Cellorigo, quoted in J. Elliott, "The Decline of Spain" in T. Aston, *Europe in Crisis: 1560–1660*, p. 193.

But there were explanations for the Spanish decline beyond those of collective sins and expiation. They were partially economic. The savage depression in the Habsburg imperium in the seventeenth century was a big factor in military defeat abroad and revolutions at home. Politically, Spanish commitments had exceeded her powers even in the sixteenth century and, by 1620, the gap was so wide that defeat could only be delayed. Efforts to prolong Spain's position as a great power simply made the final disaster worse by adding revolts to the other problems of government.

In the old regime Spain was composed of three Iberian kingdoms: Castile, Aragon and, after 1580, Portugal. Each was governed separately under its own laws. Only in Castile was the royal authority paramount, as Ferdinand and Isabella had reduced the independent power of the towns, church, and the Cortez, or Parliament. Here, the king did about as he wished, and he taxed cruelly. In Aragon and Portugal, royal power was far less extensive. Portugal retained its own administrative structure and was ruled by Portuguese. In Aragon, Parliaments retained great powers, and the king could not override them easily. In Catalonia, he could not override the Parliament at all.

"The most important thing in Your Majesty's Monarchy is for you to become King of Spain; by that I mean, Sire, that Your Majesty should not be content with being King of Portugal, of Aragon, of Valencia and Count of Barcelona, but should secretly plan and work to reduce these Kingdoms of which Spain is composed to the style and laws of Castile, without any difference."[3]

This was good advice, and Olivares as chief minister from 1621 to 1643 did his best to carry it out. But he failed. The economic disasters forced him into a series of improvisations both domestic and diplomatic, none of which had much hope of long-term success. When the resources of Castle ran out, Olivares tried to tax the other states of the Habsburg imperium. This produced revolt. On Corpus Christi Day,

[3] Memoir of Count-Duke Olivares to Philip IV, 1624.

1640, the laborers of Barcelona rose in riot and sparked a revolt in Catalonia against the government of Madrid. Later in the same year, a Portuguese national revolt broke out under the leadership of the Duke of Braganza. In 1647, the area of rebellion widened, with the revolt of Masaniello in Naples against atrocious misgovernment, high taxes, high bread prices, and unemployment. Such events made peace essential, but the Treaties of Westphalia in 1648 did not end the war between France and Spain. This dragged on, to the increasing disadvantage of the Spanish. Although the Habsburgs were able to restore government in Naples and slowly recapture most of Catalonia, Portugal was lost forever.

Peace with France in 1659 did not bring recovery to Spain. She was economically prostrate, and Castilian government had degenerated into a morass of corruption and inefficiency. The new king, Carlos II (1665–1700), could not give the leadership the state needed. He was a retarded and sickly wretch, with a jaw so large and heavy he could not close his mouth. He drooled constantly and could not control his bowels. He suffered from an astonishing variety of respiratory ailments, and constantly threatened to die. The so-called government fell into the hands of the queen mother, who ran an indolent and corrupt regime, notable only for its vicious palace intrigue. In 1680 Castile reached its nadir. A currency revaluation destroyed what remained of trade and industry and again bankrupted the crown. Royal government was nearly lifeless. It even stopped promising better times and presented a facade of quiet futility. Attempts at reform and recovery awaited the new Bourbon dynasty, who entered their paltry inheritance in 1700. And the Spanish Bourbons, though not without grave faults, were an improvement. Shorn of its power, Spain made a modest recovery in the last century of the old regime.

The circumstances of decline varied widely in the three old monarchies. Spain had a developed bureaucracy and a powerful royal army but fell prey to an excessive preoccupation with religion, the seventeenth-century depression, and unattainable imperial goals. Spain was a semimodern state that deteriorated into poverty and red tape. Poland was just the opposite. An expanding market for grain made the magnates rich but did nothing for a monarchy that possessed no army or administration. And the Ottoman Empire became an army without a state and a tribe without a country as Christians and Arabs took over nearly all the functions of government. The results, however, were the same everywhere: defeat abroad and political disintegration at home.

IV

"A great country can have no such thing as a little war," said the Duke of Wellington in 1815, after a particularly big one. In the Old Regime, the European Great Powers managed to live up to Wellington's standards as, by and large, they have since. But during the old regime, wars, although big and long enough, were seldom conclusive. Total military victory was impossible. Armies were too small, they moved too slowly, and the territories they had to conquer were too large to hold. Commanders found it difficult to administer conquered provinces. Moreover, the technology and tactics of defense were superior to those of offense. Each walled city had to be beseiged, and that often took months. Each fortified village had to be reduced. Even castles still blocked an enemy's advance. Further, an opposing army might be defeated in battle, but was seldom destroyed. It retreated into a walled town and recovered. Beyond that, armies fought by the season, campaigning in the summer when food was plentiful and retiring into winter quarters when it was not. Finally, a primitive technology limited offensive military effectiveness. Wretched roads meant that an army moving three miles a day was marching rapidly. Guns were uncertain, giving the advantage to fortifications. Armies were ill equipped to achieve victory.

Military strategy and tactics conformed to these limitations. Generals maneuvered for position, hoping to force their opponents to retreat, leaving fortified towns without hope of reinforcement. Whole campaigns were designed to reduce a single town or secure a single district. Battles were fought only when necessary. Pillage was as important a tactical weapon as battle or siege; after all, the troops must eat and enjoy. Generals measured victory in relative terms; if they ended a campaign in better position than they began it, they were well satisfied. Only the greatest commanders transcended these limited concepts of war. Eugene of Savoy, the Duke of Marlborough, or Maurice de Saxe sought to destroy the enemy. But total victory eluded even them. In spite of battles won, the technological limitations held them down. They were like speedboats trapped in the mud.

Such strategy, of course, made diplomacy more important than fighting. Since war was not fought to victory, it had to be fought to negotiations. Battles or sieges won were diplomatic counters to be used at the peace table. Diplomats traded these advantages, attempting to gain by skill in their profession what soldiers lost through incompetence in theirs.

This type of diplomacy, which dealt in limited liability, was christened "balance of power" by the English diplomat, Sir William Temple. This meant that no state could be allowed to gain a general hegemony in Europe. Should a country become too powerful, the others would combine against it, thus keeping its gains within acceptable bounds and preserving the existing state system based on national sovereignty. Temple presented this as an observation on the way things worked, but balance of power soon became a canon of plomacy, a reason constantly invoked by diplomats to justify their actions.

A second fundamental factor in the Old Regime state system was the existence of two distinct spheres of diplomacy. One was Western, comprising Spain, France, England, the Netherlands, and Austria. In this arrangement, the small Italian and German states, as well as Portugal, were seen as provinces to be conquered or as spheres of influence. Territorial aggrandizement in the West, therefore, often came at the expense of these small states. Only Spain, the weakest of the Western countries, had to part with her provinces.

Territory was not the only object of Western warfare.

Wars were fought on both land and sea, in Europe and abroad, for trade and colonies. Treaties reflected these diverse interests. They included tariff schedules and colonial adjustments, as well as provisions for European provinces and royal marriages.

In Eastern Europe the diplomatic web included the Ottoman Empire, Poland, Russia, Sweden, Prussia, and Austria. Here, diplomacy was simpler. Eastern European states were generally behind their Western neighbors in political centralization, so questions of colonies and trade were not important. Eastern powers fought only for land, for huge provinces with uncertain boundaries, few towns, little wealth, and less government. In spite of this, the military and diplomatic struggles in Eastern Europe possessed both purpose and coherence. The wars resolved themselves into one basic theme. The central issue was the disposition of three empires that had become too weak to sustain themselves—Sweden, Poland, and Turkey, an issue that eventually became known as "The Eastern Question."

Until 1740, these two spheres of war and diplomacy were generally separate. Wars were fought simultaneously, and the Austrians, who had vital interests in both halves of Europe, were frequently engaged in the East and West at the same time. But aside from this, what happened in the West seldom affected Eastern Europe, and the reverse was also true. Indeed, the Austrians, who had a habit of losing wars in the West, were usually winners in the East. In 1740, this pattern broke down, and most of the Great Powers were drawn into a single, interconnected conflict—the War of the Austrian Succession (1740–1748). And it took a dynastic crisis in the one Great Power that belonged to both diplomatic spheres to bring all Europe into the same war. The last years of the Old Regime saw a single European balance of power, thus insuring that every state would eventually become involved in the wars of the French Revolution.

In Western Europe after the Treaties of Westphalia (1648), the basic issue of international affairs was the

French attempt to establish political hegemony over her neighbors. France had emerged from the Thirty Years' War with territorial gains in Alsace, and she was also the best-organized state in Europe. French gains at Westphalia were reinforced by victory over Spain in a long and desultory war that ended in 1659 with the Treaty of the Isle of Pheasants. France added territory in Belgium as well as the Spanish province of Roussillon. By 1661, when Louis XIV assumed personal power, France was uniquely prepared for sustained expansion on a large scale.

Louis, of course, took advantage of the situation as soon as he could. After careful diplomatic preparation, he launched a massive invasion of the Spanish provinces in the Low Countries (Belgium) and grabbed it all. Such rapid and overwhelming success frightened the Dutch, who organized a coalition against France. Louis chose to negotiate rather than continue fighting and, in 1668, the War of Devolution ended. But the Sun King was still compensated for his troubles. He kept a strip of territory in southern Flanders, including the fortress city of Lille.

This was nice, but it was not enough. Louis had settled for considerably less than he wanted, and nobody likes to do that. Outraged at the Dutch success in reducing the scope of his victory, the Sun King organized a coalition against the Netherlands. In 1672 he was ready, invaded, and was only prevented from occupying the entire country when the Dutch opened their dikes. The war then settled down into campaigns of maneuver and diplomacy. The coalition against the Dutch contradicted the principles of balance of power and crumbled away within two years. By 1675, France was fighting against Spain and Austria as well as the Netherlands. By 1678, everyone had had enough. The Spanish, as usual, paid the price of peace. In the Treaty of Nijmwegen Spain ceded the province of Franche-Comté and some more Flemish towns to France. Everyone else got nothing.

After Nijmwegen, Louis XIV changed his tactics a bit, but not his aims. Instead of declaring war on his neighbors and invading them, he hailed them into French courts and invaded them. He established "Chambers of Reunion," which were to decide the true boundaries of the cities, provinces, and territories recently ceded to France. Since medieval boundaries were notoriously vague, it was possible to claim that France was owed far more land than she had received. Louis' courts solemnly claimed everything they could, and the French army occupied it, including Lorraine, Luxembourg, Strasbourg, and a good deal of the Rhenish Palatinate. There were protests, of course, there always are, but for a decade after 1678 that was all there were. For France, "Reunion" was even better than war.

The Chambers of Reunion, together with French victories in the last several wars, convinced most Western diplomats that only a powerful coalition could stop the Sun King. Therefore, England and the Netherlands submerged their colonial rivalry, and were joined by Spain and Austria in another effort to defeat France. In the War of the League of Augsburg (1688–1698) the allies did fairly well, fighting the French to a stalemate. In the Treaty of Ryswick (1698), Louis XIV was forced to make some important concessions. He recognized William III, the Dutch *stadhouder*, as king of England, thus accepting the results of the Glorious Revolution. He disgorged most of his Reunions, including Luxembourg and Lorraine.

Exhaustion was certainly a factor in the Treaty of Ryswick. France had suffered famine, depression, and disguised royal bankruptcy, and the allies were also feeling the pinch. But there was another factor, perhaps more important. It was the partition of the Spanish empire. At long last, it looked as if Charles II was finally going to die. He had no heirs, of course, and the disposition of his empire was the subject of an intense diplomatic auction. The two leading contenders, France and Austria, agreed to a Bavarian candidate, who outraged everyone by dying even before Charles II. Seeing no alternative to Austrian control of Spain, the French managed to get it for themselves. In 1700, Louis XIV's grandson became Philip V of Spain.

England, Austria, and the Netherlands could not accept that. By 1701 they were again at war with France. In the War of the Spanish Succession (1701–1713), France fought in a defensive posture. Even so, in 1704 the war turned against the French. At Blenheim, the Duke of Marlborough obliterated a French army and drove them out of Germany. Two years later, Marlborough broke through French defensive lines in Belgium at Ramillies and pushed the French back to the frontier. At the same time, Eugene of Savoy pushed the French out of Italy, and Philip V's troops barely escaped destruction in Spain. But the worst was still ahead. In 1708, Marlborough and Eugene destroyed a French army at Oudenarde and invaded France itself. The next year France was struck by the worst famine in her history, which killed over a million people.

Somehow, the French fought on. The bankrupt king managed to raise one more army by recruiting starving peasant lads who could find bread nowhere else. The French built another defense line across northern France, which the allies attacked at Malplaquet. There were over 40,000 casualties in the battle, including the French commander, Marshal Villars, but the French held and denied Marlborough his chance to march on Paris. When peace came, therefore it was, like the others, a compromise. Philip V held on to Spain, and the French surrendered a few colonial possessions to the victorious British. The Treaties of Utrecht (1713), however, masked rather than revealed the diplomatic reality. The French were badly beaten, and it would be a century before they made one last effort to dominate Europe in the wars of the Revolution and Napoleon.

In eastern Europe, during these years, the main concern in diplomatic affairs was the Turkish Menace, the most pressing aspect of the Eastern Question. The Turks controlled, more or less, a vast amount of Eastern Europe. It was a powerful empire, even though Turkish control over much of it was loose and sporadic. Most of the Eastern powers felt threatened by the Turks and were frequently at war with them. Things had been this way since the four-

teenth century when the Turks had first gained a foothold in
Europe.

In the middle years of the seventeenth century, this accustomed diplomatic pattern continued. Venice was at war with
the Ottoman Empire. It began in 1645 and gradually settled
down into an Homeric siege of Candia, in Crete. Although
the Venetians won some important naval victories, they
were unable to hold Candia, which the Turks finally took in
1669. The peace treaty in 1670 ceded the island of Crete to
the Ottoman Empire. Austria also fought the Turks continuously in the form of border skirmishes and more seriously in
a short war from 1661 to 1664. The Austrian general, Mon-
tecuccoli, won a major victory at St. Gotthard, but the Truce
of Vasvar in 1664 merely reaffirmed the existing boundaries.
Poland tried her hand at war with the Turks in 1672 and
was promptly defeated. In the Treaty of Zuravna in 1676,
the Turks gained most of Podolia, a large province with unknown boundaries and no central administration. Only the
Russians did well against the Turks. In a short war from
1677 to 1681, Turkey lost her nominal suzerainty over the
southern Ukraine to Russia.

In these desultory wars, the Ottoman Empire rarely faced
more than one Christian power at a time and fought on one
front only. Although the power of Turkey was declining, it
was sufficient to deal with such modest threats. Moreover,
Turkey's enemies only nibbled around the outer edges of the
Empire and never threatened the center. Even if the Turks
lost, as at St. Gotthard, it was not too serious. The basic
power balance remained.

In 1681, the traditional diplomatic patterns were changed.
A new Turkish vizir, Kara Mustapha, decided to invade Austria, and he provoked a general Christian alliance against
him. Austria was joined by the Papacy, Venice, Poland, and
ultimately Russia in the Holy League, whose avowed aims
were to liberate "oppressed" Christians, conquer territory,
and end the Turkish Menace.

The Turks struck first. Urged on by the French, Kara
Mustapha launched a slow and ponderous march up the Dan-

ube to Vienna. It took two years to get there but, in 1683, the Turks laid siege to Vienna. Although ably defended by Rüdiger von Stahremburg, the city might have fallen had it not been relieved by a Polish army under Jan III Sobieski.

The siege of Vienna was the high point of the Turkish efforts. As the Turks retreated down the Danube the Austrians followed. In 1686 the Austrians took Budapest, the capital of Hungary, and in 1687 defeated the Turks at Mohacs and drove them south into Serbia. At the same time, the Venetians invaded Greece, and conquered the Peloponnesian Peninsula. They even captured Athens, although in the process an ammunition dump in the Parthenon exploded and severely damaged the building.

In 1695, the Russians joined the alliance against Turkey. They besieged Azov and, after a year, took it. The Austrians were also active. In 1697, Prince Eugene of Savoy cornered a Turkish army at Zenta in southern Hungary and destroyed it. Such an overwhelming defeat persuaded the Turks to seek peace. In 1699, the treaties were signed at Karlowitz. They reflected the magnitude of the Christian victory. Austria gained Hungary, Transylvania, Croatia, and part of Serbia, while the Russians retained Azov, the Venetians kept the Peloponnesus and most of the Dalmatian coast, and Poland got Podolia. Karlowitz marked the end of the Ottoman Empire as the most powerful Eastern state, a role assumed by Austria and soon to be shared with Russia.

No sooner had war ended in the south than it broke out in the Baltic. Here, the issue was the disposition of the Swedish empire. In 1697, a young boy of 15 became Charles XII of Sweden. His neighbors, Russia, Poland and Denmark, thought it might be a good time to partition an empire that Sweden could no longer hold. In 1700 they attacked, and began the Great Northern War.

No one could know it, of course, but Charles XII was a natural military genius. In six months he had driven the astounded Danes out of the war and turned on Russia. At Narva, in November, 1700, Charles attacked 40,000 Russians with only 8000 of his own troops. The Russians were not expecting him; it was snowing and already dark when Charles attacked. People did not fight in such wretched weather. But Charles did, and he utterly routed the Russians. He then turned on the Poles and drove them out of the war in 1706.

Having dealt with Poland and Denmark, Charles turned back to Russia. But Peter the Great had used the respite to reorganize his army, and in June, 1709, Peter defeated the Swedes at Poltava. In effect, this won the war although desultory fighting and serious pillaging continued until 1721. Charles XII could never again regain the strategic initiative. The allies had been right. Sweden was too poor and small to defend her extensive Baltic empire. In the treaties of Nystadt (1721), Russia acquired the entire Baltic coast from Finland to Prussia and took her place as a legitimate Great Power.

The Great Northern War demonstrated with dreadful clarity that Poland had become a power vacuum, a part of the Eastern Question. During the eighteenth century, her neighbors intervened in Polish affairs with increasing force. As early as 1715, Russia intervened to support the nobles against the king and, by the 1730s, the Polish king was chosen abroad. In 1766, the grant of religious toleration to Protestants and Greek Orthodox Catholics brought Poland to civil war. Her Great Power neighbors moved to protect their interests in Poland, and Austria and Russia came to the verge of war. Not wishing a general conflict, Frederick the Great of Prussia proposed a partition of Poland. In August, 1772, Russia, Austria, and Prussia each grabbed a slice of Poland. This worked so well that it was repeated in 1793 with a second partition, only this time Austria was left out. In 1795, a third partition, with all three Great Powers participating, finished Poland off. Everyone except the Poles seemed pleased by this neat solution to a difficult aspect of the Eastern Question. In 1668, the retiring king, Jan Kasimir, had predicted exactly that result. Rarely has prophecy been so accurate.

In the years between Westphalia and the French Revolu-

GROWTH OF GREAT POWERS IN CENTRAL EUROPE 1648-1795

North Sea

Baltic Sea

RUSSIA

ENGLAND

Danzig

KINGDOM OF PRUSSIA

Berlin

Posen

Warsaw

SILESIA

Rhine

Prague

AUSTRIAN

EMPIRE

FRANCE

Danube

Vienna

Budapest

HUNGARY

Mohács

Zenta

Karlowitz

Belgrade

OTTOMAN EMPIRE

Adriatic Sea

- - - - Prussia in 1740
Prussia in 1795
— · — Austria in 1680
Austria in 1795

Scale of Miles
0 50 100 150 200

tion, there had been a complete reversal of the diplomatic and military relationships in Eastern Europe. In 1648, Poland, Sweden, and Turkey had controlled, in a rather disorganized fashion, huge empires in Eastern Europe. Russia was still an Asiatic state, Austria was glad to hold her defensive lines against the Turks, while Prussia was still a minor German principality. A century and a half saw all that change. Three new Great Powers—Austria, Russia, and Prussia—came to dominate Eastern Europe, largely through modernizing their armies and creating an effective civil service. They conquered vast provinces from their fading rivals and wiped one out altogether. In the process, Russia, Austria, and Prussia discovered they could gain more by cooperation than war. Russia and Austria established a cooperationist diplomacy as early as the 1720s, and Prussia joined them after 1763. The partitions of Poland signaled the change. Diplomacy replaced war as the preferred method of dealing with the Eastern Question.

After the War of the Spanish Succession and the Great Northern War, the Great Powers were exhausted. By 1715, they had been fighting almost continuously for a generation. It was time for peace. But peace only adjourned the quarrels; it did not end them. Prussia was not satisfied with the small gains from the Great Northern War. Austria and Russia hoped for more from Turkey. The Franco-British colonial and trade rivalry grew steadily worse. The British thought themselves strong enough to grab a large piece of the Spanish empire. In the eighteenth century, as today, peace was frequently a temporary expedient, a last resort when ministers could think of nothing else.

When war came, in 1739 in the colonies and 1740 in Europe, after an appropriate and recuperative interval of peace, it marked the conjunction of two separate conflicts: the continuing colonial quarrels between France, England, and Spain and the efforts of Prussia to become a Great Power. The war was immense, like the Spanish Succession and the crusade against the Turk put together. The English were reaching for colonial and economic domination, and the Prussians were trying to annex a rich and extensive Austrian province. Stakes like that brought everybody in and merged the two previously separate diplomatic spheres into one as nations sought allies wherever they could.

The midcentury war was fought in two installments with an eight-year respite between them. The first, the War of the Austrian Succession (1740–1748), was a kind of preliminary. The second, the Seven Years' War (1756–1763), saw the British and Prussians finally victorious. In between the two, there was some juggling of alliances. The French, who had been allies of Prussia in the War of the Austrian Succession, switched over and became allies of Austria for the second round. A "diplomatic revolution" contemporaries called it, since France and Austria had been enemies steadily for a quarter of a millennium. It was not really; the essential struggle remained the same. Austria was still fighting Prussia, France was still fighting Great Britain. The issues in the Seven Years' War were the same as those in the Austrian Succession.

The war in Europe, between Austria and Prussia, began with an Austrian succession crisis. Charles VI had no sons, and so he prepared to leave his empire to his daughter, Maria Theresa. To insure her succession, he had her rights acknowledged by the provinces of the realm and the major foreign powers. When Charles died in 1740, Maria Theresa assumed the thrones of Austria. At the same time, the new king of Prussia, Frederick the Great, thought it was an opportune moment to grab a piece of Maria Theresa's inheritance. He invaded and conquered Silesia. He also provoked a general European war. The French were drawn in as Prussian allies, and the British joined Austria, thus joining their colonial rivalry to the war in central Europe.

In the colonies, the Great War for Empire had begun in 1739, after two decades of nagging disagreements between England and Spain. The English had received limited trading rights in the Spanish empire in the treaties of Utrecht (1713) and, in the endless search for profits, English merchants had consistently gone beyond the letter of the law. The Spanish had retaliated by licensing coast guards to prevent illegal English trade. The coast guards were paid out of the profits from captured ships, so they captured as many as they could, regardless of what kind of trade the merchants pursued. There were protests, court cases, diplomatic representations, reparations claimed, and growing hostility between England and Spain. In 1738, Captain Jenkins, testifying before a parliamentary committee, announced an unusual and horrible atrocity. He said the Spanish had cut off his ear. It was too much. In 1739, Spain and England were at war.

When war began, the English expected to sweep the Spanish out of Latin America in a short and glorious campaign. It did not happen. The English were unprepared for war, and the Spanish, however feebly, fought back. Not until 1745 were the British really ready. Thereafter, they did well. They swept French and Spanish shipping from the seas and took Nova Scotia from the French. Only defeats in Belgium prevented the British from completing their triumph.

By 1748, both sides were ready for peace. The French were nearly bankrupt and in danger of losing their American colonies. The British cabinet was composed of nervous and petty men, who feared the war debt would mean higher land taxes. Frederick the Great of Prussia, firmly in possession of Silesia, had wanted peace for six years. Maria Theresa of Austria reluctantly concluded that her armies and treasury were to battered to go on. The Treaties of Aixla-Chapelle (1748), therefore, were a kind of truce. Except for Silesia, which remained Prussian, conquests were restored. The Great Powers concentrated on getting ready for the next round.

Part of the preparation was the search for allies. Austria, in particular, was dissatisfied with her friends. The British paid nice subsidies, but they concentrated their efforts in the colonies and their army was truly pitiful. The Austrian search for new allies ended in 1756, when Russia and France agreed to help her win Silesia back. Prussia and Great Britain, diplomatically isolated and outmaneuvered, formed their own alliance in self-defense.

Frederick the Great could see that his position in 1756 was precarious, and his enemies, at least on paper, were far stronger than he. So he struck suddenly in August, 1756, conquering Saxony and invading Bohemia before the allies were ready. Although Frederick failed to drive the Austrians out of the war with the first blow, he did maintain the upper hand for the first two years of fighting. He destroyed the French at Rossbach (1757) and forced them back over the Rhine. He held Saxony and part of Bohemia and drove the Russians back in disorder at Zorndorff (1758). By 1759, the allies' superior strength began to tell. The Russians captured Berlin, and the Austrians occupied most of Saxony and Silesia. Only the death of the Czarina Elizabeth in 1762 saved Frederick from certain defeat. Her successor, Peter III, was a great admirer of Frederick, and pulled out of the war. The French, being beaten down by Great Britain, could give no help, and Austria was too weak to win alone. In 1763, the Treaty of Hubertusburg ended the fighting on the basis of mutual restoration of conquests. Seven years of savage war had changed nothing. Prussia still held Silesia, and was, irrevocably, a Great Power.

Overseas, no one had observed the fragile interval of peace that prevailed in Europe between the two wars. The Great War for Empire continued without interruption. In India, the British and French continued fighting through the medium of native allies. In North America, Indian raids were nearly continuous along the borders of the northern English colonies. In 1753 the French occupied the Ohio Valley. They fortified Niagara and built posts on Lake Champlain. General Braddock attempted to drive the French from Fort Duquesne (Pittsburgh) in 1755 and lost his whole army. The formal declaration of war a year later changed nothing.

This time, the British fought the war with immense vigor. The little men cleared out of the way, and a great man took their place. In 1757, William Pitt became the British war leader. He was a man of incredible energy who knew just what he wanted—victory. His intensity had frightened his petty colleagues who kept him out of power as long as possible. In 1757, it was no longer possible. This war could not be fought like the last.

Pitt demanded offensive action in all quarters. He ordered his admirals in the Caribbean to capture the French sugar islands of Guadeloupe and Martinique, which they did without much difficulty. In India, Robert Clive defeated the French and their Indian allies at Plassy in 1757 and secured British domination of the subcontinent. Pitt sent armies to North America to conquer New France. He also sent the right generals. Wolfe and Amherst redeemed years of timidity and bungling by capturing Quebec (1759) and Montreal (1760), and Canada became British. In 4 years of war Pitt did what his predecessors had failed to do in 40. He had won victory everywhere.

The key to British success in the Great War for Empire was the royal navy. Naval superiority, firmly established by the victories at Lagos and Quiberon Bay in 1759, enabled the

British to maintain communications and supply, while isolating the French in little outposts that merely waited their
turn before being reduced. French shipping disappeared and
French trade collapsed. In the sugar islands the French
faced defeat by starvation before the British invasions.
Montcalm, the defender of Canada, was a competent general,
but he had a small army, no communications with home, and
his only real hope was to hold out until the British got tired
and settled for a compromise peace. Naval supremacy gave
the British a basic strategic domination that could surmount
tactical defeats, the inevitable stealing by bureaucrats and
flag officers, and the timidity of military time-servers. A
leader like Pitt, of course, put an end to all that, and the royal navy promptly won the war.

In trying to translate military victory into peace, the British faced an embarrassing and unforeseen problem. They
had won too much and had overthrown the imperial balance
of power. Something had to be given back. In the Peace of
Paris (1763), the British returned the sugar islands to the
French, Havana to the Spanish, recognized French fishing
rights off Newfoundland, and refrained from expanding
their trading privileges in New Spain. But the British kept
India, Canada, Florida, and the Ohio Valley. There must be
some reward for victory.

The treaties of Hubertusburg and Paris 1763 established
the power relationships in Europe for over a century, until
the Franco-Prussian War in 1870. British empire overseas
was balanced by four Great Powers on the continent, none of
which could dominate Europe. The result of massive war
had been to confirm the supremacy of diplomacy over fighting, to make total victory even less likely. The wars also
served to raise the concept of balance of power to the level of
sacred dogma, as the partitions of Poland, the alliance
against Britain during the American Revolution, and the
course of the wars of the French Revolution would show.
Old Regime wars, then, merely changed the names of the
Great Powers; Spain and Poland, for example, succumbed
from external defeat and internal rot while Prussia and

Russia took their places. But the state system continued unaltered. In an age of relative social, technological, and political stability, it could hardly be otherwise.

V

The French prime minister, Cardinal Richelieu, understood what government meant. He outlined a simple and ambitious program to his king, Louis XIII.

"I promised Your Majesty to employ all my industry and all the authority which it should please you to give me to ruin the Huguenot party, to abase the pride of the nobles, to bring all your subjects back to their duty, and to restore your reputation among foreign nations to the place it ought to be."

Allowing for local variations, this is exactly what happened during the seventeenth and eighteenth centuries. The state became greater than its people. Where the nobility, church, and towns had previously been stronger than the king (or king in Parliament), the reverse was now true. Thus, the state began to claim larger and larger portions of the people's resources, energies, and loyalty. The state taxed, drew people into government service and supported doctrines of patriotism and nationalism.

The state also grew bigger. It absorbed independent enclaves within its boundaries, such as appanages and ecclesiastical territories. It also extended those boundaries considerably. States fought almost constant war to annex new provinces, such as the Austrian conquest of Hungary cr French aims to conquer Belgium. Ministates like Venice or the Netherlands, no matter how rich or well organized they were, slipped behind in the race for power.

These were not inconsequential trends. They resulted in the transformation of war from a private to a public pastime. They meant that government had become more important than religion or even class. The growth of the power of the state is the most important political process of modern history. And it is not over.

BIBLIOGRAPHY

1. Primary Sources

The Duke of Saint-Simon, *Versailles, the Court and Louis XIV,* ed.
L. Norton, is a small extract of Saint-Simon's memoirs (41 vols.),
which are an immense resevoir of opinion, memory, ritual, detail,
and bile about the court of the Sun King and the Regency that
followed it. Exceptionally entertaining.

C. A. MaCartney, ed., *The Habsburg and Hohensollern Dynasites in
the Seventeenth and Eighteenth Centuries,* is a good document
collection.

A. J. Slavin, *Imperialism, War and Diplomacy: 1550–1763,* is a second
good document collection.

H. B. Hill, *The Political Testament of Cardinal Richelieu,* illustrates
clearly the philosophy of state building and divine-right absolutism.

2. General Accounts

Carl Friedrich, *The Age of the Baroque: 1610–1660.*
Friedrich Nussbaum, *The Triumph of Science and Reason: 1660–1685.*
John B. Wolf, *The Emergence of the Great Powers: 1685–1715.*
Penfield Roberts, *The Quest for Security: 1715–1740.*
Walter Dorn, *Competition for Empire: 1740–1763.*

> The above five books are part of the Rise of Modern Europe
> series, which is designed to provide a detailed narrative of Euro-
> pean history from the Renaissance to the present. The books
> are of uneven quality. Dorn is absolutely superb, and Wolf and
> Friedrich are excellent. Roberts, on the other hand, is really quite
> bad.

Leonard Krieger, *Kings and Philosophers: 1689–1789,* is another survey, more compact than the volumes mentioned above. It is an
excellent book, and the student will enjoy it.

3. Specialized and National Histories

Franklin Ford, *Robe and Sword,* is a scholarly study of the French
court system and the aristocracy in the first half of the eighteenth
century.

Hajo Holborn, *The Age of Absolutism,* is a scholarly, difficult book, the
second volume in Holborn's history of modern Germany, It is,

181

however, the best book on seventeenth Century Germany (hard cover).

John Wolf, *Louis XIV,* is a long and detailed biography of the Sun King.

B. H. Sumner, *Peter the Great and the Emergence of Russia,* is an excellent survey, and the interested student should begin with this book.

R. Rosenberg, *Bureaucracy, Aristocracy and Autocracy,* is a superb, though difficult study of the development of bureaucratic government in Prussia and its impact on Prussian society (hard covers).

C. V. Wedgwood, *The King's Peace, The King's War, and A Coffin for King Charles,* are three beautifully written studies of the English revolution.

CHAPTER
EIGHT

THE EIGHTEENTH CENTURY:
THE CRISIS OF THE OLD ORDER

"In the courts of law the laws
must speak and the ruler must
remain silent . . ."

Frederick the Great of Prussia

"It is a bankrupt business to
be a prince."

Leopold of Tuscany

The last century of the Old Regime was a time of contradictions, when European society showed contrasting aspect of health and sickness. The eighteenth was a century of sustained economic growth and prosperity. A slowly improving agricultural technology made famine less threatening. Industrialization had begun to increase the supply of goods and lower their price. There were fewer wars, and they were less destructive. Europeans were generally governed better than they ever had been.

Yet signs of decay were everywhere. After 1765 there was a series of revolutions throughout the Western world, largely the result of popular discontent with clearly improving political and social conditions. In France, the richest state on the continent, the government declined into irresolution and incompetence, the despair of minister and observer alike. An equally clear indication of trouble was the Enlightenment climate of opinion, which was highly critical of judicial torture, arbitrary arrest, legal inequalities, and social privileges, all common practices in Old Regime Europe.

By the middle of the century, the political and social structure of the Old Regime was losing its moral authority. The consensus that the existing way of doing things was right and valuable was fast slipping away. Traditional privileges and institutions, previously unquestioned, came under increasing criticism as unjust and unnecessary. Respect for ancient forms of rank evaporated. Efforts to defend privilege, divine right monarchy, or legal inequality met only ridicule and scorn. Instead, progress was preached, particularly since contemporary conditions were so monstrous. Few saw this attack on the moral authority of the Old Regime social and political institutions as an overt call for revolution. But, the criticisms hit home. The complaints convinced. The Old Regime was falling apart.

I

Criticism of social inequality and political injustice was not limited to Enlightenment philosophers. It did not escape the notice of every monarch or minister that the usefulness and legitimacy of their governments no longer commanded total respect. Kings ceased to talk of divine right, therefore, and stopped saying their subjects owed unquestioning obedience in all circumstances. They talked instead of efficiency and justice and of making the crown the focal point of reform. "I am the first servant of the state," said Frederick the Great of Prussia, and when he was thanked by a group of townsmen for replacing their burned-out homes, replied, "You had no need to thank me. It was my duty. That is what I am here for." Absolutism was abandoned as a political justification, replaced by Enlightenment ideals of religious toleration, legal equality, administrative efficiency, and social justice. This new doctrine, called enlightened despotism, also involved a generous increase in royal power and royal revenues. Reform is never cheap.

In spite of the differing circumstances in various European states, there were certain trends of reform common everywhere. The most popular, and the most clearly aligned with Enlightenment thought, was a general assault on the power, wealth and privileges of the church, something that had been going on since Charles Martel. The Spanish monarchy concluded a concordat with the papacy in 1754 which made the Spanish church practically independent from Rome. A similar agreement in 1741 had placed the Neapolitan church under state control. The campaign to reduce church independence and power was most vigorous and thorough in Austria. Emperor Joseph II (1780–1790) was an Enlightenment rationalist, and he regarded the church as an obscurantist relic of the past. He granted toleration to Protestants, established state schools, closed about 800 monasteries, and siezed great tracts of church land. An effort at personal diplomacy by Pius VI, who visited Vienna in 1782, had no effect on the emperor's anticlericalism. Destruction of church privileges continued until his death in 1790.

Monasteries and church wealth were not the only targets of reforming monarchs. The Jesuits were also an object of suspicion, largely because of their reputation as secret political agents of Rome. In Portugal, some Jesuits were implicated in the Conspiracy of Tavoras (1758) to overthrow the prime minister Pombal, and Pombal expelled the Society from Portuguese domains. This was followed in 1764 by the expulsion of the Jesuits from France and from Spain three years later. Intense diplomatic pressure on Rome finally forced the dissolution of the Society of Jesus in 1773. Whether the temporary end of the Jesuits was a triumph of Enlightenment or not, it was certainly a victory for the bureaucratic state.

Enlightened despots also tried their hand at reforming and codifying the law. Frederick the Great pushed this plan for most of his reign, and a consolidated Prussian law code emerged in 1794 as a result of his efforts. In Naples, the minister of justice Bernardo Tanucci worked on a law code, trying to mitigate barbarous punishments and reduce the traditional legal inequalities between social classes. An important part of his work, therefore, was the reduction of the numerous privileges of the nobility, and Tanucci was only partially successful before he fell from power in 1776. In general, however, codifying the immense tangle of civil law, feudal law, common law, and royal statute and harmonizing it with the best Enlightenment principles was too great a task for Old Regime monarchies, and they talked more about legal reform than they practiced it.

Allied to reform of the law was reform of royal administration. Here, enlightened despots were directly enlarging their own authority, so they put their hearts into it. Nowhere was the government more thoroughly reorganized than in Austria. After the peace at Aix-la-Chapelle in 1748, Maria Theresa and her advisors completely overhauled the central administration, clarifying the functions of various bureaus, and ending overlapping jurisdictions. The primary aim was to increase military efficiency and financial accountability in preparation for another go at Frederick the Great. This was followed in the 1750s and 1760s by greatly increasing the power of the district officials in the provinces, and instructing them to take the peasant's side against the nobles. These reforms initially applied only to Austria and Bohemia and attempts by Joseph II after 1780 to extend them to Belgium, Lombardy, and Hungary led to widespread revolt.

The Iberian states, long dormant and depressed, also experienced the winds of eighteenth-century reform. In Spain, Charles III created a new council of state to coordinate all the activities of the central administration. He abolished many of the inefficient councils that had existed since Charles V and were incapable of doing the work. Charles III also tightened up the activities of the provincial intendants and reinvigorated the Spanish colonial system. In Portugal, Prime Minister Pombal tightened royal control over an administration that had become practically an independent entity within the state. He suppressed many useless offices, and reduced the nobles' power over peasants and local government. Here, also, enlightened despotism meant an assault on the privileges of the nobility.

A final area of enlightened reform was economic and fiscal

policy. Stimulating the economy was approved by mercantilists and philosophers and was clearly seen as a royal duty. Frederick the Great subsidized the textile industry in Silesia, and induced over 300,000 colonists to take vacant lands in Prussia. He established a royal land bank to provide capital for farmers. In Austria, Maria Theresa and Joseph II were ardent mercantilists, and gave as much protection and support to industry and agriculture as they could afford. They, too, established land banks to improve agriculture. In both Prussia and Austria, the tremendous prosperity of the eighteenth century assured at least a modicum of success.

Taxation also engaged royal attention, naturally. Both Joseph II and his brother Leopold of Tuscany greatly reduced their inherited debts and did not allow royal borrowing to devour all the liquid capital of the realm. Frederick the Great did even better; not only did he end deficit financing, but he even accumulated a yearly surplus. Tax structures were also reformed. Leopold of Tuscany abolished tax farming on the double grounds that it squeezed the people without enriching the king. Even in Spain and Naples, backwaters though they were, the powers of the tax farmers were greatly reduced. Enlightened despots began to view taxes as part of an integrated royal economic policy, not merely as the art of plucking the goose with a minimum of popular complaints.

Although monarchs and ministers claimed they made enormous changes, all for the better, this was an exaggeration. By and large, the reforms were superficial, involving the appearance of things far more than their realities. Left untouched were all the vast, interlocking array of social and economic privileges enjoyed everywhere by the nobility, urban patricians, and the clergy of the established church. The legal immunities of the nobility to lawsuit, arrest, and imprisonment were only marginally lessened. Reforms in the tax system rarely meant that the clergy, nobility, or bourgeoisie paid much more than they had before, and their opportunities for evasion remained extensive. Entail and primogeniture remained, and land reform, where attempted, failed. Careers were not opened to talent but remained a function of birth and connection, both by law and custom. Privilege was simply eroded a bit around the edges, largely because it had become a hindrance and a nuisance to the increasing centralization of royal power. Talk about legal equality, and there was a great deal of this, remained just talk.

Moreover, even in those areas where progress toward legal equality was made, the law was frequently negated by custom. Royal officials could hardly be blind to rank in a hierarchical society and could not ignore the real power that noble status gave. Many royal officials were themselves nobles, all the important ones were and the rest hoped to be, and they were quite hesitant to call their friends and relatives to account. Custom everywhere supported legal privileges, and was often more respected than the law itself. As late as the 1890s, a French peasant replied to a question about his politics by saying that he was the subject of the viscount. Before the Revolution this attitude was universal. Men followed their patrons, their lords, and their betters, and attempts of reformers to alter these patterns of custom invariably failed. Social, legal, and economic privilege continued as before.

So did unprivilege. The social and legal groups that were most burdened by the privileges of others continued in that condition. Manorial and seigneurial courts, where the lord was judge and prosecutor as well as a participant in suits, were retained everywhere and insured that even the landowing peasant would remain the subject of his lord. Serfdom existed everywhere on the continent, and all attempts to abolish it failed. Seigneurial taxes were also retained, continuing as a type of permanent lien on the peasant's land. The urban laborers were totally without rights, protection, or privilege, and city fathers viewed them uneasily as criminals, bums, and fomentors of riots.

Beyond this, Old Regime governments made little progress in civil liberties. Arbitrary arrest continued as before. Censorship of books and the press was universal, and the public hangman was kept busy burning subversive literature, particularly literature produced by Enlightenment philosophers. Outrage to authority was a major crime, and those so foolish as to insult royal officials were fortunate to suffer merely exile and property confiscation. Torture was still used for both interrogation and punishment, and prisons held numerous persons accused of nothing at all. Trials themselves were conducted on the assumption that the accused was guilty; why else would the authorities have him in custody and under torture? Self-incrimination was normal. Unprivileged persons were often arrested on the grounds that they were guilty of some crime for which they had not yet been punished, or they were about to commit a crime and society profited from their timely arrest. Only a small minority thought that a citizen had natural rights which his government must not impair, and even fewer thought these ideals applied equally to the peasant and urban worker.

Finally, there was little increase in political participation to include new, less-privileged groups. The constituted bodies, such as guilds, self-perpetuating municipal and provincial councils, and local estates all resisted enlightened reforms. These corporations opposed any extension of local or provincial power and were generally successful. This pattern seldom varied, characterizing the politics of the English Parliament, the Parlement of Paris in France, the Diets of Hungary and Poland, the municipal governments of the Dutch cities and Milan, and the feudal nobility everywhere. Those with corporate political power kept it, in spite of enlightened despots' efforts to win control over the peasants from their lords or extend urban political participation beyond the circle of hereditary oligarchs. The hierarchical and traditional nature of society made change difficult, and the privileges of the nobility and bourgeoisie survived.

II

Not all of the reforms achieved or attempted by enlightened despots pleased everybody. There were individuals who demanded more legal equality, more administrative efficiency, more humanity and justice in the working of courts, and more political participation and power. There were also many who wanted less of these things, who only wanted the king to mind his own business and leave them alone. There were also individual less interested in social and political reform but who cared passionately about the new idea of nation and wanted their king to care as well. All of these people were left dissatisfied by the cautious reforms of enlightened despotism. In an era of reform, liberals and nationalists still felt their time might come, soon. When it did not, they soured on their governments. The conservative, constituted bodies feared the loss of their privileges, and therefore sponsored more militant resistance to their king. The result was a spate of revolutions, both for more reform and less of it, covering the entire Western world from Poland to America. By 1770, change was coming from below as well as above.

The first of these revolutions was a civil war between two aristocracies, two groups of legally constituted institutions —one in Europe and the other in America. The 13 colonies had grown marvelously in the eighteenth century, in size, population, wealth, experience in self-government, and consciousness of their rights. These trends did not make a sufficient impression on British political leaders, who, in 1763, after the Peace of Paris, tried to tighten the political and economic bonds of empire at the time when the external threat had vanished. These new policies were partly to be paid for in America, which was far more lightly taxed than England.

Such ideas, embodied in the Sugar Act (1764) and the Stamp Act (1765), were extremely galling to the colonial gentry, who protested that their rights as Englishmen were being violated. By 1765, Americans had come to see the British constitution differently from the British, who saw Parliament as the supreme imperial authority, able to tax and rule in the colonies as well as at home. Colonials disagreed, claiming that Parliament had no legislative authority over them at all. Governor Bernard of Massachusetts Bay put the issue succinctly in 1765:

"In Britain, the American governments are considered as Corporations empowered to make by-laws, existing only during the pleasure of Parliament. . . . In America, they claim . . . to be perfect States, not otherwise dependent on Great Britain than by having the same King."

Repeated political confrontations led to war in the spring of 1775. Early in the war the strategic equation became clear. The British, with their naval superiority, had no difficulty in capturing the major Atlantic seaports, but expeditions into the interior ended disastrously at Saratoga (1777) and Yorktown (1781). After Yorktown, the British, who were getting tired of the war, began to cast around for a way out and agreed to independence for the United States in 1783. The colonial aristocracy, having won the war, now struggled to win the peace and, with a constitutional convention in 1787, they did that as well.

At the time, the American Revolution seemed quite revolutionary indeed, far more so than it would appear after 1789. The Americans, after all, fought for the same principles of liberty, increased political participation, and an end to privilege that animated later revolutionaries in Europe. Moreover, there were a large number of Loyalist emigrants from revolutionary America, and their property was confiscated outright. There was also a certain turnover in local ruling cliques, as conservatives, less enthusiastically hostile to the king, were replaced by more radical and reliable gentlemen. Finally, there were a few legal changes in a democratic direction.

In spite of this, however, the American Revolution, from the perspective of 1789, did not seem very radical at all and, by the 1790s, respectable authorities were claiming there had never been a revolution. There was no wholesale destruction of social classes, political institutions, legal systems, or traditions. America in 1790 seemed pretty much like America in 1775. There were three overriding reasons for this. In the first place, America was democratic already by contemporary standards. Voting and landowning were quite widespread. Religious toleration was genuine and respected. There was no feudal aristocracy and no seigneurial and manorial encumbrances on the land. In America, there was much less to revolt about.

Moreover, conservative or Tory opinion in America was weak, badly articulated, and poorly presented. There was no Tory declaration of obedience, no Tory appeal to great constitutional principles. The Tories confined their case to obedience to George III, and this was not at all inspiring. The notions of the revolutionaries were more widely supported in America than elsewhere. Ideas of religious toleration, widespread political participation, legal equality, and an end to privilege were common currency over here but not in Europe. The American Revolution had less to overcome in ideological terms and was comparatively modest in its own pronouncements and politics.

Finally, the American political institutions, legally constituted and functioning, sided with the Revolution. Americans claimed they were fighting in defense of legality, not against it. This simple fact robbed the Revolution of the character of a popular uprising. It also produced a political paradox. In London, the Americans were revolting against the legally established authority of Parliament. In America, the Tories were the rebels, defying their legally constituted local authorities.

In spite of its conservatism, the American Revolution had a considerable impact on Europeans. Several European officers had gone to the New World to fight for the Americans and had come home as heroes to tell everyone about the glories of liberty, equality, and victory over the foul tyrant. Printed propaganda was equally powerful. The Declaration of Independence made a great impression abroad and seemed to promise a new government free from injustice, oppression, and noxious privilege. Finally, the unexpected

American victory seemed nearly providential, proof of the virtues of freedom and an inspiration to enlightened Europeans. It made America seem the ideal land, the inspiration of mankind, and the best hope of everyone. The reality was far less, of course, but the myth became part of the moral condemnation of the Old Regime, part of the collapse of approval in existing institutions.

The American Revolution also affected European politics. France and Spain went to war against Great Britain, and most of Europe was sympathetic to the American cause. The Dutch republic was caught in the middle of all this. Traditionally neutral, fearful of British seapower, but mindful of trade advantages in America, the Dutch government slipped into war with the British in 1780. Right from the start the war went badly. The Dutch fleet was unready, and Dutch merchants lost about 80 million gold guilders in shipping to the British. At the peace table, the British demanded new privileges from the East India Company, and got them.

Bad as the British were, many Dutch thought the attitude of their own government was even worse. The *stadhouder*, William V, an irresolute man, remained tied to the British and refused to take any real measures of national defense. William was supported in this policy by his court, many of the great nobles, and the Dutch Reformed Church, all traditional supporters of the House of Orange in its struggles with the towns.

The *stadhouder*'s policies aroused considerable opposition. The rulers of the major Dutch cities, known as regents, added this new grievance to their traditional opposition to royal power. The regents, in general, wanted to eliminate royal influence in the towns and bring the government back to a closer understanding of the needs of trade. In these times of universal criticism, however, the regents were joined by a group new to politics—the urban middle class. They found a leader in the provincial nobleman, Jan van der Capellan tot der Pol. This new liberal faction did more than merely issue manifestos. They organized into an armed militia, known as the Free Corps. In December, 1784, the Free Corps held a national meeting at Utrecht and demanded political changes that went far beyond anything the regents had in mind. The Free Corps wanted a genuine democraticization of Dutch political life. They wanted a wide increase in political participation, which was aimed at the regents as much as at the *stadhouder*. At Utrecht, the local Free Corps elected 24 of their number to supervise the city council and, a year later, dissolved the old council of regents, choosing a new one in a general election. The actions of the Free Corps at Utrecht was the program of the liberals everywhere.

Such assaults on the sovereignty of the regent oligarchy split the opposition to the *stadhouder* down the middle. The regents had only wanted a diminution of William V's power so that they could rule instead while the Free Corps were opposed to both and wanted a liberal regime. By 1786 the regents began to seek an alliance with the *stadhouder* as privileged elements drew closer together. They could only survive if the Free Corps were defeated, so the *stadhouder* and the regents began to negotiate with Prussia and Great Britain. When the Free Corps and the Dutch army fired on each other in 1787, foreign intervention was assured. The British spread some cash around and the Prussians invaded, restoring the *stadhouder* to his powers, chastising the regents, and dispersing the liberals. But the restoration solved nothing. Although the revolution failed, the *stadhouder*, failed also. He made no reforms in his government. He stood apart from his people, propped up with foreign guns and money. By 1789, kings could no longer get away with that.

The revolution in the Netherlands had a curious parallel in Poland, a land that differed from it in almost every way. As in Holland, the power of the king was a basic issue. Both revolutions took the better part of a decade to unfold, and both were crushed by foreign intervention. Both involved national as well as political and religious issues.

The differences, however, were even greater. The Netherlands was the richest, most urban, most commercial, and most middle-class state in Europe, and Poland was the least. The "aristocratic republic" that had failed to keep pace with its neighbors in the seventeenth century continued without change in the eighteenth. The elected monarch continued to agree to the "liberties" of the nobles and remained at their mercy. The "liberum veto" in the Diet continued as before; the taxes remained nominal; the bureaucracy and army were virtually nonexistent. The great magnates conducted their own foreign policy and, by the eighteenth century, foreign intervention had become customary in a state that lacked internal coherence.

Such conditions were not satisfactory to everyone, and reform sentiment, advocating changes in the constitution and a restoration of Polish glory, grew steadily during the eighteenth century. Enlightenment ideas added to the ferment. The University of Cracow became a center of nationalism, and the appearance of newspapers in the 1760s also contributed to demands for reform.

The chance for reform came in 1788, when the Russians were preoccupied with a war in Turkey, the Prussians with the Netherlands, and the Austrians with revolts and threats of revolt. The Polish king, Stanislas Poniatowski, a liberal reformer, called the four-year's Diet to discuss constitutional reform. Discuss was about all the delegates did. Not until April, 1791, did they pass the Statute of Cities, which gave the urban bourgeoisie national political rights and control over their own municipal governments. On May 3, 1791, a constitution was adopted, making the crown elective in the House of Saxony, abolishing the "liberum veto," and strengthening the king's power.

The process had taken too long, however. Inspiring as national and liberal reform was the Poles, it frightened and irritated her principal neighbors. Russia, Prussia, and Austria did not want to see a rejuvenated Poland in their midst and had put their affairs in order while the Diet deliberated. Moreover, the Eastern monarchs, seeing the explosion in France, were wary of revolutions, especially those close to home. Catherine the Great organized nobles who were opposed to reform into the Confederation of Targowica in 1792 and, using them as an excuse, invaded Poland. Prussia followed and, in January, 1793, the two great powers partitioned Poland for a second time. Enraged, the Polish liberals, led by Thaddeus Kosciuszko, rose in revolt to defend their nation and constitution. Russia and Prussia invaded again, won again and, with Austria, partitioned Poland again. The third partition, in 1795, wiped Poland out, and fulfilled the prophecy made by the retiring king, Jan Kasimir, in 1648. It also ended liberal reform in Eastern Europe until after the middle of the nineteenth century.

Between Poland and the Netherlands, both in geography and social patterns, lay the immense Austrian empire, a series of widely diverse and nearly autonomous provinces that were being ruled with increasing efficiency by the Habsburg emperors. Persistently liberal, humanitarian, and interested in increasing their own authority, Maria Theresa and her son, Joseph II, tried ceaselessly to ameliorate the conditions of the serfs and reduce the authority of the nobles. There were limits to what an enlightened despot could do by administrative pressure, however, and the career of Joseph II proved this. By 1787, the Austrian empire was wracked by revolution or, rather, by an aristocratic counterrevolution launched by the nobility of Hungary, Transylvania, Milan, and Belgium against Joseph's reforms. Austria was the first Great Power to be torn apart by the conflict between new ideas and the old social realities.

The liberties, privileges, immunities, and rights of Belgium had been confirmed in 1355 by the Duke of Brabant in a document called the Joyous Entry. It guaranteed the authority of the provincial estates, along with the powers of several specific groups within it. The first estate was represented by the abbots of the great monasteries, the second by a few wealthy nobles, and the third estate consisted of delegates from the guilds of the major towns. The society governed by these small privileged groups was basically stagnant and quiescent, the results of the great depression after the Dutch war. Dutch victory in 1609 had closed the Scheldt to Belgian commerce, which declined to depression levels and stayed there. The numerous medieval towns were accustomed by unemployment rates of 25 percent, while the industry that remained produced mainly for local consumption. The church owned about half of the land, most of it concentrated in the hands of a few large abbeys. The nobility dominated the countryside, while the guilds controlled the towns. Thousands of officials staffed the numerous medieval courts, boards, councils, and assemblies that really governed the province. The Austrian presence was limited to the viceroy, a few troops, and the lowest possible taxes, and this arrangement suited the Belgians precisely. Everything was the way it should be.

Joseph II was too energetic, too committed to reform to accept this, and the initial Belgian revolution came from the emperor himself. He decreed toleration for Protestants, suppressed a few monasteries, and reduced the rigid trade and craft monopolies of the guilds. In 1787 he went much further, reorganizing the complex network of seigneurial, municipal, and district courts. Many were abolished, judicial and administrative responsibilities were separated, and a new system of uniform appeal courts was established for the whole country.

This provoked an immense outcry from all who benefitted from the existing constituted bodies, and that was everyone in Belgium who had any political voice at all. By 1789, outrage had become revolution. A secret society—For Altar and Hearth—was organized and succeeded in driving the Austrians out. This victory promptly split the revolutionaries into two groups. The conservatives, with their power in the church and the provincial Estates, wanted to retain the existing order; they fought Joseph II only because he was changing things. The liberals supported much of Joseph's program. They wished to widen the limits of political participation and allow the urban middle classes a share of power.

These two views were irreconcilable and, in March, 1790, the conservative party won. Liberals were rounded up, and thousands fled to France. There was a general persecution, which ended only with the return of the Austrian troops in December, 1790. But the Austrians could not bring themselves to support the liberals. Reluctantly and hesitantly, they sided with the conservatives who controlled the Estates. For the time being, until the French troops arrived, counterrevolution had won.

Belgium was not the only province provoked into revolt by the reforms of Joseph II. He had the same impact on Hungary. Here, Joseph's reforms had two aims: to increase royal authority and to limit the power of the lords over their peasants. In the political sphere, Joseph tried to bypass the Hungarian Diet and county assemblies, handing over their traditional powers to civil servants appointed in Vienna. This was bad enough, but there was worse. In 1789, Joseph II issued a decree that proposed to tax all land, whether noble or peasant, at the same rate, to eliminate peasants' forced labor for their lord, and to secure the peasantry in their tenures as landowners. The nobility could not permit that, and they prepared to resist Joseph's decree. The peasants prepared to enforce it. Class war broke out in many parts of Hungary and Transylvania as peasants began to butcher their lords. Class hatreds were aggravated by ethnic ones; in Transylvania Vlach peasants were particularly brutal to Magyar nobles and generally left Germans alone.

Faced with a major social war, the Hungarian nobility in the Diet and county assemblies were unable to press their demands for political independence from the Habsburg empire. They compromised with Joseph's successor, Leopold II. Leopold agreed to surrender the bulk of Joseph's reforms, although not all, and return local government and the peasantry to the Hungarian nobility. In return, the Hungarians forgot about independence. Thus, the Belgian experience was repeated. Aristocratic counterrevolution had defeated an enlightened despot. Reform from the crown, no matter how enlightened or badly needed, could move only so far without the support of public opinion. In the Austrian empire, apart from the nobility and privileged, there was no such thing as public opinion; thus, any reform that seriously comprised existing status or privileges was bound to fail. The reforms that Joseph proposed awaited something stronger than his decrees. They waited for revolution.

III

"The constitution of England is without doubt the most perfect form of government that was ever devised by human wisdom," wrote a British literary critic in 1775. Almost everyone agreed with him. Smug self-congratulation was the common opinion, and few were bashful about expressing it. British liberty was also admired abroad. Voltaire and Montesquieu had written approvingly of English politics. Even enemies, such as Benjamin Franklin and John Adams, thought well of the British system and wished to see its virtues retained in the New World. In the minds of most people, the English were soothed by the best government ever seen or heard of.

With governments, however, even the best is not very good and, after 1763, the admirable British system began to show disconcerting signs of imperfection. A large chorus of Babbitts arose to deny this, but facts are facts, and the evidence was there. The most dramatic sign of disarray was the Wilkes case, a combination farce and serious constitutional issue that lasted a dozen years from 1763 to 1774. This was followed by the Association Movement of 1778 to 1780, which claimed that Parliament was not absolute but that the will of the people was superior to it. As the Association menace declined, a victim of riots and radicalism, the demand for electoral reform arose in Parliament and, finally, from the ministry itself. From Wilkes on, there was continual agitation for reform of the most perfect government "ever devised by human wisdom."

The Wilkes case began simply enough. The government suppressed a newspaper story that it thought insulting to the king. In April, 1763, John Wilkes published in the "North Briton" an attack on George III, calling him a fool for agreeing to the Peace of Paris. The ministry, headed by the Earl of Bute, the king's favorite, called this "an infamous and seditious libel," issued a general warrant, and had Wilkes arrested and confined to the Tower of London. When the case was considered by Chief Justice Pratt, it attracted enormous attention from Londoners, who were all on Wilkes' side. Pratt discharged Wilkes, and also declared that general warrants were illegal. Wilkes then turned upon his accusers, and sued them for damages, ultimately collecting a tidy sum.

This should have been the end of it, but it was not. Wilkes, a quarrelsome and rakish person who led a gaudy private life did not take his arrest lying down. He printed his attack on George III in book form, and appended to it an obscene poem, "Essay on Women." When Parliament reconvened in the fall of 1763, it took notice of this and expelled Wilkes from the House of Commons. Wilkes himself fled to France, only returning in 1768 to be elected to the Commons from London, where he was a great hero. He was again expelled, both as a cad and a radical. He stood again and won again. This time, the Commons not only expelled Wilkes, it seated his defeated opponent, thus explicitly stating the superiority of Parliament over the people.

This last gesture was so outrageous that Wilkes and his friends founded the Supporters of the Bill of Rights, and toured the country denouncing Parliament and calling for electoral reform. Parliament found itself faced with considerable public pressure, while Wilkes' popularity grew so great that he was elected Lord Mayor of London and sent back to Parliament in 1774. By this time everyone had had enough, and Wilkes was seated. Once back in, he carried on the attack, introducing an electoral reform bill in 1776. The bill was rejected. War had just begun in America over the rights of Parliament, and the Lords and Commons were not ready to admit that they were in any need of reform.

Although Wilkes himself faded from prominence after his return to Parliament, the issues he had raised remained. They became the program of the Association movement, which demanded increased independence of Parliament from the King and reform of electoral procedures. Under the heading of independence from royal control went the abolition of numerous lucrative and useless pensions and offices that the king had used to bribe Lords and Commons to see things his way. The other plank was for change in electoral procedures, eliminating some of the inequities of pocket and rotten boroughs. This was the more radical demand, and it involved real political changes rather than lightly retouching the surface.

The Association movement had twin foci—Yorkshire and London. In Yorkshire there was a monster meeting of the county voters in December, 1779, and about 600 attended. They urged the abolition of a number of offices, but electoral reform was far less popular and was more or less glossed over. In London, the Association met in May, 1780, and went much further, calling for a General Association from all the nation to reform the Parliament by means of the sovereignty of the people. The Association also urged universal male suffrage, an advanced concept even for the radical and godless Americans. Such ideas, naturally enough, frightened the conservative and substantial people, and they were even more alarmed at the Gordon riots that convulsed London in June. The reform movement split in two and lost momentum. No General Association ever met. No electoral reform passed. There was no sovereignty of the people or universal suffrage. Even so, there was one concrete result from it all. In 1782, Edmund Burke, of all people, guided through Parliament a bill abolishing a clutch of royal offices, thus saving small sums but failing to reduce royal influence over the Parliament.

Although electoral reform had suffered from its connection with Wilkes and the Associations, there were still many who thought it was a good idea. These included William Pitt the younger, who had just entered Parliament through the family pocket borough. In 1782, he brought in a reform bill, which was only narrowly defeated. He tried again in 1783 and lost, and supported another Member's bill in 1784. In 1785, as chief minister, Pitt tried again. It was a moderate bill. Pitt proposed to abolish only 32 depopulated boroughs, transferring the seats to larger towns and the shires. The minister also wanted to enfranchise copyholders and some long-term leaseholders. It was very similar to the bill finally passed in 1832.

Although Pitt was head of the ministry, his bill was in trouble from the start. There was no large faction in Parliament committed to reform. The king was against it. The ministry was divided. Support from the merchants in the large towns was unenthusiastic. Finally, electoral reform already had a tainted aroma, the legacy of Wilkes, the Associations, and radical rhetoric. Pitt could not overcome all this, and his bill failed by a very comfortable margin of 248 to 174. That was it. If Pitt could not carry electoral reform, no one could. The issue remained on the margin of politics until after Waterloo.

The English, by and large, escaped the horrors of reform when everyone else was succumbing to it. Only the Wilkes litigation brought any significant constitutional change, the abolition of general warrants as incompatible with the rights of Englishmen. All other proposals went down to defeat. There was no electoral reform, and the king continued to dominate Parliament and control the ministry. The Pitt ministry that went into the wars of the French Revolution was just as much a king's government as Lord North's before him, and the Members were still swayed by the king's influence.

Even so, things were not the same. There had been a great deal of loud and nasty criticism from the impious. No amount of constitution worship could efface that. Moreover, substantive issues had been raised that could not be forever postponed. There was increasing uneasiness at the king's exercise of his prerogatives, foreshadowing a day when he could no longer get away with it. Electoral reform was inevitable, considering the progress made by democratic ideas. Something had to be done about Ireland. There would be change.

Reform was considerably delayed, however, for the pressures against it were strong and articulate. There were many, like Edmund Burke, who wanted no change at all in the sacrosanct constitution. There were more who were willing to countenance some reforms, but not too many and not too fast, and not under radical pressure. They were put off by democratic proposals, by public disorder, and by theories that Parliament must be reformed by its constitutional superior—the people. The American Revolution had a lot to do with this attitude. Its assertions of popular sovereignty and the rights of the people seemed inspiring on the continent but subversive in England. The British preferred the sovereignty of Parliament and dwelt lovingly upon it. The political class clung close to the existing political system, remembering that it had brought them unparalleled power and prosperity. As threats mounted, therefore, resistance did also. Outside of an unlikely, violent revolution, change could come only by convincing the wealthy and privileged political class of its desirability. This hope faded fast after 1775 and, when war came with France in 1793, reform was adjourned indefinitely.

IV

"Nobody dreamed of a revolution, although it was rapidly effecting itself in public opinion," wrote the Comte de Ségur, son of the last war minister of the Old Regime. ". . . Every class of the old social order, undermined without expecting it, still preserved . . . its antiquated distinctions and all signs of power. The deepest foundations of the old social edifice were entirely undermined, although the surface showed no symptoms which could indicate approaching ruin. We felt no . . . anxiety for the future, and gaily trod a land bedecked with flowers which concealed a precipice from our sight." Ségur's astonishment was shared by many, who were stunned at the swift passage of events in 1789 from murmurs of reform to riots and revolution. Such surprise was

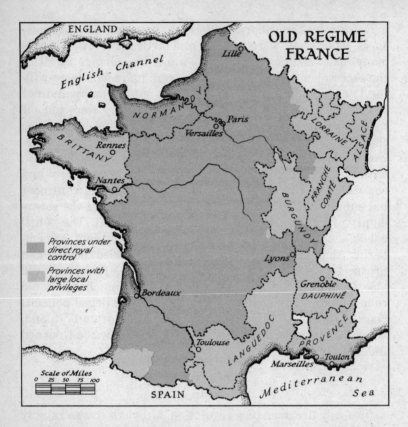

excessive. Ségur himself remarked that the words liberty and equality were heard everywhere. This included the king's ministers, who realized more than anyone that the government was inefficient, clumsy, expensive, unjust, burdensom, and profoundly irritating. Periodically, the ministers would suggest a large block of reforms of the type being promoted by enlightened despots elsewhere and publish their condemnation of current practice and their hopes for the improvement in an edict, to be posted everywhere and read from the pulpit in church. The word went out. The government was working badly, those in power knew it, and they were going to change it.

The proposed reforms, however, although often announced, never seemed to take place. Something always interfered. Some aspect of privilege always prevented the crown from reforming the administration or social structure. Louis XV was a weak and irresolute king, far more interested in women than in government, and yielding to privilege was the easiest thing to do. Although the pressure for reform was greater in France than anywhere else, few changes took place. The forces of privilege and conservatism were immensely powerful.

Privilege, in Old Regime France, had variable meanings. It was partly honorific, partly economic, partly social, partly political, and partly a form of license entitling the fortunate to enjoy immunity from the law. Many Frenchmen had varying degrees of all these types of privilege, with the wealthy nobility having the most. But privilege was not solely an attribute of nobility. Even a cursory glance at the social structure of the Old Regime explodes that myth. The carpenter or mason who belonged to a guild had a substantial grant of economic privilege because his guild excluded others from his trade and guaranteed him a living. A rich peasant who was a receiver of seigneurial dues enjoyed his lord's privileges. A poor parish priest was privileged by his occupation. In Old Regime France, not only did the nobility and clergy enjoy privilege but the entire urban middle class did also. Perhaps a quarter of the nation was privileged to some degree, and the vast majority of these were not nobles. Indeed, privilege was primarily a bourgeois phenomenon, enjoyed by craftsmen in their guilds, merchants in chambers of commerce and municipal governments, and royal officials in their positions and titles. Most merchants and officials, in fact, possessed greater privileges than the country gentry, particularly in terms of political power, legal immunities, and opportunities to make a living.

Many forms of privilege had become so entrenched that they were considered property, like land or furniture. Included among these were the seigneurial taxes and rights of justice that lords had over their manors and villages. In much of France, these ancient dues and privileges accounted for the bulk of the lord's income, exceeding what he got from the land itself. Royal offices were also a form of privilege since they were owned and could be bought, sold, or willed like any other property. There were regular quotations of the price of high offices, and people even bought blocks of them at discount and later sold them at retail. Most administrative and judicial offices were venal, and their owners, besides the salaries, enjoyed immunities to many forms of lawsuit and certain rights of graft. High judicial office, such as judgeship in a parliament, conferred noble status on its owner. Finally, royal office greatly reduced one's tax burden, leaving the peasantry to take up the slack. All in all, property derived from privilege was more extensive and valuable than land or chattels, an indication of how pervasive privilege was in the Old Regime.

The political power of organized privilege became starkly clear when the government tried to reduce it. In 1749, the comptroller-general of finances, Machault, proposed a redistribution of the tax burden. He imposed a new tax, the twentieth, to be paid by everyone with no exceptions. This would destroy the traditional tax exemptions of the privileged, which was so old that the nobility and urban patriciate believed it to be a natural and fundamental law of France. Outraged, the noble magistrates of the Parlement of Paris complained against the tax, while the clergy, meeting in 1750, declared the new tax was heresy. Everywhere in France, the privileged were reluctant to pay. Faced with an awful public uproar, Machault gave in, and the twentieth was withdrawn in December, 1751. Social and legal privilege had won a major victory over simple justice and the needs of the treasury.

The crown had no more success in dealing with provincial immunities and privileges. In 1753, it became embroiled in a prolonged quarrel with the province of Brittany. Beginning over taxes to pay for roads, the wrangling eventually covered virtually every aspect of provincial autonomy, and involved both the Parlement of Brittany and the provincial estates. By 1765, Louis XV lost patience with Breton hostility to commands from Paris. The Parlement of Brittany was dissolved, and a new supreme provincial court, more attentive to royal wishes, was put in its place. Defenders of provincial privilege were arrested. This brought the Parlement of Paris in as a defender of its sister tribunal in Brittany, and the war now extended to two fronts. By 1770, plans to tax Brittany had been dropped, the old Parlement was restored, and the provincial governor had resigned. Breton intransigence had won out. A chance to reform the archaic structure of provincial administration had been lost.

Following the pitiful conclusion of the Breton fiasco—in fact, arising out of it—came a new experiment in enlightened reform. Since Machault, it had been clear to everyone that the parlements were implacable and effective opponents of reform. All the ministers agreed the country would be better off if these vocal courts were snuffed out. Accordingly, in January, 1771, Chancellor Maupeou suppressed the Parlement of Paris. He replaced it with a new court and then started on the parlements in the provinces. By November it was all over, and the French judiciary was no longer a major political force. But the Maupeou reforms, which should have been the prelude to a systematic revamping of French political and social institutions, led nowhere. The chancellor did not disturb the multiplicity of legal systems, the procedural delays, or the endless costs of litigation. Nor did the ministers modify the gross tax inequities or the legal privileges of merchants, nobles and office-holders. The ministry gave the clear impression that it only wanted to silence criticism and was prepared to accept any injustice if no one complained.

But people did complain, and the silence of the new courts was added to their litany. When Louis XVI came to the throne in 1774, his ministers, in an effort to win popularity for the new king, decided to restore the old parlements. The magistrates soon demonstrated that three years of exile had not changed their opinions, and they were denouncing the reforms of a new enlightened minister, A. R. J. Turgot. In 1774, Turgot freed the grain trade from its numerous traditional restrictions in an effort to increase the size of the harvest. Two years later he ended the royal *corvée,* a compulsory road service that fell exclusively on the peasants and abolished urban craft guilds. The Parlement of Paris complained, and was aided in its efforts by a large bread riot in May, 1776. This combination drove Turgot from office, and his reform measures were immediately repealed.

After Turgot's dismissal the drive for reform slackened. New ministers, contemplating the fate of so many predecessors, were more cautious. But the problems continued. All of the old tax inequities stood. All forms of legal and social privilege remained. The ranks of the privileged stood ready to defend their property and status should the ministry be so foolish as to launch further reforms. But, to the ministers, royal finances were the most serious problem. By 1787, the annual deficit had grown to one-fifth of the king's income, while interest on the accumulated debt consumed 60 percent of the royal revenues. In 1787, Louis' chief minister, the Marquis de Calonne, communicated these dismal figures to the dull and astonished king. The crown was bankrupt. Large reforms were needed, not just because enlightened ministers thought they were a good idea but to save the state.

Calonne's program, in effect, was a recapitulation of the reforms of his predecessors. He wished to abolish internal customs barriers, free the grain trade, abolish the peasant *corvée* and establish a uniform land tax with no exemptions. Calonne's program was designed to do many of the things later done in the Revolution. It was a large step toward administrative uniformity. It meant the end of privileged tax exemptions, and it eased the burdens of the peasantry. It would create the largest free trade area in Europe. Most important, of course, it would avert bankruptcy and Calonne would be universally recognized as an enlightened benefactor of the people.

Calonne knew that the Parlement of Paris, which had already rejected all these ideas, was unlikely to accept them now. So he persuaded the bewildered Louis XVI to call an Assembly of Notables. The Assembly contained the most privileged men in France: seven princes of the blood royal, 14 prelates, 37 magistrates from the Parlements, 36 of the richest nobles, and other assorted magnates. The Notables were surprisingly agreeable. In general, they were willing to accept everything but the land tax that was its heart. The Notables solemnly claimed that the land tax was a wicked measure, contrary to ancient privilege, and destructive of good social order. No sort of pressure could make them approve so bad a bill.

Calonne, of course, could not survive this, and he was replaced by his most ardent and incompetent enemy, Lomenie de Brienne, one of the Notables. Brienne found it easier to get rid of Calonne than solve the problems of state. He was forced to adopt Calonne's program, and he began to feed the edicts into the Parlement of Paris for approval and registration. The magistrates reacted as the Notables had. They accepted everything but the land tax. Desperate, Brienne tried force. In August, 1787, he banished the Parlement to Troyes, but public outcry and the need for money forced him to recall it a month later.

Brienne was not content with this catastrophe. He compounded it. In May, 1788, he turned on the Parlement of Paris as the author of all his troubles. He proposed a judicial reform even more thorough than Maupeou's had been. He established new courts and made justice both cheaper and more certain. But it was too late for these things or, indeed, for any royal reforms. Frenchmen saw these measures as an assault on their liberties. A great outcry arose, and it was not confined to discussion, petitions, and pamphlets. On June 7, 1788, there was a serious riot in Grenoble, and this was followed by disorders in Brittany, Béarn, Provence, and Franche-Comté. The king called the troops out but, often as not, they refused to fire on the citizens. If that were not enough, Paris bankers refused the bankrupt government any more loans, and the clergy followed their example. In August, 1788, Louis XVI gave in. He dismissed Brienne, suspended the judicial reforms, and announced that an Estates-General would meet in May, 1789.

This was the last political decision made by the monarchy

of the Old Regime. Since 1749, the French monarchy had made consistent efforts to reform both government and society. It had tried to improve royal administration, redistribute the tax burden, and eliminate some of the grosser forms of privilege. These plans had all failed and, in the effort to carry them out, the monarchy had collapsed. The crown had resigned in favor of the people. Louis XVI would await the representatives of France. The changes that these representatives would make would not be so very different from the ones proposed by royal ministers from Machault to Brienne or attempted by Joseph II in his domains. But they were accomplished by war and terror, by a revolution that spread new doctrines across all of Europe. The people were entering the political stage and, in 1788, the astute could hear the movement described by Anatole France:

> *Wooden shoes going up the*
> *stairs of history pass the*
> *velvet slippers coming down.*

BIBLIOGRAPHY

1. Primary Sources

Thomas Paine, *Common Sense* and *The Crisis,* were both written during the American Revolution. They supported the American cause and gave popular and convincing arguments against the Tories and the British.

R. and E. Forster, eds., *European Society in the Eighteenth Century,* is a collection of documents on social classes, standards and structures.

Karl Roider, *Maria Theresa,* is a collection of letters and official documents that illuminate Austrian government in the eighteenth century.

2. Enlightened Despotism

John Gagliardo, *Enlightened Despotism,* is a small book, written expressly for the undergraduate as an introduction to the topic. Clear and simple, it is highly recommended.

S. B. Fay and F. Epstein, *The Rise of Brandenburg-Prussia to 1786,* is a short but difficult survey of Prussian institutions.

Gladys Thompson, *Catherine the Great and the Expansion of Russia,* is a good and brief introduction.

Albert Goodwin, ed., *The European Nobility in the Eighteenth Century,* is a group of short articles on the position of the aristocracy in various states. Uneven; the article on France is bad.

3.   Eighteenth-Century England

L. H. Gipson, *The Coming of the Revolution, 1763–1775,* is a short study of the breakup of the British empire by the leading scholar of imperial history. Highly recommended.

L. B. Namier, *England in the Age of the American Revolution* and *The Structure of Politics at the Accession of George III,* are both detailed and complex analyses of the English electoral structure and faction, connection, and interest groupings in the House of Commons. These are difficult books, but the student cannot understand the English politics without at least sampling them.

4.   France

C. B. A. Behrens, *The Ancien Regime,* is a short survey of prerevolutionary France, written for the undergraduate. Unfortunately, it is not as good as it might be.

Alfred Cobban, *A History of Modern France,* Vol. I, is a short and reasonably good survey of the Old Regime.

G. T. Mathews, *The Royal General Farms in Eighteenth Century France,* is a detailed study of French indirect taxation, which was burdensome, corrupt, and resented. The book is quite clear, and this is an excellent place to get a sample of Old Regime government (hard cover).

5.   Major Interpretive Study

R. R. Palmer, *The Age of the Democratic Revolution,* Vol. I, is the major recent contribution to an understanding of the decline of the Old Regime. The first volume deals with the various revolutions outside of France and presents them in a clear and precise manner. Essential and highly recommended (hard cover).

CHRONOLOGICAL CHART:

Dates	France	Great Britain	Prussia
1789	Estates-General Great Fear Bastille Declaration of Rights of Man		
1790	Civil constitution of the clergy		
1792	War with Austria and Prussia End of the monarchy Establishment of the Republic Beginning of the Terror		War with France
1793	Reign of Terror War with England, Holland, and Spain	War with France	
1794	Death of Robespierre End of Terror		
1795	Treaty of Basel Establishment of the Directory		Treaty of Basel
1796–97	Napoleon Bonaparte's Italian paign		
1797	Treaty of Campo Formio		
1798	Russia declares war on France		
1799	Coup d'état of Napoleon Bonaparte		
1801	Treaty of Lunéville		

REVOLUTION IN EUROPE

Russia	Austria	Spain
	War with France	
		War with France
	Napoleon Bonaparte's Italian campaign	
	Treaty of Campo Formio	
Russia declares war on France		
	Treaty of Lunéville	

CHRONOLOGICAL CHART:

Dates	France	Great Britain	Prussia
1801	Concordat with the Papacy		
1802	Treaty of Amiens	Treaty of Amiens	
1804	Napoleon as emperor		
1805	Third coalition against France	Third coalition against France	
1805	Battle of Trafalgar Battle of Austerlitz	Battle of Trafalgar	
1806	Battles of Jena and Auerstadt		Battles of Jena and Auerstadt
1807	Treaties of Tilsit		Treaties of Tilsit
1808	French invasion of Spain Beginning of peninsula war	French invasion of Spain Beginning of peninsula war	
1812	French invasion of Russia		
1813–14	Final coalition against Napoleon	Final coalition against Napoleon	Final coalition against Napoleon
1813	Battle of Leipzig		Battle of Leipzig
1814	Abdication of Napoleon		
1814–15	Congress of Vienna End of the Revolutionary era	Congress of Vienna End of the Revolutionary era	Congress of Veinna End of the Revolutionary era

EUROPE, 1648–1795

Russia	Austria	Spain
Third coalition against France	Third coalition against France	Third coalition against France
Battle of Austerlitz	Battle of Austerlitz	
Treaties of Tilsit		
		French invasion of Spain
		Beginning of peninsula war
French invasion of Russia		
French retreat from Moscow		
Final coalition against Napoleon	Final coalition against Napoleon	
Battle of Leipzig	Battle of Leipzig	
Congress of Vienna	Congress of Vienna	Congress of Vienna
End of the revolutionary era	End of the revolutionary era	End of the revolutionary era

CHAPTER
NINE

EUROPE IN REVOLUTION

"All titles are going to merge in
the title of citizen."

Barentin, Keeper of the Seals, 1789

"People of all nations . . . unite
with the French. Blush to wear your
chains any longer, and, in imitating
us, hasten to become worthy of
liberty."

Nouveau Chansonnier Patriot, 1794

> *Long live the fortunate moment,*
> *When everything is born again,*
> *The Kingdom is regenerated,*
> *Alleluia.*

The stanza of a popular song expressed the feelings of
most Frenchmen in the spring of 1789. The European Revolution had come to France, and democracy, gained in America, would soon grace and illuminate the French. The evils of
politics, society, and character that had plagued men were
now going to vanish. As a popular ballad announced, the
Estates-General would eradicate pride, jealousy, and drunkenness, fill the Treasury and the markets, and reconcile all
men to the new golden age. Virtue would replace vice, civic
spirit would overcome diffidence and apathy, liberty and
equality would reign forever. The renewal of the world was
here.

An ambitious program, composed of generous hopes and limitless promise, it also concealed another side to the public mood in the spring of 1789. There was impatience for reform and a deepening hostility to privilege, the result of years of Enlightenment political theory and the failure of the government to undertake any real change. Anticipation and impatience, the eagerness to embrace the New Jerusalem, all met at the first meeting of the Estates-General. When Louis XVI was late, an indignant deputy protested, "A single individual should not keep a whole nation waiting."

I

Although the king and his ministers were resigned to consulting the nation, they were not agreed on the form the Estates-General should take. Most thought in terms of the last meeting, in 1614, with three estates of about equal size, voting separately. Jacques Necker, the prime minister, heard enough popular songs to realize that this was impossible, and he obtained a concession. The Third Estate, which included everyone not a noble or a priest, would elect 600 deputies, equal to the First Estate, clergy, and the Second Estate, nobility, combined. But they were still supposed to vote separately, as Estates and not individuals. The crown had gone as far as it wanted in meeting public opinion.

The elections to the Estates-General confirmed the hopes or fears of those who wanted large social changes. In the First Estate, almost half of the deputies were peasant parish priests, who were hostile to the privileges of their noble bishops. Even in the Second Estate, about 50 liberal nobles were elected amidst a pride of poor and reactionary country gentlemen. The Third Estate was totally dominated by bourgeois lawyers, merchants, or officials who had been molded in the Enlightenment and wanted major changes.

Election was only half the process. The deputies brought *cahiers*, or statements of their constituents' grievances.

These were as important as the deputies themselves since they were supposed to be the basis of reform legislation. The *cahiers* generally reflected a liberal, reformist position. Generally, they demanded a constitution for France, freedom of the press, equality before the law, and reforms in the royal administration. The *cahiers* of the Third Estate also insisted on abolishing the fiscal privileges of the clergy and nobility. Nobles and clerics were less enthusiastic about this.

Along with elections and drafting *cahiers,* Frenchmen engaged in a lively pamphlet campaign during the winter and spring of 1788–1789. Royal censorship broke down, and a torrent of pamphlets, poems, and songs amused and aroused the public. Most denounced privilege and flayed nobles and bishops. The most trenchant was published by a cleric, Abbe Sieyes. *What Is The Third Estate?* Sieyes asked in his pamphlet, and he replied that now it was nothing.

"What does it demand? To become something . . . ."

The Third Estate, which was virtually all of the nation, wanted fiscal and legal equality, a constitution, an end to obnoxious privilege, and a share of the political power in France. The urban bourgeoisie agreed with that, and Sieyes' program found its way into many *cahiers.*

II

In the spring and summer of 1789, as the Estates-General met to set France right, there occurred four separate and distinct revolutions, each the product of different groups and classes and each concerned with different problems. At Versailles, the lawyers and deputies to the Estates-General were creating a National Assembly and beginning work on a constitution. In the streets of Paris, mobs formed in July and took the Bastille. In the countryside peasants revolted against their seigneurial lords and taxes. And, in hundreds of provincial towns, bourgeois revolutionaries took over municipal governments and forced royal officials into retirement. Together, these events formed the first of several waves of revolt that swept France during the Revolution.

In the Estates-General, the immediate issue was quite clear. How would the deputies vote, by order or as individuals? The Second Estate organized itself and announced that vote by order was fundamental to monarchical government. The Third Estate refused to organize itself or transact business, and, instead, invited the two privileged orders to join with it in a National Assembly. The First Estate, split between peasant priests and noble bishops, temporized and, finally, on June 19, decided to join with the Third, by one vote. The next day, when the National Assembly tried to assemble, they found the hall shut. Vastly indignant, and suspecting the king of siding with the nobility, the deputies met in the tennis court, and swore that they would never disband until they had given France a constitution. The Tennis Court Oath symbolized the deputies' demand for reform, and attempts by the king to override it failed. On July 27, Louis gave in and accepted the National Assembly.

Having won the procedural question, the liberal deputies turned to what they thought was their main task—giving France a constitution. A constitutional committee was organized, and debate began on what sort of constitution it should be. Every politician had a speech to make, and many had quite a few, and debate dragged on in an endless chain of pompous orations, seeing delegations from the provinces, and reading patriotic letters and addresses. Nonetheless, the deputies actually made progress and, on August 26, adopted a fundamental document, "The Declaration of the Rights of Man and the Citizen." A short and general document, the Declaration stated the natural rights of man, which were not to be curtailed by the state. These included freedom of religion, habeas corpus, abolition of torture, guarantees of due process of law, and careers open to talent, not merely birth. The Declaration combined an affirmation of natural rights derived from Enlightenment philosophy combined with a prohibition against some of the most grating and degraded features of Old Regime government.

While the deputies spoke at leisure about dignity and imperishable principles, the people of Paris faced a more basic problem. Starvation stalked the city as bread prices had been at famine levels for a year. Uncertainty accompanying the collapse of the old monarchy had held up grain shipments to the capital, since farmers, fearing they would not be paid and hoping for even higher prices, kept their grain back. In June, rumors of royal troops marching on Paris added to the anxiety and fear. On July 12, Paris exploded. Mobs pillaged markets and shops in search of bread and wine and sacked public buildings looking for guns. The municipal customs barriers were burned, and the city government was overthrown. Many of the troops joined the people and, on July 14, a neighborhood mob took the Bastille, destroying the symbol of royal power in Paris as it had previously ended the reality.

Although the mob violence was satisfying and brought sharp changes in municipal government and police, capture of the Bastille had not meant more bread. Prices remained high, and stocks stayed low. People were still starving. On October 5, a crowd of hungry and angry women marched through a cold, steady rain 20 miles to Versailles to present their grievances to the king and National Assembly. The next day, the women insisted that the king and Assembly move to Paris. Unprepared to resist, both Louis and the deputies agreed. At the time, the move to Paris seemed an insignificant concession to calm a frightened and turbulent city. It turned out to be far more than that. After October, the course of the Revolution was tied to the moods and politics of Paris, while the wishes of the rest of France fell into the background. After October, it was more the Paris Revolution than the French Revolution.

When the news from Paris reached the provincial cities, it provoked an immediate reaction. In hundreds of cities, the old municipal and provincial bureaucracies simply collapsed, to be replaced by self-constituted committees of bourgeois, who took over local administration and formed national guards for police and defense. Sometimes violence accompanied the change. At Tours and Bar-le-Duc men were murdered. Most often, however, the change was peaceful, even quiet. The centralized state French kings had been building for seven centuries dissolved in one month.

The fourth revolution was in the country, a national uprising of peasants against enclosures, the manorial system, and royal taxes. Having been asked to state their grievances in the *cahiers,* the peasants assumed that the king meant to end them. Isolated instances of rural unrest and violence had occurred throughout the spring of 1789. Peasants refused to pay manorial dues and attacked chateaus. Provincial authorities fought back; at Macon, 33 peasants were hanged. After Bastille, however, the uprisings became too general and the government too disorganized to save the detested manorial privileges. Between July 18 and August 6, the Great Fear, six separate and independent peasant revolts, churned the French provinces. Roused by the cry, "The brigands are coming!," peasants armed and, when no brigands appeared, they turned their attention to manorial dues and land enclosures. Local authorities were helpless, and the only response from Versailles was an evening session on August 4 when privileges already lost were formally renounced. The manorial institutions of France, which originated during the fall of Rome, were destroyed. Of all of the revolutions of 1789, the peasant revolution succeeded most completely.

III

During the cold and rainy winter of 1790, the pace of revolutionary change slowed appreciably. Instead, there was sharp debate, both in the country and Assembly, on what was to be done. The basic issues had changed after 1789. Manorial dues, class privilege, and the old government—all these institutions were gone beyond recall. Now, men clashed over the place of the Roman Catholic Church in the new France, the role of the king, and the increasing threat of war. None of these questions was easily solved, and the process of confronting them led the French into further renewed revolutions, counterrevolution, wars, and the Reign of Terror.

The most serious problem faced in 1790–1792 was religion. Everyone agreed that the Roman Catholic Church must abandon its privileged position in the state, and most agreed there should be freedom of religion. These things were done and, in July 1790, the Assembly passed the Civil Constitution of the Clergy, which was to be the institutional framework of the French church. The Civil Constitution required priests and bishops to be elected by their people. The number of dioceses was reduced from 135 to 83 corresponding to the departments, which were the new administrative units of provincial government. Finally, bishops were forbidden to recognize the institutional supremacy of Rome. The ties to Rome would be doctrinal and sentimental, nothing else. The Civil Constitution of the Clergy was the culmination of efforts by French kings to establish a state church, which dated at least from the fifteenth century. The revolutionary deputies completed the policies of the old monarchy.

In Rome, of course, this all went down badly. Relations with the papacy worsened when the Assembly imposed an oath of obedience on the French clergy. Half of the priests and all but seven bishops refused to uphold the Civil Constitution. Strengthened by this French resistance, the pope condemned the Civil Constitution of the Clergy in March 1791. This swung the king against the Revolution. Louis was a man of deep, although simple faith. Now Louis sought relief from his religious and political woes through flight from France. In July he tried to escape to Germany but was captured and returned to Paris. Having exposed his treason, he was no longer really king but an object of suspicion and contempt. The growing conflict over religion had dragged the crown in as well as the church, and was soon to become the focus of counterrevolution.

The National Assembly also followed the policies of the Old Regime in dealing with government bankruptcy, which had been the immediate cause of the Revolution. The deputies first confiscated church lands, a favorite royal remedy from Charles Martel to Henry VIII. When this failed to fill the treasury, the Assembly issued paper money, called *assignats,* which differed only in name from the various notes and bills of the Old Regime. As the new government could not collect its taxes, the deficit grew, and the Assembly, following hoary precedent, debased the money by issuing *assignats* at will. The resulting inflation had the serious political repercussion of helping keep bread prices high.

In spite of the burdens of running a disorganized country on a daily basis, the National Assembly made slow progress on a constitution, and finished in September, 1791. It was a poor document. The deputies of the National Assembly disqualified themselves, so the new Legislative Assembly consisted of entirely new men. Ministers were excluded from the Legislature, making it easier for deputies to fight the king than help him. Only the bourgeoisie got the vote, so the new Legislature lacked a broad political base. In political terms, with the restricted franchise, religious division, distrust of the king, and an inexperienced Legislature, the new government was going to have to fight for simple survival.

The Legislative Assembly met on October 1, 1791, and from the start failed to direct events. The chamber was badly divided into factions and was unable to cooperate with the king. Bickering replaced debate. Bread prices continued to rise, reflecting both political uncertainty and inflated money. Religious hostilities grew, as the government drove "refractory" clergy, who had not sworn to support the Civil Constitution, from their parishes. There was a steady dribble of emigration, as men foresaw trouble and took themselves and their cash to safety. Everyone knew the king was intriguing with foreign powers. In April, 1792, France drifted into war with Austria and Prussia, and the war went badly. The army was disorganized, officers fled to the enemy, frontier fortresses surrendered at once, and the allies slowly occupied must of eastern France. The Legislative Assembly seemed helpless, paralyzed by problems it could not solve. The French people became more and more restless and scared, demanding the government do something. In Paris, the public mood swung erratically to the left, while the provinces became more conservative, an ominous split that mirrored the ancient hostility between capital and country. In the provinces, men wanted peace, the old priests, and to be left alone to run their own affairs. In Paris, citizens talked of plots and traitors, wanted a defense of the Revolution and nation, cheaper bread, and an end to the suspect and ineffectual monarchy. In the summer of 1792 Paris became more turbulent and moved rapidly toward a new spasm of revolution.

IV

On August 9–10, 1792, the anger and fears of Parisians exploded into revolt. A well-organized mob occupied City Hall and dispersed the municipal government. A new and more radical government, the Commune, was formed from delegates from the Paris sections (electoral wards) and dominated by a rising revolutionary personality, Georges Danton. The next day the mob invaded the royal palace and made the king a prisoner. The Legislative Assembly bowed to these events and called a National Convention to draw up a constitution for now republican France. The monarchy was over.

The August Days did nothing to end the problems the old government had failed to face. People were still hungry, and a foreign army was still marching on Paris and threatening dire revenge on revolutionaries. As the days passed, and nothing was done, Paris tempers and fears began to rise again. Now it was rumored that the huge number of aristocratic and ecclesiastical prisoners were planning an immense jailbreak, which would be the signal for a slaughter of patriots. On September 2, armed mobs formed. They proceeded to the prisons and began a methodical execution of prisoners. For five days the massacres went on. Over 1200 prisoners were slaughtered, half of those held in Paris jails. Then, for the moment, Paris seemed calmer, but the savage butchery had signaled a new era of revolution, a time of terror.

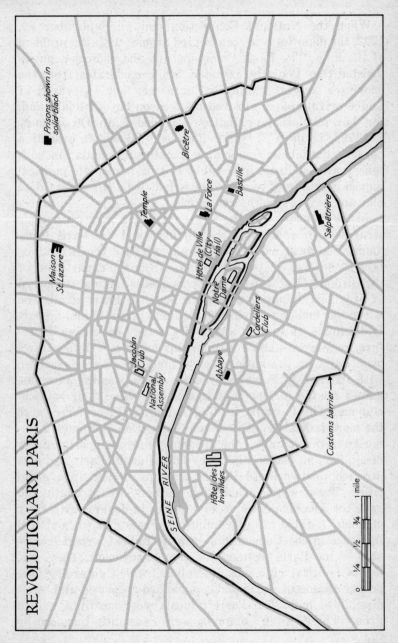

REVOLUTIONARY PARIS

Prisons shown in
solid black

Bicêtre

Temple

La Force

Bastille

Salpêtrière

Maison
St. Lazare

Hôtel de Ville
(City
Hall)

Notre
Dame

Cordeliers
Club

Jacobin
Club

Abbaye

National
Assembly

Customs barrier →

SEINE RIVER

Hôtel des
Invalides

0   ¼   ½   ¾   1 mile

When the National Convention met on September 20, 1792, the deputies were confronted at once with the problem of the king. The Paris Commune and the radical deputies insisted that Louis be executed, while moderates from the provinces sought frantically for a way out. A search of Louis' private papers proved his treason beyond doubt and, for that, revolutionary justice demanded death. On January 21, 1793, Louis XVI was guillotined. The king's execution had great symbolic importance, making reconciliation with conservatives almost impossible. But its immediate political impact was slight because Louis had long since ceased to play any real role in the government.

In the months after the Convention met, several factions struggled for control of the chamber and the Paris Commune. The most moderate group was called the Girondins, because several of its leaders came from the department of the Gironde (Bordeaux). This was a loose faction, composed of provincial deputies with no support in Paris at all. The Girondins had only the loosest political program and no party discipline. In spite of a majority in the Convention, therefore, they were unable to turn this advantage into control over Paris or the national government. A second faction, with strength in Paris and the provinces, was the Jacobins, named for the former Jacobin convent where their political club met. The Jacobins, led by Maximilien Robespierre, were the more radical deputies of the Convention. Although a minority in the chamber, the Jacobins enjoyed superior party discipline and leadership. They had allies in Paris and also directed a network of local Jacobin clubs in many provincial cities. These were considerable elements of strength and gave the Jacobins decisive advantages in dealing with their enemies. A third group, confined to Paris and without real influence in the Convention, was the radical, urban leadership of the Paris sections and city government. They, too, had a political club, the Cordeliers, which controlled the poorer section of Paris and commanded an armed and semi-disciplined mob. The Paris radicals were hardly a unified group. Those in the Commune were constantly menaced by more extreme politicians from the sections and the streets. Even so, the armed force of their mob made them a serious political power.

In the months after the September prison massacres, faction politicians struggled to control the state and meet the problems of war and revolution. In this contest the Girondins steadily lost ground to the Jacobins. While they held their majority in the Convention, the Girondins were blamed for military defeat in Belgium and Germany. They were denounced as traitors and monarchists and food hoarders. Thus, the power of Jacobins grew steadily as the mistakes and misfortunes of their enemies accumulated.

In the city, a similar political evolution occurred. High bread prices and fears of a counterrevolutionary plot undermined the moral authority of the Commune. Radical orators from the sections took advantage of this. A foolish attempt by the Girondins to arrest some of the leading radical Paris politicians sparked a new revolt. On May 31, the city government was overthrown, to be replaced by the Revolutionary Commune, a collection of Paris politicians somewhat louder and more radical than their predecessors. Two days later, on June 2, the Convention bowed to Parisian demands for a purge of 29 Girondin deputies. Once again, an organized Paris mob had overthrown both the municipal and national government.

Although workers and shopkeepers from the poorer sections of Paris had made the *coup* of May-June, 1793, the real victors were the Jacobin politicans in the Convention. Having defeated their Girondin enemies, even if by proxy, the Jacobins created a strong and successful revolutionary government over the course of the next year. The instrument they used was terror. Imitating the Paris example, the Jacobins made terror into a system of government. Terror became an acceptable substitute for strong local administration and took the place of the departed royal bureaucracy. It filled the army with recruits, encouraged officers to do their duty, and persuaded peasants to release their grain to the market at an acceptable price. Terror punished counterrevolutionary and food hoarder alike. It was used as an instrument of daily administration as well as revolutionary security.

Terror had a number of advantages over traditional means of government. It freed the government from dependence on reports and red tape and allowed it to make rapid and flexible decisions, appropriate for the emergency conditions. The law's delay meant nothing now. A sense of urgency was reinforced by the guillotine. The government was brutal, but it was also efficient.

Although terror was the mainspring of government, the Jacobins also built institutions to carry out their policies. At the center, the Convention abdicated most of its executive power to the Committee of Public Safety. The Committee consisted of 12 able men, dominated politically by Robespierre. Within the Committee, the men worked in quasi-ministerial fashion. Lazare Carnot, a former regular army captain, directed the creation of the revolutionary armies and earned the title, "Organizer of Victory." Bertrand Barère, the most astute parliamentary politician in the Convention, managed the chamber. Jean-Bon Saint-André, a former Protestant pastor, became a sort of minister of the navy. Together, their energy and efficiency dominated French government as no ministry had since Chancellor Maupeou in the 1770s.

The Committee of Public Safety's orders were carried out largely by three groups: the army, the network of local Jacobin clubs, and deputies of the Convention sent on missions to the provinces or the front. Of the three, the deputies on mission were the most important. Sent out on the Committee's orders, their task was to recruit men for the army, collect grain for Paris, purge unreliable local officials, execute subversives, and monitor the activities of the army. "I found this department religious, royalist, Girondin, public spirit killed, a small group of patriots molested, scarcely daring to call themselves Jacobins," wrote Taillefer, the deputy on mission to the department of Cahors. "I de-Christianized, republicanized, Jacobinized, regenerated it . . . ," he added. It was just what the Committee expected him to do.

Many of the deputies were not too particular about the means they used to do these things. At Nantes, Carrier drowned over 1200 prisoners, sinking them in the Loire River in large rafts. At Lyons, after the Jacobin army captured the city from the Girondins, Fouche shot about 2000 "counterrevolutionaries." Milder men often began their work with arrests and an execution or two, to set the proper tone of seriousness for their mission. Occasionally, the deputies and local Jacobins could not cope with the opposition and had to call in the army. In such cases, of course, the slaughter was appreciably increased.

In spite of the provincial revolts, the Jacobin Committee paid particular attention to Paris, an attitude of great political wisdom. To deal with the countless subversives everyone believed infested the city, the Committee relied on the Revolutionary Tribunal. Trial procedure was simple. The accused was permitted no defense. Hoarding grain and counterrevolutionary activities were the usual crimes. Between the execution of Louis XVI and the one of Robespierre in August, 1794, the Revolutionary Tribunal condemned 2672 persons to the guillotine, imprisoned some, and even acquitted 857. The Tribunal was assisted in this patriotic work by watch committees in the 48 Paris sections, most securely under the control of loyal Jacobins. The Committee also watched the Paris municipal government and gradually purged it of enemies, replacing them with Jacobins. On the whole, Jacobin rule in Paris worked well, and complemented growing Jacobin control in the countryside.

The basic problem faced by the Committee was the war. On the frontiers the spring of 1793 had brought serious defeats. On April 5, the Girondin commander in Belgium, Dumouriez, deserted to the Austrians who then drove the disorganized French back across the border. In July, two key fortresses surrendered, and it appeared that the Austrians were about to march on Paris. In Lorraine and Italy, French troops were also in retreat or on the defensive. Carnot and his associates reversed that and turned defeat into victory. By autumn, Carnot's new armies were ready. At Honde-shoote and Wattignies the French defeated the Austrians and began another invasion of Belgium that culminated in the victory at Fleurus in July, 1794 and opened the Low Countries to French conquest. The civil war also went well for the Jacobins. In April, 1793, a royalist-clerical revolt had begun in the Vendée in western France and it was soon seri-ous enough to require regiments from the frontiers. Fur-thermore, in July, 1793, a federalist revolt, tied to the expul-sion of the Girondin deputies from the Convention, broke out in many of the large cities of southern France including Bordeaux, Lyons, Marseilles, and Toulon. Again, the regular army was needed. The Jacobins pushed the campaigns against counterrevolution with energy and brutality. In De-cember, at Savenay, the army caught up with the Vendéans and defeated them. In the south, the major cities were recap-tured. It was all accompanied by reprisals and butchery. Suspects were executed without trial, and prisoners were shot. The Jacobin deputies on mission showed what revolu-tionary justice really meant.

The instrument of victory was a new army, organized and equipped by the Jacobin Committee. Lazare Carnot directed this effort, and his general orders were simple, far different from the cautious strategy of the Old Regime. Seek battle, he commanded,

". . . keep the troops in constant readiness . . . use the bayonet on every possible occasion, and follow up the enemy without pause until he is completely destroyed."

Carnot's recruiting methods were also revolutionary. He was not content with convicts and bums but drafted sturdy peasant youths for his regiments. Command no longer went automatically to incompetent nobles. Carnot sought ability. Unlucky and defeated generals were cashiered and guillo-tined. Others took their places, including Napoleon Bonaparte and eight of his marshals. Carnot's 14 armies, animated by nationalism and revolutionary fervor, to say nothing of the guillotine, were victorious everywhere. In one year they repressed revolt and conquered the Rhine frontier. It was a superb and immense achievement, the real beginning of national armies and modern war. It also made the other European powers exceptionally nervous.

Victory in war would be meaningless if the Revolution were overthrown internally by its enemies. The Jacobins, who had come to power by conspiracy, were extremely sensitive to plots and rumors of plots. Everyone must be loyal to the Revolution. There was no room for dissent. The emergency demanded total vigilance. Nobles, priests, food hoarders, slackers, and defeatists were all subversives. As the gray and rainy winter of 1793–1794 closed in on Paris, with political tension high and bread prices higher, these sentiments were translated into executions and purges.

The first to perish were the Girondins. Already compromised in the federalist revolts, the Girondins were also implicated in a suspected although imaginary counterrevolutionary plot. Hailed before the Revolutionary Tribunal, they were guillotined on October 31, 1793. The Paris radicals came next. Their demands for total price controls were opposed by Robespierre. Arrested without warning, the radicals were executed in March, 1794. Immediately, Robespierre turned on a dissident Jacobin faction. Georges Danton and his friends were arrested on charges of corruption and hostility to the Committee of Public Safety. They were unquestionably guilty on both counts and were guillotined on April 5.

Extermination of the factions, however, did not end the Terror. Instead, it became worse. The executioners never lacked work. The Republic of Terror now added a new dimension to its public philosophy. Madame la Guillotine would do more than enforce political conformity. In their season of triumph, the Jacobins would establish the Republic of Virtue. Virtue, in the Jacobin state, was given a civic cast. It meant a willingness to fight for the revolutionary government and ideals, to care for them, and to sacrifice for them. Idleness was prohibited, and hoarding of food became crimes as black as royalism. *Civisme* was a badge of honor and loyalty, while *incivisme* merited death and often got it. The New Jerusalem was at last at hand. A final effort, and the corrupt would be cast down, while the virtuous, once downtrodden, the stone the builder had despised, would inherit the Kingdom.

> *Long live the fortunate moment*
> *When everything is born again.*

Psychologically, the French Revolution had come full circle.

For the faithful, for the true believers in the Jacobin vision, a Republic of Virtue was awesome and inspiring. They applauded such laws as the edict of November 10, 1793, which prohibited the worship of the Christian God. Good Jacobins supported discarding the traditional Christian calendar in October, 1793 and replacing it with a patriotic and revolutionary one. Certainly, Jacobins approved of the law of 22 Prairial, II (June 9, 1794), which made it possible to execute corrupt deputies to the Convention and greatly extended the range of *incivique* crimes. But to others—to priests and nobles and to federalists and sceptics—the Jacobin paradise was a vision of hell. For Jacobins who had quarreled with Robespierre, the law of 22 Prairial was a death warrant. So, a plot was hatched by dissident Jacobins to end the Terror. Some, like Billaud-Varennes, were on the Committee of Public Safety; others, like Fouché, were deputies in the Convention. On the ninth of Thermidor, II (July 27, 1794), Robespierre and a dozen supporters were arrested. The next day they were executed. Robespierre was shocked at being taken in a *coup,* and he protested violently. But execution at the hands of fellow conspirators is a common end for revolutionaries, and it is also appropriate.

Politically, the *coup* of the 9th of Thermidor was the turning point of the Revolution. In the years since 1788, the Revolution had been supported by fewer and fewer people as the groups in power drifted farther away from the generous ideals of 1789. At the same time, the political factions became better and better organized and enjoyed the total support of their adherents. The execution of Robespierre checked this trend. It was, in effect, the triumph of general opinion over political organization, and it was the first time during the Revolution this had happened.

Robespierre's death also ended the Reign of Terror. Practical men, who were untouched by the Jacobin vision, thought the Terror was no longer needed. Once, it had been necessary for survival. Terror had fed Paris, overthrown the factions, defeated enemies both foreign and domestic, and had held France together. But those days were over. It was time to stop. Men doubted the promises of the Republic of Virtue, doubted that the Jacobins could lead France to perfect liberty, equality, fraternity, and justice. They believed that the continuation of the Terror was horrible and inhuman and, what was worse, pointless. Did the Jacobsins want the horror to continue forever? Nobody wished that. Frenchmen were tired of heroism and sacrifice, tired of the faith and fear that accompanied the Jacobin heaven. In a debate in the Convention, a Jacobin called for justice only for patriots. But France wanted justice for everyone.

V

With the war going well and the Terror ended, the Convention turned to its ostensible task and drew up a constitution for France. The Constitution of 1795 (year III) was extraordinarily complex, designed to keep the people at bay and prevent the government from governing. Executive power was given to five Directors, for whom the Directory was named. The Legislature was bicameral consisting of a Council of Elders of 250 and a lower house called the Five Hundred. Each chamber had one-third of its members elected annually by a restricted electorate that excluded workers and poor peasants. It was a middle-class constitution, designed to uphold bourgeois values, virtues, property, and power.

The Directory never really established itself, however. It was plagued by *coups,* as the habits of conspiracy and faction died hard. In 1796, a proto-Socialist simpleton named Gracchus Babeuf led his Conspiracy of Equals against the regime. Its aim was to abolish private property. The government suppressed this puny putsch with ease and executed Babeuf, who was later canonized by Marxists as a sort of Socialist John the Baptist. The second *coup* came from the Directors themselves. On September 4, 1797 (18 Fructidor, V), three republican Directors exiled their two conservative colleagues, including Carnot, and purged their friends from the legislative Councils. A third *coup,* in 1798, followed this pattern. The Directors annulled the elections, which they had lost, and appointed their cohorts to the Legislature. It all went smoothly enough, but the third resort to extralegal means in as many years revealed the political bankruptcy of the regime.

The Directory also failed to solve the social problems inherited from the Jacobins. The most insidious was the inflation of the *assignats,* which had fallen to less than a penny on the dollar. Consequently, bread prices remained artificially high. Efforts to deflate the *assignats* and assign them a fixed value only brought about a depression in 1798–1799. Nor was the Directory able to do anything about the religious divisions in France. The regime neither renounced the de-Christianization of the Jacobins nor settled its differences with Rome. Instead, the government intermittently persecuted both priests and Jacobins. These loathsome practices helped discredit the Directory in the eyes of decent and moderate Frenchmen, as indeed they should have.

The most serious problem, however, was the rampant and cynical corruption that characterized the Directory. All the politicians could be bought, although this is not unusual, and business with the government was normally conducted by bribery and influence peddling. The degraded psychology of the *nouveau-riche* businessman pervaded the regime. People assumed that everyone had his price and that politics was simply the art of finding it. These attitudes extended to women. It was an era of courtesans, not the least talented of whom was Josephine Bonaparte. Fashionable ball gowns consisted of gauze draped tastefully over a nude body. Parties given by the Director, Paul Barras, were elegant orgies, which everyone enjoyed attending. For a brief period, this open and public corruption was exciting, sophisticated, and fashionable. After a few years, however, it disgusted the middle-class Frenchmen who were the regime's main support. It was a moral revulsion that finally doomed the Directory.

Yet the Directory was not without its successes. Its legislation laid the basis for Napoleonic administrative reforms and anticipated Napoleonic edicts in law, education, and finance. Most important, the Directory won the foreign war. In 1796, a young general—Napoleon Bonaparte—was appointed to command in Italy, an advancement he owed to the political and sexual intrigues of his wife, Josephine. Napoleon promptly attacked the Austrians and defeated them. He drove the Austrians out of Italy in a series of brilliant campaigns and, in October, 1797, negotiated the treaty of Campio Formio. It reflected the magnitude of the French victory. Austria recognized the French conquest of Belgium and the new French client states in Italy. Even the Sun King had not won such a victory.

Military victory and the beginnings of institutional consolidation were not enough to save the Directory. It had never inspired much loyalty or commanded much fear. Its politicians and generals thought in terms of overthrowing the regime. The last *coup* came on November 9, 1799 (18 Brumaire, VIII), when the most successful general, Napoleon, aided by the Directors themselves, captured the machinery of state. There was no resistance. France was apathetic. Most citizens simply wanted an end to adventure and revolution. With the advent of Napoleon France came full cycle, from an incompetent monarchy to an effective one, from a floundering king to an enlightened despot who meant to end revolution at home while extending it abroad.

VI

The new regime, the fifth since 1789, bore a surface resemblance to the ones it followed. There was a written constitution that contained the usual provisions for a legislature, legal equality, modest political liberty, and a plural executive. The constitution created three Consuls, with only the First Consul, Napoleon, having any real power. There were four legislatures, with their functions strictly divided. The Legislative Body voted on bills, but could not debate them. The Tribunate debated bills, but did not vote. The Senate decided on the constitutionality of bills, while the Council of State drafted legislation, but neither body debated nor voted on it. The electoral laws were as carefully manipulated. All adult males voted, thus keeping faith with the Jacobin tradition. But they voted only for the commune list, who then chose one-tenth of their number as the department list, who chose one-tenth of *their* number as the national list. From these came the members of the legislature. The whole system was designed to concentrate all real power in the hands of the First Consul. It was eyewash for dictatorship. But it was not unpopular. A plebiscite in 1800 ratified the constitution by a vote of 3,011,107 to 1657, a comfortable margin.

The man who devised the constitution was born into a petty and turbulent Corsican family, with loads of brothers, sisters, debts, and feuds. Napoleon was an unmanageable boy, so his family packed him off to military school, a solution that has since occurred to many American families, although not with such spectacular results. In due time, the troublesome and moody Corsican got his commission. He was even promoted to captain, in spite of an abrupt and abrasive personality and numerous absences without leave. He was destined for unhappy obscurity until the Revolution. By sheer

luck, he was at the seige of Toulon when the artillery commander was wounded. Posted to his slot, Napoleon set up his
guns and took the town. This display of military aptitude,
plus some opportunistic Jacobin oratory, persuaded Carnot
to make him a general. When the Jacobins went down Napoleon went with them, but Josephine restored him to grace
and obtained for him command of the army of Italy. It was
considered a poor post, with little chance for glory. Director
Paul Barras gave it to Napoleon as much in pity and contempt as anything else, just to satisfy Josephine, get the im-
portunate young man out of town, and bury him in a minor
but honorable position. For the elegant and cynical Barras,
the appointment to Italian command was a form of dismissal; for Napoleon, as he surveyed his ragged and complacent
troops, it was the beginning of everything.

Once in power, Napoleon turned immediately to domestic
reform. He swept away some of the debris of the revolution,
and included elements from both the Old Regime and the five
revolutionary regimes that preceded him. He had two basic
aims: an efficient government and one that would inspire
loyalty. Anything less, and Napoleon would lose power as
others had before him.

Peace with Rome was probably Napoleon's most popular
achievement. He indicated his intentions his first month in
power by returning churches to the priests for worship. He
reestablished Sunday. He began negotiations with the pope,
and reached an agreement in 1801. The Concordat incorporated many of the characteristics of the Old Regime, Gallican
church. The government (Napoleon) appointed the bishops, who took an oath of loyalty to the state. The government also controlled the seminaries and paid the salaries of
priests and bishops. The church acquiesced in the loss of its
lands and gained the right to accept gifts and bequests.

In spite of some complaint from anticlericals, the Concordat was generally popular. It reassured Frenchmen that
they could keep their church lands, and it ended the squalid
religious persecution. Grateful for that, the church constant-

ly praised Napoleon and his government and even included some of this praise in the catechism. The Concordat was also popular with Napoleon, which is what counted. He believed that a state supported by the church would be seen as legitimate, and this sense of permanence was what he wanted most.

Having settled with God, Napoleon turned to the civil administration. Building on the work of the Directory, he created a civil service that surpassed both the Jacobins and the Old Regime in administrative centralization. In the finances, Napoleon reverted to the system of the old regime. He partially repudiated the *assignats*, in imitation of countless royal swindles. He reinstated the Old Regime land tax and excise taxes, although without tax farming and aristocratic exemptions. He founded the Bank of France and established a firm budget and accounting system, all of which had eluded the Bourbon kings. As a result of these reforms, Napoleon received about 400 million francs a year, about what Louis XVI had coming in, but he did it with the most efficient and honest tax system the French had known since the fall of Rome.

Finally, Napoleon completed the codification of French law, a project begun during the Revolution. Napoleon pushed this project hard and, in 1804, the Civil Code was approved. Two years later came the Code of Civil Procedure, in 1807 the Commercial Code, then a Code of Criminal Procedure and, finally, a Penal Code. As with his other domestic legislation, the law codes contained both revolutionary and Old Regime legislation, as well as Napoleon's own ideas. It was also in the tradition of Old Regime enlightened despotism, of which Napoleon was the heir. Continuity in politics is as instructive as change.

Domestic reforms, which never occupied more than a fraction of Napoleon's attention, were designed to keep him in power. That power was to be used for war. Basically, Napoleon was a soldier, and he thought war was the only profession worthy of his talents. Once his *coup* was complete, and domestic reform begun, Napoleon went to the front. His presence made a decided difference. The French offensive of 1800 was extremely successful. Napoleon defeated the Austrians at Marengo and drove them from Italy for the second time. Defeat in Germany also convinced the Austrians to sue for peace. At Lunéville, in 1801, Austria again abandoned Italy and the left bank of the Rhine to France. With Austria out of the war, Great Britain lost her last continental ally. British diplomats began to think of peace. After long negotiations, France and Britain ended a decade of war with the Peace of Amiens in 1802.

This was the most critical time of Napoleon's career. He had defeated his enemies and concluded pace. He had established a firm regime at home. At Amiens and Lunéville, Napoleon had reached the limits of conquest that the European state system, based on the balance of power, could concede and accept. "A conqueror, like a cannonball, must to on," wrote the Duke of Wellington of Napoleon. After Amiens, Napoleon chose to become a conqueror, pursuing the goal of European domination that was forever unstable, that was doomed by a single defeat. His sense of realism abandoned him. He moved into the realm of dream.

This decision was symbolized for all to see by Napoleon's coronation as emperor of the French on December 2, 1804. It was a stupendous ceremony, with the pope himself attending. Afterward, Napoleon I created a brilliant court. He made kings and princes of his family and friends and established an elaborate etiquette to emphasize his grandeur. It was a creditable imitation of the Sun King, less grandiose perhaps, but certainly an effective statement of Napoleon's intention to be the embodiment of France and the arbiter of Europe.

Napoleon's expansion began again less than a year after the Treaty of Amiens was signed. In 1803 he undertook the reorganization of the ramshackle Holy Roman Empire. Most of the ecclesiastical states and imperial cities were destroyed, along with the smaller imperial dignities. Although not immediately affected, the British saw clearly enough where this blatant aggression must lead, and they declared

THE EXPANSION OF THE REVOLUTION
Napoleon's Empire
in 1810

French Empire
Dependent States
Allied States
x Battle sites
□ Treaty towns

Volga

St.Petersburg

○ Mosco

Borodino x

RUSSIA

Black Sea

Constantinople

OTTOMAN EMPIRE

Danube

Baltic Sea

Tilsit

PRUSSIA

Berlin

Warsaw

x Leipzig

x Austerlitz

AUSTRIA

Vienna

Campo Formio

North Sea

Amsterdam

Auerstadt

Jena

Rhine

Luneville

○ Milan

Rome

Naples

ENGLAND

London

Waterloo

Amiens

Paris

FRANCE

Mediterranean Sea

Atlantic Ocean

Salamanca

Madrid

SPAIN

Lisbon

Scale of Miles
0 100 200 300 400 500

war on France in May, 1803. In 1805, they were joined by
Russia and Austria in a third coalition against the French
emperor.

The allies won their only battle at sea, but it was a permanent strategic victory. On November 25, 1805, Lord Nelson
destroyed a Franco-Spanish fleet at Trafalgar. French hopes
of defeating the British went down with the navy. Napoleon
would never invade England.

On land, Napoleon, who was at the height of his powers,
did much better. On December 2, 1805, the first anniversary
of his coronation, Napoleon annihilated a combined Austro-
Russian army at Austerlitz. This disaster drove the Austrians out of the war and the Russians out of Germany. Again,
Napoleon reorganized the smaller German states, this time
into the Confederation of the Rhine, a bloc of satellite kingdoms. At this point, when it was too late, Prussia joined the
allies. In October, 1806, in the twin battles of Jena and
Auerstadt, Napoleon crushed the Prussian army. Moving
fast, the French emperor took Berlin and marched east
against Russia. At Friedland, in 1807, Napoleon completed
his triumph by soundly beating the Russians. That was it.
Only the British could go on. Russia and Prussia asked for
peace.

The peeace negotiations were carried on at the highest
level, with Napoleon, Czar Alexander I, and Frederick-William III of Prussia acting as their own negotiators. Napoleon proved less apt in diplomacy than in war. His terms, although not unrealistic in view of the magnitude of his victories, made any permanent peace impossible. Russia was
treated rather leniently and actually gained some territory.
But she was forced to recognize Napoleon's German settlement, as well as the Grand Duchy of Warsaw, a Napoleonic
client state on her borders. Prussia paid the price of peace.
She lost most of Polish lands to the Grand Duchy of Warsaw
and all of her provinces east of the Elbe River. Prussia was
forbidden to keep an army of more than 40,000 men and was
condemned to pay a huge indemnity and admit French occupation troops to her fortresses. The Treaties of Tilsit

dropped Prussia from the ranks of the Great Powers. They also involved Napoleon in Polish affairs, which Russia had traditionally regarded as vital to her national interests.

Peace at Tilsit left only the British still in the war. Invasion was impossible, so Napoleon tried to defeat the British by cutting off their trade. In 1806 and 1807, he issued the Berlin and Milan Decrees, which closed continental ports to British goods and ships. By these means, Napoleon hoped, Britain would be driven to bankruptcy and peace. Such a grandiose scheme was bound to have holes in it. Portugal, a British economic satellite, refused to join the Continental System and, in November, 1807, the French occupied the country. Great Britain could not permit its oldest ally to be absorbed by Napoleon. A British army under the Duke of Wellington landed, and the war in the Iberian peninsula began.

The peninsula war widened in March, 1808, when Napoleon invaded Spain. Unexpectedly, the Spanish fought back. When the French tried to extend the benefits of revolutionary church reform to Spain, there was a massive popular uprising—the Vendée revolt on a huge scale. The war was fought in the best modern tradition—peasant insurgents against a regular army. It was also fought by modern methods, mainly against civilians, by pillage, murder, and burning, by torturing priests, by shooting prisoners, and by raping the women. The French made gains against the insurgents but were unable to drive the British from the peninsula. By 1811, the British were clearly winning. They had driven the French from Portugal and were advancing into southern Spain. In July 1812, Wellington destroyed a French army at Salamanca and obliged the French to abandon Madrid and fall back toward the Pyrenees.

Spanish problems might have remained a nagging, although hardly fatal difficulty if Napoleon had not begun to drift into enmity with Russia. The czar was unhappy with the French in Poland, was unwilling to live within the Continental System, and was dissatisfied with the French attitude toward Russia's war with Turkey. Remembering past defects, however, he was reluctant to break openly with

France. Napoleon saved him the trouble. The French emperor felt that one more war, one last and mighty conquest would force the British into peace and secure the Napoleonic system. In June, 1812, the French invaded Russia with a huge army of about 600,000 men. At Borodino he met the Russians. It was a hideous and bloody battle in which Napoleon abandoned all of his own tactical maxims. Instead of trying to flank the Russian position, he ordered an infantry charge against the center of the line. The Russian guns cut the French to pieces but, when the day was over, the Russians retreated. A month later, the French occupied Moscow. The Russians refused to concede that they were beaten. Instead of negotiating, they burned Moscow. Instead of dictating peace terms, Napoleon began a ghastly retreat toward the frontier. As his starving army stumbled toward Germany, it was constantly harassed by Cossacks and pursued by the Russian regulars. Winter came early and hard, and thousands perished in the cold. Equipment and guns were abandoned, and stragglers were left to be shot by the Russians. At the icy Beresina River the army fought its way across a bridge, but a large part was cut off and destroyed. The retreat collapsed into a rout, after which less than 100,000 men survived.

When the magnitude of his defeat became clear, Napoleon's artificial diplomatic alliances began to crumble. In March, 1813, Prussia deserted the French and joined the Russians. Even so, Napoleon was not completely finished. In May, he defeated the allied armies at Lutzen and Bautzen and drove them out of Saxony. The Russians and Prussians, fearing that Napoleon would recover, accepted Austrian mediation and offered Napoleon a generous peace. The emperor refused. It was a monstrous blunder. Austria joined the allies in August, 1813, and turned the power balance against the French for the first time since 1794. Napoleon did what he could. He won an initial victory at Dresden over the Austrians, but the allies massed their forces anyway. In a three-day battle at Leipzig Napoleon was decisively beaten and driven back to the Rhine. As he abandoned Germany, Napoleon received some unwelcome news from Spain. The

British under Wellington had crossed the Pyrenees into France.

Although Napoleon was clearly on the run, the allied generals were still wary of him. On November 8, they offered peace again, conceding France the Rhine frontier. Napoleon again refused. The war continued with an allied invasion of France. In his defensive campaign, Napoleon fought as well as he ever had. In February, 1814, he defeated various detachments of the allied armies in six rapid battles, driving them back in some disorder. Again he was offered peace, this time with the frontiers of 1792. Again Napoleon refused. Twenty years of continuous fighting and negotiation had badly eroded his grasp of strategic and diplomatic reality. He was greatly outnumbered; he might win tactical victories but not the war. Each of the allied offers had been generous, as everyone but Napoleon could see.

After Napoleon's last refusal, the allies pushed on to Paris. They entered the city on March 31, 1814, 22 years after the first Austro-Prussian invasion had set out for Paris to end the revolution and restore a Bourbon to his throne. Although the Bourbon Restoration had been delayed, it was not forgotten. Louis XVIII, old, fat, safe, and complacent, was placed on the French throne, and Napoleon was packed off to Elba. Except for the picaresque drama of the Hundred Days, which ended in the catastrophe at Waterloo, the Napoleonic era was over.

VII

The heavens themselves, the planets and this centre
Observe degree, priority and place
Insisture, course, proportion, season, form,
Office, and custom, in all line of order . . .
Take but degree away, untune that string,
And, hark, what discord follows.

When William Shakespeare wrote *Troilus and Cressida* he described values that seemed secure in men's thoughts as well as the social structure. By the end of the eighteenth century such approval had vanished. Order, hierarchy, privilege, and rank, these essential attributes of Old Regime society and government, were badly mangled by the Revolution and wars. Nobles, clerics, and kings could be pardoned for seeing the Revolution as satanic and the Napoleonic wars as a crusade against them.

Certainly, the Revolution had been more successful than the enlightened despots in clearing out the remaining centers of Old Regime private political power. Aristocratic, ecclesiastical, municipal privilege had generally withstood the best efforts of Old Regime reform. The old constituted bodies —whether guilds, parlements, manors, or churches—had not done so well after 1789, however. Such privileges had been destroyed or damaged in much of Europe. The government now faced most of its citizens without noble or privileged intermediaries. A basic result of the Revolution was the immense and permanent growth in the power of the state.

Equally important were the changes in the way men thought. In the long interval of war and revolution society had become more egalitarian, more individualistic, and more secular. Liberalism was a popular ideology even in 1815, and the traditional social conflicts between the privileged and the commoner were by no means over. Ideas of legal equality and careers open to talent eroded allegiance to traditional concepts of social hierarchy and status. Even worse was the new secular religion—nationalism. The French had rallied to defend their nation in 1793 and then drove all Europe to do the same 20 years later. The relatively decorous contests between dynasties were being replaced by the degraded and savage struggles between peoples. Without wishing it, the Revolution and Napoleon had created a Europe of nations.

The revolutionary era, therefore, witnessed the triumph of the two basic political forces of modernity: the state and the people. Not everybody—certainly not the former masters of society—was pleased with this or with the prospect of more of it. "No one who has not lived before 1789 knows how sweet life can be," commented the French foreign minister Prince Talleyrand, and he expressed the spirit of 1814. It was the voice of the past.

BIBLIOGRAPHY

1. Primary Sources

Edmund Burke, *Reflections on the Revolution in France,* A Conservative Englishman's hostile commentary on the French Revolution. Burke's book was sharply and specifically attacked by

Thomas Paine in *The Rights of Man,* which defended the Revolution and resulted in Paine's exile to France.

J. H. Stewart, *A Documentary Survey of the French Revolution,* is a large collection of the salient, official documents from 1788 through 1799 (hard cover).

2. General Accounts

Albert Goodwin, *The French Revolution,* is a short narrative, which ends with the death of Robespierre in 1794. It is excellent for the beginning student.

J. M. Thompson, *The French Revolution,* is a long detailed, difficult, but outstanding study of the Revolution. It, too, ends in 1794. It is not for the casual reader.

Albert Mathiez, *The French Revolution,* is a general survey by the leading admirer of Robespierre. Like Thompson, it is a difficult book.

Alexis de Tocqueville, *The Old Regime and the French Revolution,* is an essay, not a narrative history. It is brilliant, well written, and clear and presents a liberal, democratic view of the Revolution. Written in 1852, it is still, in many ways, the best book on the Revolution. Highly recommended.

Crane Brinton, *Decade of Revolution,* goes to 1799 and gives a fairly detailed account of the Directory. In general, however, this is not an outstanding book.

Georges Lefebvre, *The French Revolution* (2 vols.), is an outstanding book, and should be consulted by the serious student (hard cover).

3. Detailed Studies on the Revolution

R. R. Palmer, *Twelve Who Ruled,* is a brilliant study of the Jacobin Committee of Public Safety. The student must already be familiar with the events of the Terror to get the maximum benefit from this book.

246

Georges Lefebvre, *The Coming of the French Revolution,* is the single best study of the events of 1788–1789. No student can afford to miss this brilliant, clear, and concise book. Highly recommended.

George Rude, *The Crowd in the French Revolution,* is a study of Paris crowds and mobs during the major riots of the Revolution. A sociological study, it will repay careful reading (hard cover).

Charles Tily, *The Vendée,* is also a sociological study, this time of the serious counter revolution in western France. The book's thesis is that religion was not a major cause of the Vendee rebellion, and then it proceeds to prove that religion was a basic factor. Hard to read but exceptionally interesting.

Alfred Cobban, *The Social Interpretation of the French Revolution,* is a series of semidetached essays on various aspects of the social history of the Revolution. Exceptionally good and highly recommended.

4.   Napoleon

Felix Markham, *Napoleon and the Awakening of Europe,* is a short and adequate narrative of the Napoleonic years. It concentrates, of course, on war and diplomacy.

Robert Holtman, *The Napoleonic Revolution,* presents the very doubtful thesis that Napoleon was responsible for the lasting effects of the Revolution. Also included excellent coverage of Napoleon's domestic accomplishments.

5.   Major Interpretive Account

R. R. Palmer, *The Age of the Democratic Revolution* (2 vols.), presents the thesis that the French Revolution and Napoleon are part of a general era of revolution, which begins in Geneva in the 1760s and includes Latin America, the United States, Ireland, Belguim, Prussia, Holland, Poland, most of the Austrian Empire and, of course, France. This age of revolutions grew out of the general prosperity and general misgovernment of the eighteenth century, as well as the beguiling ideas of the Enlightenment. This is a brilliant book, well written, clear, and extremely convincing. The serious student of eighteenth century revolutions should begin here, and should reread this book periodically (hard covers).

Technological Change in the Early Industrial Revolution

Mining and Metallury

1702–1712	Development of the Newcomen atmospheric pump
1709–1730	Development of coke by Abraham Darby
1759–1761	James Brindley built the Worsley Canal to take coal to the sea. First of the great English canals
1775	James Watt invented the steam engine
1784	Henry Cort invented the puddling and rolling process
1802–1803	Richard Trevithick invented the high-pressure steam engine

Textiles

1733	John Kay invented the flying shuttle
1765–1770	James Hargreaves: spinning jenny
1769	Richard Arkwright: water frame
1775	James Watt: steam engine
1784	Samuel Crompton: Crompton's mule
1785–1787	Edmund Cartwright: power loom
1785–1787	James Watt and Claude-Louis Berthollet: developed industrial chlorine bleach
1789	Nicolas LeBlanc: soda furnace to make industrial alkali
1800	John Monteith: steam-driven factory of power looms

CHAPTER TEN

INDUSTRIALIZATION

"... that decisive interval in
the history of a society when
growth becomes its normal
condition."

W. W. Rostow, *Stages of Economic Growth*

When a mechanic named John Kay invented the flying
shuttle, making the weaving process more efficient, his
neighbors denounced him and drove him into exile in
France. His invention would put weavers out of work, they
said. Only the rich merchants would benefit, as was usual
when things changed. It was better to keep to the old ways.
At least the poor would find work. But the old ways were
slipping from men's grasp. Kay's invention was just a straw
in the hurricane. The irrevocable and continuous process of
industrialization had begun.

Industrialization is not an event, like a battle or the passage of a law—something that occurs once and not again. It
is a continuous process, endless as far as we can tell, of apply-
ing more and more sophisticated technology to the production, distribution, and use of goods, services, and ideas.
While natural resources such as coal or oil are limited, technology appears not to be, making the entire process one of
continuing innovation in certain basic areas, such as the
transportation of goods, the dissemination of ideas, or the
manufacturing process itself. Thus, the railroad was an improvement over the stagecoach, which was better than the
ox cart, which was better than a backpack. A single industry
experienced substantial technological change and, after
1750, this process became quite a rapid one.

The implications of this process of industrialization are genuinely stupendous. In the place of a stable social system there has come mobility. Continuous and rapid economic growth has replaced a static economy. Affluence has become more common than poverty. Governments have used the new technology to increase their power over the citizen and were far more successful at this dismal business in the century after Napoleon than in the millenium before him. Science and technology slowly replaced religion as the informing principle of Western culture. Instead of continuity, Westerners have had to accustom themselves to endless change. The process has made us rich and given us comfort and power beyond anything our ancestors dreamed of. I wish I could say it has also made us happy.

I

Industrialization had diverse origins, like all major historical trends. Some were cultural, others were political and social, and still others were rooted in the economic history of the sixteenth and seventeenth centuries. In England alone, however, these historical trends led toward industrialization. Elsewhere, in Prussia or Austria, even the most devoted support given agriculture and manufacturing by mercantilist ministers did not provide the impetus necessary to move from a traditional economy to an industrial one.

The economic origins of English industrialization go back into the great depression of the seventeenth century. Although the English had suffered from depression and civil war, recovery after 1660 had been extraordinarily rapid. As the Dutch economy leveled off, the English forged ahead. The English also profited from the French depression of 1683 to 1725 and from the extremely slow recovery in central Europe and the Mediterranean Basin. As a result, the English economy began to diverge rather sharply from its continental neighbors.

A basic difference came in the rate of capital accumulation. After the Civil War, the English began to acquire capital at a rate similar to that of the Dutch in the years before 1650. By 1700, the English were fitted out with their own national debt, the Bank of England, and marine insurance companies, all in imitation of Amsterdam. But, whereas Dutch fiscal institutions had ceased to grow very much after 1660, the English expanded with only small interruptions throughout the entire century and a half from Cromwell to Napoleon. Thus, the English possessed a vast source of capital, which they invested in canals, roads, industry, trade, and technology. The costs of industrialization were immense, on a scale larger than any Old Regime commercial or colonial venture. Only the English had that sort of capital.

A major factor in English capital accumulation was the increasing concentration of overseas trade in English hands during the eighteenth century. Although English merchants faced rugged competition from the French and Dutch in such things as the slave, spice, and sugar trades, they dominated commerce in manufactured goods. They could not keep up with the demand. Growing markets first forced English manufacturers to supply more labor, still using the traditional methods of production. That did not suffice. By the middle of the eighteenth century, therefore, there were solid economic reasons for Englishmen to search for new ways of making things, for a new and more efficient technology.

Economic origins and causes of industrialization were probably less important than cultural ones. Market pressures, after all, existed everywhere in Western Europe, but only in England did they lead to technological change. Perhaps the most important cultural factor in England was the habit of tinkering with machines and techniques. This went back into the sixteenth century and was supported by the government. The first royal patent for smelting iron with coal was in the reign of Elizabeth I. Dozens of subsequent patents were granted in the seventeenth century for the same process; alas, none of them worked. But inventors kept at it and one of them, Abraham Darby, eventually succeeded. It was the same with steam engines. The first two practical models were both invented by Englishmen, Thomas Savery

(1698) and Thomas Newcomen (1706). Gadgets to improve spinning and weaving were offered to the public—at a price, of course—long before the crucial innovations of the eighteenth century.

These habits of tinkering interested men far above the usual social level of mechanics and, in the stratified society of the Old Regime, aristocratic patronage was essential for success. Noble owners of estates interested themselves in "improvements," which included new types of farm machinery. The first canal was financed by a duke, and James Watt's steam engine attracted the capital and business acumen of a successful manufacturer of buttons. Even the American scientist and inventor Benjamin Franklin found friends and encouragement from the English aristocracy.

Added to this were the habits of business and investment acquired in centuries of foreign commerce. Trade had attained social acceptance as a legitimate and worthy occupation. Englishmen of all classes invested their savings in commerce, and there were neither laws nor customs that prevented the aristocracy from engaging in trade. In this, England differed from all continental countries except the Netherlands. Not only did the nobility and gentry invest in commerce, but many others did as well. The number of smaller investors was also in contrast to the continent, where the government was the principal source of risk capital. In Austria, for example, the largest industrial and agricultural investor was the emperor, Franz-Stefan. His activities were not the result of conviction, however. His wife, Maria Theresa, would not allow him any role in government, so he invested to give himself something to do.

A final factor in the development of industry in England was the government. As with all Old Regime governments, the English adhered to the tenets of mercantilism and put great emphasis on state aid to industry and commerce. Direct government investment in England fell far behind France, Prussia, Austria, or Russia, but the English put great emphasis on the navy that in the long run, was probably the most useful thing the crown could have done. Beyond this the English government was particularly sensitive to commercial interests, which were expressed in the House of Commons and in merchant's petitions. These latter were responsible for most of the Navigations Acts. Finally, the government supported trade and industry by winning its wars, something that the French neglected to do. The fruits of victory, and they were substantial, passed to the English. No government is perfect, however, or even very good, and the English promptly squandered their advantages and lost them in the American Revolution. Even so, the English recovered rapidly and, when they next fought the French, managed, after some difficulties, to emerge a winner at Waterloo.

The aforementioned factors were all vital parts of the origins of industrialization, but it is more crucial to see that they all occurred together. There had been previous periods of large capital accumulation and a remarkable concentration of trade, as in thirteenth century Venice, Milan, Florence, or Flanders, but this had not led to the cluster of technological innovations that mark industrialization. Colbert had mobilized the resources of seventeenth century French states in the cause of trade and industry, but the technology has remained almost static. Hellenistic Alexandria had been the site of considerable capital accumulation and sustained research into science, mechanics, and mathematics, all without industrialization. Only in eighteenth century England were all the factors present, and even in England technological change and industrialization was slow and sporadic and not fully established until the 1780s.

II

The industrial revolution was more than factories and machines. Mechanization of industry was accompanied by four other social movements, each an integral part of industrialization: (1) there was a sharp population rise in the eighteenth century, (2) along with a sustained and remarkable expansion of English trade, (3) England also experienced a complex agricultural revolution and (4) a general reconstruction of her transportation system. These four areas of change were indivisible from the mechanization of industry and the rise in production. They were as important as invention to the progress of industrialization.

English population at the beginning of the eighteenth century hovered near six million. It did not begin to climb until the decade of the 1740s, when the rate of increase grew from less than 1 percent to over 3 percent a decade. By the 1780s, English population was growing at 11 percent a decade and, after Waterloo, it grew at over 16 percent a decade. This was a phenomenal increase, only partly explained by the general absence of epidemics, a long run of good harvests, or an increase in agricultural output. Industrialization also played a part. The new machines provided additional jobs, additional goods, and a generally rising Gross National Product. For much of the population, it also meant a rising standard of living and, for almost everyone, more opportunities.

The population rise also affected the process of industrialization. It provided a constant pool of labor and meant that labor was cheap, a major consideration for the inadequately capitalized factories of the early industrial revolution. A growing population also added to the number of consumers, thus widening the market at the precise time when manufacturers were producing more goods than ever before. People were as basic a resource of industrialization as coal or iron or cotton and were just as ruthlessly exploited.

Along with the spectacular growth in population came a slow but genuine revolution in the methods and output of English agriculture. Agricultural change had several facets. It involved the introduction of new crops and new machinery. Farmers slowly discarded the ancient methods of crop rotation. They began to plant artificial meadows and experiment with improved stock breeds. There was also large-scale enclosure of the land, both the wastes and commons and the medieval strips of arable. Each of these contributed to a general result, a continuous rise in agricultural productivity, which meant more food.

The introduction of new implements spanned the century, beginning with Jethro Tull's seed drill, developed about 1700. The seed drill enabled the farmer to plant his seed in straight rows, far enough apart to allow continuous cultivation between them. The weeds were kept under control, the expenditure of seed was reduced, and the yield was increased. In the 1730s the Rotherham steel plow was invented. The Rotherham plow allowed the farmer to use two horses in place of the eight ox-two man team inherited from the Middle Ages. To these were added threshing machines, first produced in the 1780s. These were only the first steps on a continuous road of change in agricultural technology, but they broke the old medieval patterns of farming.

The English also developed new crops during the eighteenth century. The most famous was probably the turnip, tirelessly extolled by an amiable eccentric, Turnip Townshend. More important, however, were the legumes and grasses that made up artificial meadows and replenished the soil, thus permitting the farmer to cultivate all his land all the time. Along with new meadows came experiments in cattle breeding now that the land could support them. The new crops did not supplant traditional ones, such as wheat, rye, barley, or oats but were added to them, enabling the English to use more land and to use it more efficiently.

In spite of their manifest advantages, all of these new crops and equipment made slow progress against the ingrained conservatism of the countryside, the lack of capital that plagued most farmers, poor transportation, and the medieval patterns of land ownership and use. Indeed, many of the new tools and techniques, which could be quite expensive, brought real profits only on large farms that produced for the market rather than subsistence. Since the population rise after 1750 guaranteed good profits from large farms using the improved methods, many lords and squires consolidated their holdings, a process known as enclosure.

Enclosures of both arable and common lands had been known since Tudor times, and there had been quite a rash of them during the prosperous years of the Restoration. The scattered strips of arable had been consolidated into units, with each farmer getting approximately his original acreage. Frequently, the waste, pastures, and commons of the village had also been enclosed and divided proportionately. Such an event made the lord's fortune since he could now farm for the market, and it was catastrophic for the cottager who needed his rights on the common and waste to survive.

In the eighteenth century, rural magnates used acts of Parliament to force enclosures on their reluctant tenants and villagers. In the years after 1750, when agricultural prices rose consistently, there was an increasing volume of parliamentary enclosures. Between 1760 and 1815, there were about 1800 individual Enclosure Acts and, in 1801, Parliament passed a General Enclosure Act that made the process much easier. One and a half million acres were enclosed between the Peace of Paris and Waterloo, a considerable chunk of the English countryside.

Enclosures, which primarily benefitted the large farmers, made the transition to new agricultural methods almost inevitable. Profits alone would insure that, but pride was also involved. It was a time when George III, in his fleeting moments of sanity, called himself "Farmer George" and maintained a model farm and breeding station. Great landlords did likewise, and provided their estates with the latest crops and equipment. Agricultural societies encouraged this trend. Year by year, English agriculture slowly shifted away from medieval patterns toward modern, heavily capitalized farms.

Agricultural modernization would have taken even longer than it did had not the English also improved internal transportation. God knows, it needed it. English roads in the early eighteenth century were supposed to be the worst in Europe, trails of mud or dust according to the weather. After 1750, however, there was a sustained effort to improve them. Unlike France, where such activities were undertaken by the government, English road building was largely the result of private enterprise. Turnpike companies were formed, received a charter from Parliament to improve a section of public road, and charged tolls for its use. Between 1750 and 1810, Parliament passed from 40 to 60 Turnpike Acts a year, and most of the major English roads were affected.

Some improvements were marginal, merely fixing the worst ruts at the least expense, and charging the highest tolls possible. Other roads were completely remade. The engineers used methods copied from the Romans, putting down layers of rock and gravel that settled into a hard surface. Such expensive repairs were in the minority, but they were concentrated on the main roads. Travel times between London and the main provincial cities were cut by about one-third, and the number of stagecoaches went up astronomically. By 1820 there were about 1500 coaches leaving London each day over the improved roads. Costs of land transport went down also, but not so far as to compete with waterborne traffic. That development would await the railroads.

Although the improvement in roads aided industrialization, the major element of the transportation revolution was canals. Commerce by water was far cheaper and faster than by land, and the canals tied England together into a single market and allowed exploitation of resources previously unusable. Like turnpikes, canals were built with private capital, only a far greater amount was required. The first canal was financed by the Duke of Bridgewater, and it cost him over a quarter of a million pounds. It was to carry coal from the duke's mines at Worsley to Manchester. The canal was designed by James Brindley, an almost illiterate engineer, who made all of his calculations in his head, using the powers of memory and concentration. Unable to explain to the duke his canal plans, Brindley carved a model in soap. Work began in 1759, and was completed two years later. It was a gigantic achievement, containing a tunnel at Worsley and a huge viaduct over the Irwell river at Barton.

The Worsley Canal was a stupendous success. It cut the price of coal at Manchester by one-half, made pots of money

for the duke, and established Brindley as a great man. The
people who lived in the district were also caught up in the
project. They painted the canal boats bright colors and held
annual competitions for the most beautiful coal boat. On
Good Friday, families would picnic at Barton, in the shadow
of the viaduct. People spoke of Brindley and the Duke of
Bridgewater in Biblical accents, as great and wondrous men
who had brought fame and prosperity to their district. Today the canal is no longer in use, but it is still kept up as a
public monument to times and glories past.

The canal at Worsley also set off a wave of canal building
elsewhere in England. Brindley himself designed the Grand
Trunk Canal, which connected the Irish and North Seas,
though he did not live to see its completion in 1777. By Waterloo, the country was tied together by almost 4000 miles of
internal waterways, which connected all the major ports,
mines, and industrial cities.

Canals were the highways of the early industrial revolution because they made it possible to move bulk items such
as wood, stone, grain, coal, and iron to any spot in the country. Land transportation was still too slow and expensive,
and the roads could not accommodate the vast amounts of
coal and iron the new factories needed. The canals thus over-
came the localism of the thousands of petty markets and
economies. Industrialization could not have occurred without
them.

The final dramatic change that accompanied industrialization was in trade. During the eighteenth century British
overseas trade grew dramatically, particularly after 1780.
With the wars of the French Revolution, the British acquired virtually a monopoly of international trade. The numbers of ships increased along with trade volume and, by the
1790s, every major port was starting an extensive program
of dock construction. The seventeenth century mercantilist,
Thomas Mun, had declared that England's treasure was by
"forraign trade" and, by the end of the eighteenth century,
this seemed truer than ever.

The boom in foreign trade after 1780 was more than sim-

ply a commercial bonanza, however. It was also connected
with the processes of industrialization. Overseas trade created a continuing and growing demand for British manufactures, as well as the habit of buying them. The English domestic market, although the deepest in the world, was still
too small to absorb all of the products of industrialization.
Foreign commerce took up the slack. It also gave the English
access to needed raw materials that would not grow or were
not found at home. Cotton from India and the southern
United States was a prime import, as was high-grade Swedish iron ore. Beyond that, the English imported dozens of
items for resale abroad, mostly to Europe. These included
rice, tobacco, and sugar. Moreover, commerce produced a
large capital surplus, much of which found its way into industrial investment, rather than back into trade. Canal
building was financed largely from the profits of commerce.
Finally, trade was a major factor in building a business eth-
ic and the institutions to support, such as banks, insurance
companies, and a stock market. Because of trade, London
was the financial capital of the world, and the habits of investment built up in trade were transferred to the expansion
of industry.

III

The process of industrialization itself, taken in isolation
away from associated social and agricultural movements,
can best be described as a clump of technological innovations, some processes, and some inventions that change the
way things are made and change them sharply and rapidly.
Time is important. Both printing and radio radically altered
communications, but they did it half a millennium apart, and
no one considers these two inventions as part of a single "industrial revolution"—a single shift from a primitive economy to an industrial one. "Clustering" or "convergence" of
technological innovation was a basic factor in the dramatic
and irrevocable economic shift that occurred in England toward the end of the eighteenth century. It was the short

time-span in which they occurred, as much as the nature of the innovations themselves, that had such a revolutionary effect in English industry.

These clusters of innovations occurred in two distinct industries—the manufacture of iron and textiles. These industries occupied a strategic location in the English economy. Textiles, particularly woolens, had been a basic English export since Henry I, and iron products had joined them in the sixteenth century. Both products enjoyed international as well as home markets, and both were plagued by insufficient production and inadequate quality. Technological change in these industries, therefore, had a disproportional impact on the English economy, far greater than if the changes had taken place in the manufacture of paper or even shipbuilding.

Textile manufacture in 1750 followed traditional lines, similar to production patterns on the continent and those of medieval Europe. The domestic, or putting-out, system was common, wherein the worker owned or rented his machinery and worked in his house. Manufacturing was thus scattered about in the villages, with the peasant supplementing his agricultural income with industrial labor. The supplies of wool, flax, or cotton were brought to the village by a merchant-industrialist, who paid by the piece to have it made into thread and then cloth, picking it up when the work was done. Much of the labor was concentrated in rural areas in order to escape guild regulations that, on the continent at least, were extremely strict.

There were several social advantages to the domestic system. It spread the work around. If no one got rich, almost everyone could eat. It also kept the peasant in his village, where life was familiar and comprehensible, where he enjoyed the dignity of working the soil and, perhaps, owned a scrap of land. Domestic manufacturing required only a modest capital outlay. No factory need be built, the merchant paid only for the raw materials, and the workers, more often than not, could afford their own looms and spinning wheels. Finally, it fit into the hierarchical structures of Old Regime society, preserving the traditional relationships between peasant and gentry, worker and master, and townsman and countryman. It was a comfortable system, and most people spoke well of it.

There were disadvantages also, and they became more acute as the eighteenth century wore on. First, the quality of work done by yeoman weavers and spinners was excruciatingly modest, if that good. Quantity was inadequate also; the market snapped up all cloth made, no matter how shoddy. Agricultural work interfered with manufacturing, and supplies of cloth were periodically interrupted. The disadvantages were mainly economic and technological and were complained of by the merchants, while the benefits were essentially social, conferred, as it turned out, mainly on the poor. Under these conditions, it is obvious that there would be a massive effort to improve the way cloth was made.

Within the traditional textile industry, there existed a basic imbalance that no juggling of supplies or organization of labor could solve. This was the gap between spinning and weaving. Using hand looms and wheels, weavers could do more work than the spinners. It took four, sometimes six women working at their spinning wheels to supply thread for a single weaver. This imbalance was aggravated in 1733 when John Kay invented the flying shuttle, which could be attached easily to existing looms. The flying shuttle did two things. It enabled the weaver to dispense with his assistant, and it also made him more than twice as efficient as previously. Now, he could absorb the work of a dozen women. For these very reasons, the flying shuttle was attacked as being destructive of good social order. As a result, the flying shuttle spread very slowly and was not at all common until the 1770s. But it did spread, and it did make a spinning machine absolutely necessary. It was either that, or the English were going to have to import a great many women.

Efforts to invent a spinning machine had begun in earnest as early as the 1720s, and by 1730 a mechanic named John Wyatt had come up with one. Between 1732 and 1742, Wyatt and his partner, Lewis Paul, tried to exploit the invention.

They did not succeed. In the first place, they lacked the capital and, in the second place, the machine was defective. The need for such a machine continued to grow, of course, and in the 1760s two inventors succeeded. In 1765, James Hargreaves, a weaver and carpenter, invented the spinning jenny, which he named after his daughter. It was a simple machine, rather like a spinning wheel set on its side. A movable wooden frame contained a number of spindles, allowing the operator to twist the thread and draw it at the same time. The jenny was more efficient than the spinning wheel, and it produced finer quality thread as well. Finally, it was designed to be used at home, thus fitting into the framework of the domestic system.

The other inventor was Richard Arkwright, a ". . . bag-cheeked, pot-bellied . . . much-inventing barber," Thomas Carlyle called him. In 1768, Arkwright invented the water frame, patented it at once, and began to produce a coarse but strong thread by means of water power. The water frame was simply a huge, vertical jenny, but it produced thread strong enough to be the warp as well as the weft of cotton cloth, which neither the jenny nor the spinning wheel could do.

Both the jenny and the water frame were immediately successful. Ten years after Hargreaves' death in 1778, there were said to be over 20,000 of his machines in England, and the smallest of these had six or eight spindles. The water frame, producing its strong thread, was also indispensable, so much so that others took it up, in defiance of Arkwright's patent, fighting him in Parliament and in court, ultimately winning a legal decision in 1785. But Arkwright was not defeated. He may have had an unprepossessing appearance, but he was also a man of exceptional business skill, and his establishments were the best managed and most profitable in all of England. His original mill, established at Cromford on the Derwent River in 1771 had, within a decade, grown to several thousand spindles and employed 300 workers. Arkwright himself worked constantly to improve his mills, extend his education, and increase his fortune. He was knighted by George III, became high sheriff of Derby, and died in 1792 leaving an incredible fortune of half a million pounds (about 250 million dollars in modern purchasing power) and a legend for industry, astuteness, and achievement.

Arkwright's invention was significant beyond the immediate increase in thread. His was the first machine that did not fit into a cottage and that did not come to the worker but demanded instead that the worker come to it. The water frame meant factories. At one stroke, the worker lost ownership of the machines, control over his own working conditions and hours of labor, and his agricultural pursuits. All these passed to the owner of the mill. The textile worker was transformed from an independent petty producer into a hired hand, with all the loss in autonomy and status that this implies. On the other side, the entrepreneur was obliged to lay out immensely greater amounts of capital. He must build the factory, construct the machines and maintain them, purchase huge quantities of raw materials, pay wages in cash, and be able to ride through periods of slack demand when his expenses outran his income. The owner must also know how to manage his business, talents that Arkwright possessed but that many others did not. In return, however, there was the chance of getting rich.

Thus the worker and the owner, who had once been partners of a sort, who had once belonged to contiguous social classes, who had once shared risks and the capital outlay, now became opponents. The factory worker saw his interests as opposed to the owners. The worker wanted higher wages and shorter hours, and owners usually did not want them to have these. Owners wanted newer and more efficient machines, while the men who ran them feared being thrown out on the street. These changing attitudes spread only slowly as the implications of the factory system became clearer. But with the spread of factories, the new social attitudes came to dominate older conflicts between lord and peasant, layman and cleric, and town and countryside.

The next spinning machine, the "mule" of Samuel Crompton, was a combination of the jenny and the water frame.

Developed between 1774 and 1779, Crompton's mule produced thread both fine and strong, and thus improved upon older machines. Within a decade, the mule had been hooked to both water and steam power, while the number of spindles per machine had been increased from a few to a few thousand. By 1800, the mule was the basic spinning machine, and remained such. It completed the technological evolution of cotton spinning and the transformation of that industry from domestic production to the factory.

These new machines radically increased the supply of thread and its quality as well, and thus reversed the traditional imbalance between spinning and weaving. Now, it was the weavers who could not keep up. By 1790, skilled weavers were being paid in pounds instead of pence. William Radcliffe, a contemporary entrepreneur, wrote that, about 1800, ". . . there was not a village within thirty miles of Manchester . . . in which some of us were not putting out cotton . . . in short, we employed every person in cotton weaving who could be induced to learn the trade." That could only mean a weaving machine. And one was invented, by Edmund Cartwright, the youngest son of a country gentleman. In 1785, Cartwright produced a very crude machine, which had a distressing tendency to break down. He kept at it, however, and two years later had made a much better model. By 1789, he had hooked it to a steam engine. The first factory, at Manchester, was burned to the ground by hostile weavers, and Cartwright lost everything. But the logic of the machine was irresistible and, in 1800, the Scottish industrialist, John Monteith, established a power loom mill, which was the prototype for the hundreds that followed. By Waterloo, both spinning and weaving were mechanized, with complicated machines hooked to steam engines, housed in factories, and owned by great capitalists. And it had all happened, by and large, within 40 years.

Industrialization of both spinning and weaving again shifted the pressure point in the manufacture of cotton. It was now raw material, the cotton itself, that was in short supply. Neither India nor America, nor both together, could keep up with the insatiable new machines. A Yankee gun-smith, visiting the Georgia plantation of General Nathanial Greene, solved the problem. In 1793, Eli Whitney invented the cotton gin, which replaced the slow and laborious separa-tion of cotton fiber from the stalk. Whitney's machine had immediate and powerful results. It increased the supply of raw cotton to the point where it could not all be used, and it gave the American slave system a new lease on life. The English were certainly pleased with the first, although Americans have had some difficulty in adjusting to the lat-ter.

Some of the results of this industrial transformation we have already mentioned: factories, new social classes and re-lationships, and changing social attitudes. There were other results, equally significant. One, already hinted at, was the sharp increase in the quality of cloth. There is a myth today that handmade goods are better than those made by ma-chine. Usually, the reverse is true. The machines were more consistent than man, made fewer mistakes, and eliminated the coarse and fragile patches that characterized handmade products. The quantity produced went up, of course; that was the main reason for the new machines. But it kept going up, with no end in sight. No matter how much the factories produced, the market absorbed it. Growth seemed endless and fantastic to men accustomed to the static economy and inelastic demand of preindustrial days. Finally, most won-drous of all, the price of cloth dropped. Prices for cotton cloth were slipping steadily before Waterloo, and afterwards they fell by three-fourths again. Mass production meant low-er costs, lower prices, a greater market, better goods, sus-tained economic growth, and all of these things, so astound-ing to contemporaries, were as much a part of the "industrial revolution" as the technology itself.

Cotton was not the only industry that experienced radical technological change during the eighteenth century. Iron-mongering did also, and its technological and economic de-velopment, while less spectacular, was probably the more important industry. Certainly, the development of metallurgy made it possible for other industries to move beyond the stage of simple wooden machines powered by hand.

Englishmen had long recognized the importance of the combined industries of mining and the manufacture of iron products. From cannon to horseshoes, the iron industry was essential to the nation's power and prosperity. It was also sick and had been for some time. There was plenty of domestic iron ore, but it was of inferior quality. So the English imported, largely from Sweden or Russia. Between 1710 and 1720, the ore imports were between 15,000 and 22,000 tons a year, and by 1765 this figure had risen to over 55,000 tons. These two facts meant that the production of pig and bar iron was small and on a small scale. During the first half of the eighteenth century there were never many more than 60 blast furnaces, some producing less than 150 tons of pig iron a year. The iron was expensive, and the operation suffered from the distinct disadvantage of requiring a great deal of capital investment for a small return.

An additional problem was the general technological backwardness of iron mining. The iron ore mines were little more than dog holes, a few yards deep. Mining was mainly scraping the ore from the surface. One furnace in Surrey even used slag from Roman foundries, rather than ore from new mines. None of these were signs of a healthy industry.

The metal finishing industries reflected these sad conditions. They, too, were organized into small shops, on the domestic system. Most craftsmen worked in their own homes, with their own tools. Guild regulations still survived, particularly in the north with the Holy Fellowship and Company of Cutlers and Makers of Knives within the Lordship of Hallamshire in the County of York (1624). Few other English guilds exercised the control over their trade as did the Holy Fellowship, and this control was directed toward finding work for the masters, keeping others out, and freezing the technology of metal working at its current, unsatisfactory level.

Beyond all of this, the worst problem was fuel for smelting the ore. Charcoal was used, and it presented serious problems. It was in short supply and extremely expensive. It was also hard to ship, and so the ore diggings had to be near forests, not where the best ore might be. Thus, the forges drifted across England, hunting for oak trees, and leaving slaughtered forests behind them. Since wood was the basic material for construction, wagons, ships, and machines, such timber butchery had evil economic consequences. Forests were also necessary for the survival of small farmers who used them for poaching, grazing their pigs, firewood, and construction. Forests massacres had evil social consequences as well. Finally, when the forests ran out, the iron industry would die. By the eighteenth century, that day was not far off.

The answer to this problem was at hand, and everybody knew what it was. Coal must replace charcoal as the fuel for smelting ore. Since the sixteenth century, men had been trying to find a way to use coal for refining iron. All attempts sank on the same reef. English coal had a high sulfur content, which the burning coal released and which the molten iron absorbed. Sulfur in the iron made it extremely brittle, and pig iron refined with coal was useless. Not until the eighteenth century was this problem solved, and then only slowly. A Quaker ironmaster, Abraham Darby of Coalbrookdale, conducted numerous experiments, smelting iron with cooked coal, or coke. It was all trial and error, the chemistry behind the process was completely unknown. Between 1709 and 1713, Darby got excellent results, smelting a good pig iron using coke and cutting his costs by about two-thirds. He died in 1717, however, before the process was perfect, and the experiments were not taken up again until 1730 when his son, also Abraham Darby, took over the furnace. The second Darby extended the range of his tinkering. He improved and enlarged the bellows, thus making the fire hotter, and he began adding limestone to the molten ore to add to the purity of the pig iron. By the 1760s, the whole process—coke, lime, and bellows—was a distinct economic and technological success and had greatly increased English production of pig, or cast iron.

This was all to the good, but it did not solve the iron industry's problems completely. The bottleneck moved from fuel to the refining process itself. Pig iron could be produced in large quantities, but it still remained too full of impurities, too brittle for every use. A further refining step was needed. The pig iron must be heated and hammered, again and again and again, into wrought or bar iron. This cost time and money, and some pig iron was so impure, so contaminated with carbon, that heating and hammering would not work. Thus the English, even after they had increased their production of pig iron, were still importing bar iron from Russia and Sweden. This in itself was bad enough, but a sharp rise in the price of Baltic iron after 1770 made things even worse. A technological revolution in forging bar iron had become as great a necessity as one previously had been in smelting pig iron.

In 1783, two men found the answer simultaneously. One, Peter Onions, was an obscure ironworker at Merthyr Tydvil in Wales, but the other, Henry Cort, had influential friends and could publicize his process. Cort took out a patent in 1784 for his invention, called puddling and rolling. The pig iron was first refined again over a coke fire, which drove some of the carbon off. It was then put into a furnace with clinkers containing iron oxides, which combined chemically with the carbon given off by the molten pig iron. The whole mess was stirred (called puddling) then hammered and finally rolled into a long metal strip. The process both purified the iron and rolled it into a usable sheet. It solved at one blow all the major existing technological problems in the iron industry.

Although Cort's process was an immediate and spectacular success, many of the biggest ironmasters remained unconvinced. James Watt, inventor of the steam engine, was outraged at their blindness and stupidity and wrote, "Cort is treated shamefully by the business people, who are ignorant asses, one and all." Only up to a point, however because when Cort lost his patent in the bankruptcy of his backer, they all converted to puddling and rolling at once, now that it was free.

The final invention that transformed metallurgy was the steam engine, which found two primary uses. It powered bellows far larger than man or horse could move and thus made possible larger furnaces and more efficient smelting. Steam engines were also used in the mines. The need for both coal and iron ore could not now be satisfied with strip mines, dog holes, and the like. But deep mines flooded and could not be used in the rainy season, which in England is always. Watt's steam engine, finished in 1775, enabled miners to pump water out of the mines faster than God put it in. The English could now mine at any depth, and they increased the production of coal and iron ore so fast that they were exporting both by the time of the French Revolution.

The results of these inventions and changes were momentous, as contemporaries could clearly see. As with textiles, the quality of the product, both pig and bar iron, improved dramatically, and the price fell as well. England ceased importing and began to export iron, not merely ordinary iron, but the highest quality metal that competed favorably with the Swedish. Again, as in textiles, the new innovations meant a concentration of the industry, and signaled the doom of domestic metal workers. Iron had always required large amounts of capital, and now it demanded even more. But it began to pay better. Some ironmasters became almost feudal lords of an industrial empire. John Wilkinson fit this mold. He was progressive about technology and was one of the first to use the new Watt steam engine. He owned coal and iron mines and built blast furnaces all over England. In 1777 he established the Indret iron works near Nantes, France, which were the most advanced and efficient in that country. He made his own coins, which showed his face and majestic inscription, "Wilkinson Iron Master." He ran all of this with a high and hard hand, even driving his brother out of the firm, but his abilities were great and his decisions usually correct. He led the world in finding new uses for his product, including an iron bridge, iron canal boats, and iron pipes. Equally large and important, although in another field, were the Carron iron works, established in 1760 by John Roebuck. He, too, used the most advanced technology and produced goods famous in all the world. They were guns, guns so efficient and deadly that "carronade" became a European synonym for cannon fire.

A final consequence of the improvement in ironwork was its enormous impact on all other industries. Before puddling and rolling, every industry used wooden machines.; iron ones were too expensive and fragile. Now, that was no longer true. Metal machines replaced wooden ones in the textile industry rapidly after 1800, since they alone could tolerate the power output of steam engines, and now they cost less. The machine-tool industry also dated from puddling and rolling. In 1797, Henry Maudslay invented the screwcutting lathe, the basic tool and die machine. It was an invention that awaited high quality and low-cost metal. Thus, innovations in metallurgy affected the entire economy as the technological transformation of the textile industry had not. The changes in ironworking were basic to the entire process of industrialization.

IV

Most of the innovations in processes and machinery made during the first half century of industrialization in England were the result of trial and error tinkering, conducted by men who actually constructed and repaired existing implements. No formal scientific or technical training was required. Tinkering, that was what counted—a curiosity about how the machine worked, an itch to take it apart and put it back together, and an ability to learn from the machine itself how it worked. John Kay, for instance, was a weaver and a mechanic who fixed looms and had no formal education in science and technology at all. Richard Arkwright was an itinerant barber who could read somewhat and whose great skill was in recognizing the value in other men's inventions. James Hargreaves was a weaver and carpenter. Abraham Darby was both an owner of a foundry and a worker in his own plant. Peter Onions had risen to the rank of foreman at Merthyr Tydvil, a position also occupied by Henry Maudslay the year he invented his screwcutting lathe. None was a scientist, all were skilled in working with machinery. They lacked theories; Darby, for instance, was totally ignorant of the chemical reactions that had kept ironmongers from smelting with coal. But they knew machines, which was what mattered.

There were a number of reasons for this separation of science and technology, which seems so strange to us today. A basic cause of it was social. In the highly stratified society of the Old Regime, workers and mechanics were light years away from the aristocrats who went to the universities and studied "natural philosophy," as science was then called. The lower classes did not go to school, and weavers, mechanics, barbers, and tinkerers were part of the lower classes. The Greek prejudice against people who worked with their hands was still strong. Beyond that, there was the state of science. Chemistry was virtually unknown until the last quarter of the eighteenth century; oxygen was not identified until 1775. Physics dealt more with planets than with strength of materials. Most scientific disciplines were not yet enough of a coherent body of knowledge to be useful in practical problems of technology. Finally, there was the nature of the innovations themselves. Most were rather simple, a reorganization of elements or techniques already known. Theoretical knowledge was far less important than lots of experience. "It's all in knowing how," runs the worker's epigram and, in the eighteenth century, it spoke the simple truth.

This separation of science and technology, while quite substantial, was not absolute even in the earliest phases of industrialization. The chemical industry, particularly, benefited from the knowledge of scientists. Glassmaking and the manufacture of soap, alkalis, and chlorine bleach were all transformed by the work of scientists. The development of chlorine bleach involved James Watt, inventor of the steam engine, whose interests were almost universal. Chlorine bleach itself was first described by Claude Louis Berthollet, one of the great chemists of his day and a collaborator with Antoine Lavoisier. In 1785, Berthollet published a five-page article in the *Journal de Physique*. Watt learned of the research the next year from Berthollet himself and began experimenting in his father-in-law's Glasgow textile shop. After about 18 months of effort, Watt succeeded in producing chlorine from sulphuric acid and salt in quantities large enough for commercial use. Watt was also involved in the production of industrial alkali, having begun experiments in 1766 and continuing then intermittently for four years. He succeeded, after a fashion, but large amounts of inexpensive industrial alkali awaited Nicolas Leblanc's experiments with the soda furnace, which were completed in 1794, the year of the Terror.

The greatest invention of the age was also the work of a scientist. It was the steam engine, the work of James Watt. Watt came from a background far different from most of the inventors of the late eighteenth century. His grandfather was a teacher of mathematics, and his father a municipal magistrate, architect, shipbuilder, and a skilled craftsman who built navigational instruments. Watt himself showed an early scientific bent and chose the profession of maker of scientific instruments. He went to Glasgow and set up his workshop in the university. In 1762 he began experiments with steam power and, by 1764, he had fixed his attention to improving Newcomen's rather inefficient steam engine. Watt worked at this for five years, and took out a patent for his own steam engine in 1769. He also interested John Roebuck, owner of the Carron iron foundry, in supporting an effort to make Watt's invention a commercial success. The project took longer and cost much more than either man had anticipated. Roebuck's financial difficulties, as well as defects in the machine, led Roebuck to surrender his rights to Matthew Boulton, a button manufacturer whose shops had the latest and best machine tools. Watt and Boulton made the new steam engine work and in 1775, after the expenditure of the enormous sum of 50,000 pounds (perhaps 25 million dollars), Watt took out a new patent for the invention that made him immortal. Boulton and Watt formed a company to exploit this fantastic device, and within a quarter century it had begun to shift every English industry toward a changing and sophisticated technology. It also made a fortune for the partners.

Watt, of course, was the way of the future. The connection between scientific theory and technological application was small in his time, but it was growing. Innovations became more complicated as the problems to be solved were themselves more complicated. Tinkerers and mechanics still understood what had to be done, of course, and the career of Thomas Edison demonstrated that they could also solve the problems, on occasion. But, steadily and inexorably, technological innovation demanded the disciplined application of scientific insight and mathematical knowledge. The connection between the shop and the laboratory became ever closer. Today, we can hardly tell them apart.

V

"Novus ordo seclorum," a new order of the world, reads the motto on the American dollar bill, once a valuable piece of paper. Whether America was that new order or not has been debated, but no one doubts that technology and industrialization was. The old order was dissolved by a solvent so pervasive and powerful that no church, no king, no aristocracy, and no people could put it back the way it was. Nor could they even stop the flow of change or even seriously deflect it. Change had become rapid and permanent, something that the generation of 1800 was slow to accept and even slower to act upon.

Industrialization also demanded a new approach to the antique problem of order. Previously, when contemplating the right order of the universe or the well-ordered society, philosophers and theologians had recourse to the theories of long-dead authorities. They quoted Aristotle, Plato, Cicero,

Aquinas, Augustine, Newton and, on very rare occasions, Jesus. They rummaged through stately speculations, searching for a sentence or an idea that would help them discover the secret of order. It lay in there somewhere, that elusive secret, and if one could only find it, then everything would be clear, and the proper order of the world would be exposed to view. This was the common method of all philosophers from Philo to Rousseau and, if it had ever worked, it did no longer. Order was not to be found that way, not after the changes by technology and industrialization. Now, it is different. ". . . The principle of order is not something existing outside ourselves, something ready to hand . . .," wrote Jules Romains in *Men of Good Will* (Vol. V), ". . . but rather that it is something which we ourselves have got to apply. . . . It is not a question of recognizing order, but of creating it."

BIBLIOGRAPHY

1. General Accounts

Paul Mantoux, *The Industrial Revolution in the Eighteenth Century: The Beginnings of the Modern Factory System in England,* is a long, detailed, but exceptionally clear account of English industrialization to about 1815. It includes a good deal of information about English farming, trade, and transportation, as well as dealing with the standard themes of invention and urbanization. Highly recommended.

Phyllis Deane, *The First Industrial Revolution,* is a clear, concise, su perb book on industrialization. It emphasizes the role of clusters of innovations, and describes industrialization as a continuing process, not an event. Not as detailed as Mantoux, it covers the same ground. Highly recommended.

David Landes, *The Unbound Prometheus,* is a superb survey of technological change and industrialization. The first 120 pages deal with industrialization in England, and they are outstanding. Highly recommended (hard cover).

2. Specialized Studies

M. Dorothy George, *London Life in the Eighteenth Century,* is an exceptionally interesting study of urban life in a city beginning to undergo the pangs of industrialization. It is particularly good on the urban poor, both industrial and pre-industrial variety. Highly recommended.

A. E. Musson and E. Robinson, *Science and Technology in the Industrial Revolution,* is a series of 15 articles on various facets of industrialization, with particular emphasis on a vital problem: the connection between science and technology. These are difficult, scholarly articles but are presented in a clear, clean manner, and a good student can grasp them, if he concentrates (hard cover).

CHAPTER
ELEVEN

EPILOGUE : 1814

"America's present need is not heroics but healing, not nostrums but normalcy,"

announced Warren Harding, a typical politician who, on this one occasion, rose above the general mediocrity of his dismal trade. He expressed the precise opinion of most Europeans in 1814, as well as the hopes of diplomats and monarchs. The monster Napoleon had been packed off to Elba, there to ponder his fate gradually and be forgotten. God willing, it was the end of revolutions and adventures.

For most people, healing and normalcy meant peace. An end had come to alarms and sieges, to drafts, destruction, and slaughter. It was a pretty spring in 1814 and, by the end of May, there were 10,000 English in Paris to savor its entertainments and gaze at its monuments. There was a moment of excitement when the Prussians threatened to blow up to Pont du Jena, which commemorated a Prussian defeat. The restored Bourbon king, Louis XVIII, gained a brief popularity by promising to sit down in the middle of the bridge to prevent its destruction. Czar Alexander I of Russia stayed at Talleyrand's house, where he was manipulated both by the great diplomat and Baroness Julie de Krudener, a religious mystic who thought of the czar as the Second Coming. Parisians and visitors were delighted to learn that Alexander was more or less convinced. Allied officers strutted around Paris, marveled at its beauties, and brought a genuine prosperity to the cafes and prostitutes.

For others, however, there would be no healing, and normalcy meant revenge on the Revolution and all its works. As French soldiers and administrators streamed home from Italy and Germany, their places were taken by monarchs returning from exile. In Spain, Ferdinand VII restored the Inquisition and began a savage persecution of people who had supported the French. In Naples, Ferdinand I called back the Jesuits, restored monastic lands, reestablished the Inquisition, and had a chief minister who believed that ". . . the first servant of the crown should be the executioner. . . ." In Rome, the pope maintained a vast system of police spies and jailed hundreds on suspicion of liberalism. Everywhere, the French law codes were discarded, along with legal equality and careers open to talents. In France itself, there were ominous signs of reaction. Ardent royalists conducted a "white terror" in the provinces, persecuting revolutionary officials and men who had bought church lands. Louis XVIII, spoke of the renewed alliance of throne and altar. Napoleonic officers were put on half pay, and aristocrats just returned from exile took their place. The white flag of the Bourbons replaced the tricolor of the Revolution. Suddenly, priests and elderly émigré nobles were seen everywhere. There was talk of giving the church its land back and restoring feudal dues. The Old Regime, so remote only a few months ago, seemed on the verge of revival by July, 1814.

But could that be? Had not too many years, too many changes divided the Estates-General from Elba? In 1814, there was no answer to that question. The two Europes faced each other, one strong in tradition, religious sanction and military victory, the other the product of a quarter century of revolution, the rights of man, and nationalism. Whatever the future might be, in 1814 there was no sure sign that foretold the victor.

Index